Analyzing Social Settings

A Guide to Qualitative Observation and Analysis

SECOND EDITION

John Lofland
Lyn H. Lofland

UNIVERSITY OF CALIFORNIA,
DAVIS

D0023851

Wadsworth Publishing Company
A Division of Wadsworth, Inc.
Belmont, California

Sociology Editor: Sheryl Fullerton
Production Editor: Leland Moss
Designer: MaryEllen Podgorski
Copy Editor: William T. Reynolds
Technical Illustrators: Marilyn Krieger, Salinda Tyson
Cover photos: © Eileen Christelow (sides), Barbara Paup (center)/Jeroboam, Inc.

Printed in the United States of America
2 3 4 5 6 7 8 9 10–88 87 86 85 84

ISBN 0-534-02814-4

Library of Congress Cataloging in Publication Data

Lofland, John.
    Analyzing social settings.

    Bibliography: p.
    Includes index.
    1. Sociology—Research. 2. Social sciences—Research.
3. Sociology—Methodology. I. Lofland, Lyn H. II. Title.
HM48.L63 1984   301'.072   83–10346
ISBN 0-534-02814-4

To Erving Goffman

1922–1982

Credits

Agatha Christie, *Murder in Three Acts,* New York: Popular Library, 1934; material on page 39 reprinted by permission of Dodd, Mead and Company, Inc. and Hughes Massie Limited.

Melville Dalton, *Men Who Manage,* New York: Wiley, 1959; material on pages 86–87 reprinted by permission of John Wiley & Sons, Inc.

Erving Goffman, *Asylums,* copyright © 1961 by Erving Goffman; material on pages 88 and 102 reprinted by permission of Doubleday & Company, Inc.

Ritchie P. Lowry, *Who's Running This Town?,* New York: Harper & Row, 1965; material on pages 54–55 reprinted by permission of Ritchie P. Lowry.

Sarah H. Matthews, *The Social World of Old Women,* © 1979 by Sage Publications, Inc.; material on pages 55–56 reprinted by permission of Sage Publications, Inc. and Sarah H. Matthews.

Julius Roth, "Comments on 'Secret Observation'," *Social Problems,* Winter 1962; material on pages 23, 24 reprinted by permission of the Society for the Study of Social Problems and Julius Roth.

Barrie Thorne, "Political Activist as Participant Observer," *Symbolic Interaction,* Spring 1979; material on page 35 reprinted by permission of the Society for the Study of Symbolic Interaction.

Rosalie H. Wax, *Doing Fieldwork,* Chicago: The University of Chicago Press, 1971; material on pages 16, 27, 32, 36, 46 reprinted by permission of The University of Chicago Press.

William F. Whyte, *Street Corner Society,* Chicago: The University of Chicago Press, 1955; material on pages 41, 42 reprinted by permission of The University of Chicago Press.

Contents
in Brief

Contents

2

FOCUSING DATA   *69*

Chapter 7 / Asking Questions *93*

3   ANALYZING DATA   *129*

GUIDING CONSEQUENCES *153*

List of Figures

Preface

People familiar with the initial edition of this manual may find it helpful to have an explanation of how this revision is similar to and different from it.

Our primary goal is still to assist people in *doing* qualitative data collection and analysis. The most conspicuous change in our approach to this goal is the reordering of the materials into a sequence of tasks, to be performed roughly in the order they become problematic in research. This is quite different from the original edition, which discussed qualitative analysis at the outset, followed by data collection techniques and the mechanics of analysis.

In this resequencing, none of the basic topics covered in the original have been deleted. Rather, we have enlarged this edition to include several new topics, and the discussions of many of the old topics have been expanded. The principal additions and enlargements are as follows:

▶ The initial edition said very little about the social relations aspects of participant observation and intensive interviewing. We have included a full-scale treatment of these aspects in the new chapters called "Getting In" and "Getting Along." Here, we have especially tried to address ethical questions.

▶ A new first chapter ("Starting Where You Are") stresses the importance of *personally* caring about what is being researched.

▶ A new concluding chapter ("Guiding Consequences") strives to set the research process in larger social and ethical contexts of *relevance* to the researcher.

▶ The question "what is interesting research?" is now raised (in Chapter 8).

▶ This edition's Part Two ("Focusing Data") contains basically the same material as the old Part One ("Qualitative Analysis"), but it has been extensively rearranged and—we believe—simplified. The six "units" described in the old Chapter 2 have been assimilated into the eleven more sophisticated "thinking units" of Chapter 6. The "static" and "phase" analysis ideas from the old Chapter 2 have been consolidated with the "causes and consequences" of the old Chapter 3 to become part of the seven questions around which Chapter 7 ("Asking Questions") is organized.

▶ Throughout, we have revised the prose, deleted examples that are now out of date, and called on the best of the most recent studies and methodological commentaries.

▶ Unlike the original, this edition has a comprehensive and current bibliography.

Otherwise, and to repeat, virtually all of the original *Analyzing* is still here. We have simply expanded the coverage and streamlined the presentation. It is our earnest hope that previous users will find these revisions and enlargements helpful.

Acknowledgments

The debts we wish to acknowledge vary as to how specific they are to this book.

We desire first to express gratitude for the support of a number of colleagues who have not been specifically involved in producing this particular work. However, through conversations, admonitions, off-hand remarks, publications, and examples, they have had an important hand in it "once removed." For brevity's sake, we list only their names: Herbert Blumer, Fred Davis, Barney Glaser, Erving Goffman, John Irwin, Anselm Strauss, Jacqueline Wiseman and Morris Zelditch, Jr.

This volume is dedicated to Erving Goffman, our mentor and friend, who died in 1982 at age 60. He was to us the most outstanding practitioner of, and advocate for, naturalistic inquiry in social science. We grieve his premature passing.

As indicated in the preceding notes, this edition has been considerably revised from the original. These revisions have not arisen in a vacuum, but have grown in the course of working with students struggling to do qualitative field research. This book is a direct product of our efforts to help such students—it is a distillation of what we have learned from them about what has seemed most useful and important. Thus, perhaps our most important debt is to the hundreds of undergraduate and graduate students at the University of California, Davis, who have, over the course of more than a decade, "tried out" and reacted to a succession of formulations of these materials. We wish to thank them for all their patience and tenacity and to express regret that there are too many of them to name individually.

A manual of this sort can emerge only out of the accumulated data collection and analytic experiences of generations of naturalistic researchers. We owe a special debt to all the men and women whose writings have formed the "data base" for our efforts. They are listed in the bibliography.

Finally, a number of persons have provided very direct assistance. Kathy Charmaz painstakingly and expertly examined the entire manuscript in detail, provided much salient commentary, and rescued us from many misstatements and ambiguities. The detailed and constructive suggestions of James Cramer, Gary Hamilton, Patrick Jackson and Carl Sundholm on the "Focusing Data" chapters were extremely helpful. Several anonymous reviewers have assisted us significantly in sharpening the text. We thank them and the two editors who arranged their assistance, Larry J. Wilson and William Oliver. Mary Arbogast and Bill Reynolds edited our too often involuted and excessively qualified prose into cleaner and more pointed text. Leland Moss guided us through the production process with grace and tact. And Doris Craven patiently and precisely typed and retyped our multicolored scrawlings on complicated and pasted-up draft pages.

Analyzing
Social Settings

Introduction:
The Aim and Organization
of This Guide

This book offers a practical guide to the analysis of ongoing social settings through **qualitative social research.** Qualitative research uses the data *collection* techniques of participant observation and/or intensive interviewing and data *analysis* techniques that are nonquantitative.

I. AUDIENCES

Although by training and affiliation we are sociologists, our manual treats qualitative social research as a trans- or inter-disciplinary activity and *not* as the special province of sociologists. Indeed, the research practices we describe are used in at least a dozen theoretical and applied disciplines with excellent effects. Aside from anthropology, political science, and history, qualitative research methods are used in such diverse fields as administration, communications, criminal justice, labor relations, nursing, and social work.

II. OVERVIEW: FOUR CLUSTERS OF ASPECTS

Based on our own teaching experiences and on suggestions made regarding the first edition of this book, we have found it useful to divide the research process into eleven "aspects," which are themselves grouped into four "clusters" of concern. These clusters and aspects are discussed in roughly the same order they become problematic in an investigation.

The first cluster addresses the *gathering* of data in natural settings (Part One).
The second cluster is concerned with *focusing* the data in a social scientific fashion (Part Two).

The third cluster concentrates on the processes of *analyzing* data and organizing them into reportable form (Part Three).

A last "cluster," consisting of a single aspect, deals with *guiding the consequences* of qualitative social research (Part Four).

III. ELEVEN ASPECTS OF QUALITATIVE SOCIAL RESEARCH

In order to provide a holistic overview of the research process, the eleven aspects may themselves be "capsulized."

1. Qualitative social research encourages you to *start where you are*— to use your current situation or past involvement as a topic of research. The advantages and disadvantages of doing this, and related matters are discussed in Chapter 1.

2. Some settings are more amenable to particular research techniques than others; therefore, a process of *evaluating data sites* in terms of appropriateness and access is necessary. Guidelines for doing this are given in Chapter 2.

3. Sometimes *getting into* a relevant site can be problematic. The mode of entry must be decided in terms of the social, political, legal and ethical considerations discussed in Chapter 3.

4. Once you have begun, the relationship between the research and its setting will provide a continual array of problems for you to deal with. These problems of *getting along* are considered in Chapter 4.

5. The main substantive activity of the researcher is *logging data.* Two principal logging methods are interview write-ups and field notes. Chapter 5 provides detailed instructions for doing both of these.

6. In Chapter 6, we call attention to the need to decide the level or form of social setting that will be the focus of the analysis. To this end we describe eleven basic *units* of social organizations in ascending order of "scale," including such familiar entities as social roles, groups, and lifestyles.

7. It is necessary to ask one or more *questions* about whatever unit or units are selected. Seven major classes of possible questions are outlined in Chapter 7.

8. Creativity is a factor that is difficult to depict but indispensable in doing research. In Chapter 8 we discuss the problem of *being interesting* and suggest some generic techniques commonly employed to engage audience interest.

9. While focusing the data, the researcher is simultaneously and subsequently *developing the analysis* by means of certain physical devices, such as coding or filing small pieces of the analysis. These and related tasks are explained in Chapter 9.

10. The process of *writing reports* has a logic and a social psychology of its own. In Chapter 10 we offer some physical and organizational

"tricks" to facilitate this work and suggest features to strive for in written reports.

11. Finally, you have the task of *guiding the consequences* that may follow from your research. In Chapter 11, we discuss these consequences at the levels of the researcher's personal life, immediate associates, the people studied, the foes of the people studied, social knowledge, and the wider world.

IV. COMPETING LABELS FOR QUALITATIVE SOCIAL RESEARCH

We have labeled the matters just described as *qualitative social research*. However, not all social scientists use the same labels in the same ways. Social science is a terminological jungle where many labels compete, and no single label has been able to command the particular domain before us. Often, especially in political science and occasionally in psychology, researchers simply "do it" without worrying about giving "it" a name. Anthropologists provide us with the term for which, historically, the strongest case can be made, and that term is *fieldwork*. But as matters have developed in anthropology and other disciplines, *fieldwork* no longer captures all the salient qualities that we consider relevant. In sociology, our own discipline, the *fieldwork* label has some currency, but there are many competitors that connote important additional ideas: *qualitative methods, fieldwork interactionism, grounded theory, the Chicago school of ethnography, naturalism,* and *West Coast interactionism.*

We point to the existence of this nomenclature chaos in order to help orient those readers who delve into items we cite and into other publications on specific topics being researched. Being aware of the "terminological jungle" should make it possible to look beyond the labels to the activities in which the researchers actually engage. (Brief histories of this many-labeled tradition are provided by R. Wax, 1971: Chapter 3 and Burgess, 1982; Emerson, 1981a reviews some recent developments within it.)

V. NATURALISM

Among the diversity of labels we could use, *qualitative social research* is probably the most general, encompassing, and widely accepted; therefore, we employ it often in this guide (cf. Bogdan & Taylor, 1975). Personally, however, we have a fondness for the term *naturalism,* or *naturalistic research.* This term has a tradition (for example, Matza, 1969; Blumer, 1969; Denzin, 1971; J. Lofland, 1967) and possesses transdisciplinary neutrality. Further, it suggests an appropriate linkage to *naturalist,* as that word is used in field biology. From the realms of philosophical discourse, it has acquired the connotation of minimizing the presuppositions with which one approaches the empirical world—a laudable resonance indeed. Moreover, as a literary genre, *naturalism* involves a close and searching description of the mundane details of everyday life, a meaning we seek to foster in the social science context. Both denotatively and connotatively, then, we consider it a richer and more significant label than *qualitative social research*.

In these chapters we pay homage to more general usage by referring often to *qualitative social research* and sometimes to *fieldwork*. However, we also frequently use our personal favorite. We trust that these minor inconsistencies will not prove confusing.

PART ONE

Gathering Data

Five aspects of gathering data form the initial phase of naturalistic research:

The readiness to start where you are (Chapter 1)

The preference for rich sites of direct, face-to-face engagement where intimate familiarity is acquired (Chapter 2)

The need to deal with difficulties in entry (Chapter 3)

The existence of serious problems in relating to the people being studied (Chapter 4)

The logging motif of data collection (Chapter 5)

Starting
Where You Are

The naturalistic approach to social research fosters a pronounced willingness, even commitment, on the part of the investigator to orient to her or his own extrasocial scientific concerns; that is, to the concerns which you *bring to* the situation of doing social analysis. Your concerns may overlap or be the same as the codified concerns of social science, certainly. But you must first determine what it is you care about *independent* of social science. If that determination coincides with what is already deemed of interest in the relevant disciplines, fine. If it does not, that is fine, too.

These extrasocial scientific primary concerns may be of one of two types or both. There are the concerns born of the *accidents of current biography*, and there are the concerns born of *accidents of remote biography and personal history.*

I. CURRENT BIOGRAPHY

A job; a physical mishap; the development, loss or maintenance of an intimate relationship; an illness; an enjoyed activity; a living arrangement—all these and many other possible circumstances may provide you with a topic you care about enough to study. It is important to emphasize that it is not only that these accidents of current biography may give you physical and/or psychological *access* to social settings, (although this is crucial—see Riemer, 1977, on varieties of what he calls "opportunistic research"; see also Prus, 1980:134–5). Such access becomes the starting point for meaningful naturalistic research only when it is accompanied by some degree of *interest* or concern.

Many social science research projects have had their genesis in current biography. Some particularly striking examples are listed in Figure 1-1, where we have also tried to show the variety of situations out of which social analyses grow.

II. REMOTE BIOGRAPHY AND PERSONAL HISTORY

The concerns you bring to the doing of social analysis may also arise from accidents of remote biography and personal history—of residence, ethnicity, gender, sexual preference, past identities or experiences, family customs, class of origin, religion, and so forth. For example, the fact that most of the work on gender roles is currently being done by women is hardly coincidental. John Irwin's interest in *The Felon* (1970) and in *Prisons in Turmoil* (1980) was intimately related to his own felony conviction at the age of 21 and the five years he spent in a California state prison. Samuel Heilman's study of *Synagogue Life* (1976)

was made easier . . . by the fact that I had all my life participated in the life of Orthodox Jewry . . . [and the study] was an opportunity both to examine my own traditions in ways I had never before considered and to present them to students of society in a novel way. (Heilman, 1976:x, xi.)

In Heilman's study, current and remote biography were fortuitously combined, for he had joined the synagogue he studied some time before the research was even conceived. And Helena Znaniecki Lopata tells us that her interest in American women as members of a unique, highly urbanized and industrialized society

undoubtedly came from my having been socialized in a different society, Poland, and from having come to this country during World War II. As a budding sociologist, I became fascinated by the gap between the image American women had of themselves and others had of them, on the one hand, and the competence and creativity with which they performed their roles, on the other hand. (Lopata, 1980:68.)

Out of her interest have emerged such works as *Occupation: Housewife* (1971); *Widowhood in an American City* (1973); and *Women as Widows: Support Systems* (1979).

It is often rumored among sociologists that, as sociologists, we "make problematic" in our research matters that are problematic in our lives. With the proviso that the connection between self and study may be a subtle and sophisticated one, not at all apparent to an outside observer, we would argue that there is considerable truth to this rumored assertion. In fact, much of the best work in sociology and other social sciences—within the naturalistic tradition and within other research traditions as well—is probably grounded in the remote and/or current biographies of its creators. That such linkages frequently are not publicly acknowledged is understandable—the norms of scholarship do not require that researchers bare their souls, only their procedures.

Figure 1-1 Examples of "Starting Where You Are"

This person:	starting where he or she was:	developed this published social analysis:
Jacqueline Wiseman	a long-time patron of secondhand clothing stores	"Close Encounters of the Quasi-Primary Kind: Sociability in Urban Second-Hand Clothing Stores" (1979)
Julius Roth	a patient in a tuberculosis hospital	*Timetables: Structuring the Passage of Time in Hospital Treatment and Other Careers* (1963)
Barrie Thorne	an antiwar activist in the Boston area during the 1960s	"Protest and the Problem of Credibility" (1975a) and "Women in the Draft Resistance Movement" (1975b)
Fred Davis	working as a cab driver while in graduate school at the University of Chicago	"The Cabdriver and His Fare: Facets of a Fleeting Relationship" (1959)
Catherine Schmidt	a travel agent trainee with an agency in Centereach, New York	"The Guided Tour: Insulated Adventure" (1979)
Max Heirich	a graduate student in sociology at the University of California, Berkeley when the "free speech" movement began there	*The Spiral of Conflict: Demonstrations at Berkeley 1964–65* (1971)
Marvin Scott	a horseracing aficionado	*The Racing Game* (1968)

III. TRADITION AND JUSTIFICATION

Within the naturalistic tradition, the positive evaluation of "starting where you are" has a long history. Speaking of Robert Park—one of the founding fathers of the naturalistic tradition—and of his work with sociology graduate students at the University of Chicago in the 1920s and 1930s, Everett Hughes has related that

Most of these people didn't have any sociological background. . . . They didn't come in to become sociologists. They came in to learn something and Park picked up whatever it was in their experience which he could build on. . . . He took these people and he brought out of them whatever he could find there. *And he brought out of them very often something they themselves did not know was there.* They might be Mennonites who were just a little unhappy . . . about wearing plain clothes . . . girls who didn't like to wear long dresses and funny little caps; . . . or children of

Orthodox Jews who really didn't like to wear beards anymore (that was a time of escaping a beard, the beard was the symbol of your central Russian origin and you wanted to get it off). And he got hold of people and emancipated them from something that was inherently interesting but which they regarded as a cramp. *And he turned this "cramping orthodoxy" into something that was of basic and broad human interest.* And that was the case for a lot of these people. *He made their pasts interesting to them, much more interesting than they ever thought they could be.* (L. Lofland, [ed.], 1980:267–268, emphasis added.)

As we shall see in following chapters, starting where you are may cause methodological and ethical difficulties. We believe, however, that any such difficulties are a small price to pay for the very creative wellsprings of the naturalistic approach. "Starting where you are" provides the necessary meaningful linkages between the personal and emotional, on the one hand, and the stringent intellectual operations to come, on the other. Without a foundation in personal sentiment all the rest easily becomes so much ritualistic, hollow cant. Julius Roth (1966) has written persuasively of the dangers of "hired hand research," of the dismal work performance of alienated labor in the scholarship business. But alienation is not limited to occasions of following someone else's agenda. If *your* agenda is not personally meaningful, you may be alienated from it as well. Unless you are emotionally engaged in your work, the inevitable boredom, confusion, and frustration of rigorous scholarship will make even the completion—much less the quality—of the project problematic.

Evaluating
Data Sites

Having identified a personally meaningful interest—in a group, a situation, a setting, a question, a topic, whatever—the naturalistic investigator must then decide how best (in the sense of "how most fruitfully") to pursue this interest. This requires an assessment of the most appropriate or most feasible "wheres" and "hows" and "whens" of the research.

We do not mean to suggest that all decisions regarding the research are, even initially, "up for grabs." As a student, for example, you may be required to write about a particular setting; that is, the "where" of your research may be largely predetermined. Or your interests may logically imply one sort of "how" rather than another.

Nonetheless, regardless of the degree of freedom you have, the process of evaluating data sites is crucial. If it is not crucial in making your own decisions, it may at least be important in terms of understanding the implications of decisions that are already made.

I. THE OVERALL GOAL

Your overall goal is to collect the *richest possible data*. Rich data mean, ideally, a wide and diverse range of information collected over a relatively prolonged period of time. And for the naturalist, that collection is achieved, again ideally, through direct, face-to-face contact with, and prolonged immersion in, some social location or circumstance. You wish, that is, to earn "intimate familiarity" with that sector of social life which has "tickled" your interest (J. Lofland, 1976:Chapter Two).

The naturalistic penchant for *direct* observation and apprehension of the social world reflects a certain **epistemology**, that is, a theory of knowledge. The central tenents of this theory are (1) that face-to-face interaction is the fullest condition of participating in the mind of another human being, and (2) that you must participate in the mind of another human being (in sociological terms, "take the role of the other") in order to acquire social knowledge. Whatever the barriers to the validity of direct knowledge of others (and they may be numerous), they are as nothing compared to the difficulties engendered by indirect perception. (For important segments of this epistemology, see Schutz, 1967, especially Chapter 4 and Sections C and D; Bruyn, 1983; Berger & Luckman, 1967, especially pp. 28–34; and Cooley, 1926.)

As noted in the Introduction, we shall, in this manual, be concerned primarily with those two interrelated methods most closely associated with the naturalistic preference for direct apprehension: participant observation and intensive interviewing. We recognize, however, that many matters of interest to potential investigators, many questions or topics or settings or situations, will simply not be available through these methods. There will be matters that you cannot "reach" through direct apprehension—historical settings or events, for example, or the actions of very large units, like political systems. For these research problems, other manuals are to be recommended. (See, for example, Bertaux, [ed.], 1981; Brewer & Hunter, 1983; McCoy, 1974; Shafer, 1969; Smelser, 1976.) There will also be matters whose direct apprehension requires neither participant observation nor intensive interviewing, as these terms are traditionally understood. If you are interested in the themes of symbolic productions—conceptions of women, say, or images of urban life—you might be best advised to use novels or works of art or television shows or magazine advertisements for your data (see, for example, Goffman, 1979). For that sort of research, some of what we discuss in the following pages ("getting in" and "getting along" especially) will be of little value. But most of the matters discussed here should apply equally well to analysts of human cultural *productions* and to researchers of human cultural *producers*.

II. PARTICIPANT OBSERVATION AND INTENSIVE INTERVIEWING

Also known as "field observation," "qualitative observation," or "direct observation," **participant observation** refers to the process in which an investigator establishes and sustains a many-sided and relatively long-term relationship with a human association in its natural setting for the purpose of developing a scientific understanding of that association. This may not be the person's sole purpose for being present in the setting, but it is at least an important one. **Intensive interviewing,** also known as "unstructured interviewing," is a guided conversation whose goal is to elicit from the interviewee rich, detailed materials that can be used in qualitative analysis. In contrast to "structured interviewing" (such as opinion polling), where the goal is to elicit choices between alternative answers to preformed questions on a topic or situation, the intensive interview seeks to *discover* the informant's *experience* of a particular topic or situation. Among other contrasts, the structured interview seeks to determine the frequency of preconceived kinds of things, while the unstructured interview seeks to find out what kinds of things exist in the first place.

The literature on qualitative methodology has traditionally distinguished rather sharply between participant observation and intensive interviewing (see, for example, Becker & Geer, 1970; J. Lofland, 1976), frequently viewing the former as the preeminent method, the latter as a pale substitute. We believe this distinction to be overdrawn and any invidious comparison unwarranted. As many anthropological accounts make clear, doing participant observation in another culture involves a great deal of native informant interviewing (Berreman, 1962; Golde, 1970; Powdermaker, 1966; R. Wax, 1971). And as W. Gordon West has noted, a review of sociological field reports suggests that "the bulk of participant observation data is probably gathered through informal interviews and supplemented by observation" (1980:39).

Classic participant observation, then, always involves the interweaving of looking and listening (Schatzman & Strauss, 1973:Chapters 4 & 5), of watching and asking—and some of that listening and asking may approach or be identical to intensive interviewing. Conversely, intensive interview studies may involve repeated and prolonged contact between researchers and informants, sometimes extending over a period of years, with considerable mutual involvement in personal lives—a characteristic often considered a hallmark of participant observation (Bodgan, 1980; Charmaz, 1981; Rubin, 1981). Additionally, as we shall see, many social situations can be directly apprehended *only* through intensive interviewing. Thus, rather than being a poor substitute for participant observation, intensive interviewing is frequently the method of choice.

For these reasons, then, we wish to emphasize the *mutuality* of participant observation and intensive interviewing as the central techniques of the naturalistic investigator. In what follows, we shall distinguish between them where it is necessary to do so, but most of our discussion is applicable to both. (A considerable number of general treatments of participant observation, intensive interviewing, or both are available. Among these are: Bogdan and Taylor, 1975; Burgess, 1982; Dexter, 1970; Douglas, 1976; Emerson, 1983; Glazer, 1972; Gordon, 1975; McCall & Simmons, 1969; Schatzman & Strauss, 1973; Schwartz & Jacobs, 1979; Smith & Manning, 1982; Spradley, 1980, 1979; Williams, 1967.)

III. DETAILED ASSESSMENT OF DATA SITES

Assuming, then, that you wish to gather the richest possible data, using participant observation, intensive interviewing, or some combination of the two, potential data sites need to be evaluated for appropriateness, for access, and for ethics.

A. Evaluating for Appropriateness

Questions constrain research locations; research locations constrain questions; methodological preferences and topics constrain both, and so on. The point is that "starting where you are" is likely to set some parameters around what will be appropriate, and these need to be assessed. While the naturalistic tradition in social science puts a premium on flexibility, it is simply a fact that some questions, research locations, topics or methods logically necessitate other questions, locations, topics or methods. If you have decided to rely solely on observation of persons in public places, for example, you will not be able to collect many useful data on emotional states and processes. Or, if you are interested in body management strategies in public interaction, intensive interviewing is hardly an appropriate tool, since the data you need are largely outside individual awareness. Doing research with children in a nursery school will yield little of value about day-to-day interaction of school administrators. And you will not be able to learn about the grief experience by participant observation in a group with a low death or other attrition rate.

All of this may seem obvious, if not simpleminded. Yet, as anyone who has read any reasonable number of *unpublished* social science works (by professionals as well as by students) can testify, a fair portion of research appears to proceed without any noticeable awareness of, or appreciation for, the problems of appropriateness.

The circumstances of potential research projects are too diverse to yield many specific "principles" of appropriateness. We can, however, offer three general rules.

First, participant observation, used alone, is probably most fruitful when the question, topic or situation you are interested in is physically located somewhere, at least temporarily. If you wish, for example, to study a new housing development (Gans, 1967), to observe behavior in some public space (Karp, 1973; Sundholm, 1973), or to investigate the way staff members of an intensive care unit handle death (Coombs & Goldman, 1973), observation will likely yield the richest data most efficiently.

Second, and conversely, you may be interested in what Joseph Kotarba has called "amorphous social experiences—those facets of everyday life that are unique to individuals and not [to] specific kinds of settings . . . [those] existential experiences of self, rich in their social forms. . . ." (1980:57). In that event, intensive interviewing or interviewing combined with limited observation may be the most felicitous, possibly the *only* way to proceed. Examples of amorphous social experiences include having chronic back pain (Kotarba, 1977); being the widow of a suicide (Wallace, 1973); being chronically ill (Charmaz, 1980); being a mugging victim (Lejeune & Alex, 1973) or performing a mugging (Lejeune, 1977); and returning home from Vietnam (Faulkner & McGaw, 1977).

Third, always consider the possible appropriateness of new or little-used variants of the standard research methods. Zimmerman and Wieder (1977), for example, have reported on the field procedure of the **diary/diary-interview** method. The technique uses diaries as observational logs maintained by the person being studied, which are then, in turn, used as a basis for intensive interviews. They recommend the technique in situations "where the problems of direct observation resist solution or where further or more extended observation strains available resources . . . [that is,] when the investigator is unable to make firsthand observations or wishes to supplement those already collected" (1977:481). As another example, you might consider **group interviews** in place of, or as a supplement to, one-to-one interviews (see, for example, Irwin, 1970:4–5). Group interviewing may be most productive on topics that are reasonably public and are not matters of any particular embarrassment. It has the advantage of allowing people more time to reflect and to recall experiences; also, something that one person mentions can spur memories and opinions in others. Moreover, by allowing moments of not having to talk, of being able to listen to others, group interviewing allows each person to rethink and amend any initial account that, upon reflection, seems in need of amplification, qualification, amendment, or contradiction. Finally, people may not agree with one another on matters of opinion, providing instances of interchange between contrasting perspectives. (For further reading on evaluating for appropriateness, see Schatzman and Strauss, 1973:19–21.)

B. Evaluating for Access

We, as liberals, humanists, Christians, or whatever, like to believe that all humans have equal access to the minds of all other humans—that in our shared humanity, we are more like than unlike. But a realistic appraisal of any proposed research necessitates our recognizing that, in combination, the attributes of the investigator, of the setting or situation to be studied, and/or of the persons to be learned about may create barriers to the acquisition of rich data. As part of your general task of evaluting data sites, then, you must be concerned with the possible existence of such barriers, with assessing their seriousness, and with considering if or how they can be overcome. In fact, in the literature of qualitative methodology, **access** is probably one of the most written about of topics—understandably so, for it remains problematic throughout the entire period of research. As such, we shall be encountering it again in subsequent pages, especially in Chapters 3 and 4. Even then, however, we shall not have exhausted the topic, for the possible combinations of investigator, setting, and participant attributes generate an almost endless litany of discrete "access situations." Our more limited and realistic goal here and in later pages is to provide you, the investigator considering your own particular access situation, with some "food for thought."

In the current context of data site evaluation, we shall consider three problem areas: investigator relationship to setting; ascriptive categories of researcher and researched; and difficult settings.

1. **Investigator Relationship to Setting.** In a penetrating and insightful essay, Fred Davis (1973) has written about two opposing orientations or stances a researcher might take toward what he or she is studying. Conceived metaphorically as the "Martian" and the "Convert," these stances capture the "dilemma of distance" encountered by all researchers. The "Martian" sees distance as a passageway to knowing, the "Convert" views it as a barrier.

The Martian . . . yearns to grasp the human situation with wholly fresh or, better yet, strange eyes, in a blush of wonderment as it were. In order to do this he wants to divest himself completely of the vast array of unwitting cultural assumptions, rules of thumb, modes of sensibility and—were it somehow possible—the very language, which comprise the "cognitive stuff" of our everyday worlds and beings. . . . In contrast to the Martian's desire to escape and stand wholly outside the social ontological frame of his subjects in order to see how the frame is constructed, the Convert's overriding impulse is to immerse himself ever more deeply *within* the frame so that the distinctive subjective currents of the group may forcibly and directly reveal themselves to him. (F. Davis, 1973:336, 338.)

Davis's metaphorical creatures represent very real methodological preferences and debates about those preferences within the social sciences. More profoundly, however, they symbolize a tension which many researchers feel *within themselves*. To ask questions of, to "make problematic," to "bracket" social life requires distance (Martian). To understand, to answer questions, to make sense of social life requires closeness (Convert). The sensitive investigator wishes not to be one or the other but to be *both or either* as the research demands.

The point for the prospective investigator assessing for access is simply this: If you are already (or will become) a member in the setting, you almost "naturally" possess (or will possess) the convert stance. You have easy access to understanding. You need, therefore, to seek mechanisms for distancing. Conversely, if you are an outsider to the setting, a stranger to the social life under investigation, your access to questioning will be equally natural. You need, then, to seek mechanisms for reducing that distance. The moral is this: Be neither discouraged nor overconfident about your relationship to the setting. Whatever that relationship, it is simultaneously an advantage and a drawback.

2. **Ascriptive Categories of Researcher and Researched.** Many social orders define ascriptive categories—for example, gender, age, ethnicity—as important points of difference among people. Therefore, in this limited sense, "who" the researcher is, in contrast with "who" the researched are, may throw up barriers to the acquisition of rich data. As Rosalie Wax describes the problem:

. . . Many tribal or folk societies not only maintain a strict division of labor between the sexes and ages, but the people who fall into these different categories do not converse freely or spontaneously with each other even when they eat, sleep and live in the same dwelling. For example, a young male anthropologist might live in an Indian household and even carry on with the Indian girls and yet learn very little about what women—old or young—think, say or do. . . . Conversely, I, as a middle-aged woman, was never able to converse openly or informally with either the old or the young Indian men at Thrashing Buffalo. The older men, even when I knew them fairly well, would tend to deliver lectures to me; the younger men, as was proper, were always too bashful or formally respectful to say much. With the Indian matrons, on the other hand, I could talk for hours. (R. Wax, 1971:46.)

Wax is writing about a special situation of doing research with tribal or folk groups, but her general point is equally applicable to doing research among modern populations in industrialized societies. If you are black, studying Ku Klux Klan members and sympathizers will probably not be feasible. Nor are you likely to reach the desired "intimate familiarity" if you are male and attempting to study a radical lesbian group. (See further Easterday, et al., 1977; L. Lofland, 1975; Mann, 1970; Warren & Rasmussen, 1977.)

While identity category barriers to acquiring rich data are unquestionably real and should be taken into account in planning your research, they should not be *overemphasized*. Just because you are not "identical" to the persons you wish to study, you should not automatically conclude that such research is impossible, or even unusually difficult. The literature of the naturalistic tradition resoundingly contradicts any such conclusion. Being female, for example, did not prevent Carol A. B. Warren from performing a sensitive analysis of gay men (1974). Being an adult did not deny Gary Fine intimate access to the world of small boys (1980, 1979, 1976; Fine & Glassner, 1979; Kleinman & Fine, 1979). Being young was not an insurmountable barrier for Sarah Matthews in learning about old women (1979, 1976), nor for Victor Marshall in studying a retirement community (1976, 1975). Being white did not prevent Elliot Liebow (1967) from producing a classic ethnography of the world of black streetcorner men. Being Jewish proved no particular difficulty to Sherryl Kleinman in her research with ministerial students of the United Methodist Church (1981, 1980; Kleinman & Fine, 1979). And the rich literature of anthropology is certainly convincing testimony to the human capacity to transcend ethnic and cultural differences.

3. **Difficult Settings.** Some settings or aspects of social life are easier to research than others. Gathering rich data through observation in bus depots or other open public settings (L. Lofland, 1973, 1972) or in bars and taverns (Allon, 1979; Cavan, 1966; LeMasters, 1973), for example, can usually be accomplished with a minimum of misadventure. Doing so in a highly conflict-ridden prison (J. B. Jacobs, 1974), in the midst of political strife (R. Wax, 1971:Part IV), or during civil war (Joseph, 1983, 1978)—that is, in situations of conflict internal to the setting—may be extraordinarily difficult. Conflicts between the people being studied and the larger society may also generate "difficult settings." The suspicion, fear, protectiveness or demand for allegiance that are the by-products of such conflict are very likely to interfere with data collection (see, for example, J. Lofland, 1977:Appendix; Thorne, 1979). But even in the absence of immediate conflict, pieces of social life may be so shrouded in mystery that merely knowing about them, much less gaining intimate familiarity with them, may be problematic. Examples include the day-to-day workings of a segment of the Central Intelligence Agency, the details of the business dealings of the economically powerful, and the arcane rituals of such otherwise innocuous groups as Masons and Greek letter societies.

While we consider it appropriate for the prospective investigator to assess the possible difficulties inherent in the setting of interest, we do not wish to suggest that you should necessarily avoid difficult settings. The difficulty may, on closer inspection, turn out to be illusory. But even if it is real, difficulty does not necessarily equal impossibility. And if the setting or situation is an especially significant or interesting one, even a partial study of it will be better than none at all. The well-known belief in social science that it is easier to "study down" than to "study up" (that is, to study the less powerful rather than the more powerful) probably has some basis in fact. But that belief has also undoubtedly discouraged the execution of studies that would contradict it. Premature foreclosures such as this do a disservice to social science and to social knowledge in general and should be avoided. You should bear in mind that numerous social groups popularly presumed to be difficult to "get to" have been studied well—for example, physicians (Freidson, 1970), elite surgeons (Bosk, 1979), middle-class "closet" gay males (Warren, 1974), corporate managers (Kanter, 1977), and the higher echelons of the American liquor industry (Denzin, 1978).

C. Evaluating for Ethics

Ethical problems, questions and dilemmas are an integral part of the research experience (especially the naturalistic research experience)—no more than in everyday life, certainly, but also no less. We shall repeatedly be concerned with ethical matters in following chapters, for they are especially acute, or at least acutely *felt*, while the research is in progress. Here, in the context of data site evaluation, two critical and closely related questions require the prospective investigator's serious consideration. First, should this particular group, setting, situation, question, or whatever be studied by *anyone?* Second, should this group, setting, situation, question, or whatever be studied by *me?* In asking these questions of yourself, you are assessing the *potential negative consequences* (see Chapter 11) that the research or its publication might have for various parties (including yourself) and your ethical evaluation of these consequences.

Traditionally in social science neither question was problematic. Rather, the conventional wisdom held that knowledge was *always* better than ignorance and that, therefore, everything that could be studied should be studied by anyone who had or could obtain access. In recent years, however, that conventional wisdom has been challenged.

Relative to the question of *anyone* doing a particular study, two kinds of challenges have been made. First, some have argued that under conditions of economic and/or political oppression of some populations by other populations, the protection of the less powerful may demand that knowledge about them not be made available to the more powerful (for example, Glazer, 1972; Sagarin, 1973; Sjoberg [ed.], 1967). Second, some studies have been called ethically unacceptable because they are "trivial" (for example, aspects of everyday life) or because the subject matter is "immoral" (for example, the act of mugging, Posner, 1980; see replies and commentaries by Lejeune, 1981, 1980; Sagarin, 1980; Cohen, 1980). This second challenge, apparently emanating from a kind of social science "moral majority," we find frivolous and—if taken seriously—a threat to free inquiry. However, in our view, the first challenge is much less easily brushed aside.

In any event, the decision on whether to study or not to study some aspect of social life, and the ethical basis or bases for that decision, are matters that must be left to the individual researcher. This question touches on your particular and personal relation to the group or setting or question, on your value structure, and on the values of other significant and supportive persons. We urge only that your decision be *consciously* made and that you clearly *articulate* to yourself the basis or bases for your decision. We should point out that expressions of personal pain over, serious doubts about, or even regret for having performed research studies have begun to appear in the literature of qualitative methods (for example, Glazer, 1972;

Heilman, 1980; Pepinsky, 1980; Thorne, 1979). Some of these researchers would undoubtedly "do it again," but others would not. We consider it well worth your time to at least ponder the question "whether me" before committing yourself to a specific field project.

IV. A CONCLUDING WORD OF CAUTION

The foregoing words of advice should not be construed as suggesting that problems, issues, ethical dilemmas, strategies for surmounting barriers, and so on, can all be resolved or determined beforehand and that you can then simply proceed, tidily and without difficulty, to put your research plan into practice. Nothing could be further from the truth. Naturalistic research is first and foremost *emergent.* Today's solutions may become tomorrow's problems; tomorrow's problems may provide special research opportunities the day after. "Who" you are at the beginning of the research is not necessarily the same "who" that will emerge at the end. Ethical decisions made before entering the field may prove moot; other unforeseen and perhaps unsolvable dilemmas may arise. This emergent character is what gives "being in the field" its edge, its complexity, its vigor, and, for many people, its excitement (R. Wax, 1971); it also necessitates *flexibility* on the part of the investigator.

You evaluate data sites, then, not because doing so will make your life as investigator a bed of roses. You evaluate data sites because doing so may help to remove a few of the thorns.

Getting In

The process of deciding what is meaningful to study and whether you have (or can gain) ethical and appropriate access to rich data may involve conversations and consultations with others, but the decisions themselves are *personal*. When decision is translated into action, when your intention to do research is translated into beginning that research, then you encounter the first truly *social* moment of naturalistic investigation: **getting in**—gaining the acceptance of the people being studied.

It is one thing to decide for yourself about interest, appropriateness, accessibility and ethics; it is quite another to get all the interested parties to go along with your plan.

In some forms of research, the investigator has considerable power over the research "subjects." Laboratory animal research or medical research with captive human populations are extreme examples. But in the main, naturalistic social research is not one of these forms. In this tradition, you look at and/or listen to people either because the people freely agree to it or because they don't know they are being studied. And since there is little or nothing to stop them from refusing to be interviewed, from denying an observer entree into their lives, or from throwing out or shutting out a secret investigator who is "uncovered," getting in naturally concerns all potential researchers.

The specific form of relationship a prospective investigator has or will develop with the people or setting of interest generates its own set of problems, ethical questions, and solutions regarding the process of entry. The varieties of such relationships have been diversely formulated. Buford Junker's (1960) well-known typology of fieldwork roles—the complete observer, the participant observer, the complete participant, the observer participant—is one example. Schatzman and Strauss (1973) distinguish watching from the outside, passive presence, limited interaction, active control, the observer as participant, and participation with hidden identity. Such elaborate formulations are quite useful in some contexts. But for our purposes, a simpler set of distinctions will suffice.

We shall consider the "getting in" aspect of naturalistic research as experienced (1) by *unknown investigators*, either in *public/open settings* or in *closed settings*, and (2) by *known investigators* who are either *full participants* in the setting or outsiders whose *research role is primary*. We will conclude this chapter by discussing two additionally relevant problems: legal and political barriers, and the question of anonymity.

I. THE UNKNOWN INVESTIGATOR

Getting in is not really a problem if you are not known as a researcher to the people you are studying. You simply take up or continue playing a role in the setting and begin logging data "on the sly." What is problematic is the *ethical status* of covert research itself.

In this section, we consider three types of hidden research. Probably the least controversial form is research conducted in public and open settings. Doing research in a closed setting in which you are already a member is more marginal. The most controversial research arrangement involves taking on a role in a closed setting for the secret purpose of researching it.

Two qualifications are in order before we proceed. First, some forms of naturalistic research cannot be conducted secretly. It *is* possible to interview persons who do not quite understand your exact role as interviewer. (For example, a number of Rosalie Wax's early interviewees in a Japanese internment camp believed that she was a sympathetic newspaper reporter [1971:53].) It is also possible to interview "informally" without letting on that one is doing so (Riecken, 1969). However, it does *not* appear possible to do intensive interviewing (as we define it) covertly. Therefore, the following discussion applies only to participant observation.

Second, while the distinctions we make in this chapter are useful, maybe even necessary, for clarity, actual researchers and settings do not fall into such discrete categories. In the real world, what is a public and open setting and what is a closed one may not be all that obvious. Indeed, as we shall see, the line between open and secret research gets fuzzy when examined closely.

A. Public and Open Settings

If a setting is public and open, that is, defined in law and tradition as a place where "anyone" has a right to be, it is a very simple matter to enter it for purposes of doing research. When Lyn Lofland (1972, 1973) observed public places (for example, waiting areas of bus depots and airports), she simply entered and sat down. In the observational stage of David Unruh's study of a coffee shop (1979b), he began by frequenting the place. Partly because getting into public and open settings presents so few problems, such settings are frequently the training sites for untrained and "unleashed" undergraduates, to use James Myers's term (1969:155).

While it can be argued that such research is clearly unethical—it does, after all, involve deceit by omission if not commission—serious ethical debate seldom lingers on this research situation. Presumably the impossibility, if not the ludicrousness, of removing the deception is one reason. As Julius Roth has noted, "When we are observing a crowd welcoming a hero, it is obviously absurd to say that we should warn everybody in the crowd that a sociologist is interpreting their behavior" (1970:279). The presumption that no harm can come to any of the people observed is another reason. A third, perhaps, is the frequent "ho-hum" attitude of people when they learn they are being researched. Natalie Allon's experience is typical:

When I expressed my intellectual curiosity about the [singles] bars, quite a few male and female patrons laughed me off. They said that I had a most sophisticated, protective defense if I did not wind up meeting a man whom I liked and who liked me. After all, whether or not I succeeded in meeting a man, I would always succeed in collecting information. Some said that doing research was a most clever introductory greeting, and they were going to try such a line as they met others. Some told me to relax and take it easy—I was single and drinking and so a member of the scene just like everybody else. They said that everybody in the scene had ulterior motives and mine happened to be research. (Allon, 1979:68–69.)

B. Closed Settings

The serious ethical questioning about covert research begins when the researcher moves out of the public realm and into the private, that is, into a closed setting, access to which is not granted to just "anybody." Gary Fine has referred to this situation as "deep cover":

In research studies in which subjects are not aware that they are under investigation, the position of the researcher is structurally equivalent to that of the undercover intelligence agent, although presumably there is a different set of motives. In that situation, the researcher may witness a wide variety of behaviors but simultaneously may find it difficult to inquire about any of these behaviors without the cover being suspect. A cover that is blown in such a situation—when subjects discover that their *new member* is actually a professional observer—may have profound implications. This uncovering discredits not only the research . . . but the researcher as well, and perhaps the entire scientific enterprise. (Fine, 1980:124, emphasis added.)

It is precisely the "spy" quality of covert research in closed settings that raises questions about its propriety in social science. In fact, some persons argue that an investigator who takes a position for the purpose of secretly researching the setting is committing the most unethical research act in the naturalistic tradition. Interestingly enough, however, if the research project arises after you have become part of the setting—a frequent corollary of "starting where you are"—the moral onus seems less severe.

Thus some social scientists who equivocate about secret research in settings where one is already "in place," and who find no moral difficulties with doing it in public and open settings, are adamant that entering a setting for the purpose of secret research should not be allowed (Erikson, 1970;

Gibbons & Jones, 1975:Chapter Nine; but see Hilbert, 1980 for a different view). Julius Roth's comments on what might be viewed as moral hair-splitting among social scientists are apt:

> Does the manner in which one comes to be a secret observer affect the morality of the situation? Is it moral if one gets a job in a factory to earn tuition and then takes advantage of the opportunity to carry out a socio-logical study, but immoral to deliberately plant oneself in the factory for the express purpose of observing one's fellow workers? If the outcome is the same—e.g., if the manner in which the observations are used is the same—I for one, see no moral difference in these two situations, but I find some of my colleagues do not agree with this position. (Roth, 1970:279.)

Our view is that there are very serious, perhaps damning, ethical problems in *all* covert research if the presumed immorality of deception is the overriding concern. Deception is no less present in public and open setting research than in preplanned, "deep cover" research in closed settings. On the other hand, if other concerns are also important (for example, lack of harm to those researched, or the theoretical importance of a setting which can never be studied openly), then we can find no more justification for abolishing *all* deep cover research, preplanned or not, than for abolishing secret research in public settings.

As in all other ethical dilemmas of naturalistic research, we believe that the ethically sensitive, thoughtful and knowledgeable investigator is the best judge of whether covert research is justified. The key words here, however, are *sensitive, thoughtful,* and *knowledgeable.* We would suggest that you undertake no covert research (at least none in closed settings) before you have acquainted yourself with the problems, debates and dilemmas associated with such research. You should, at minimum, be familiar with the code of ethics (if any) of your discipline. Beyond that, the following book chapters and sections are recommended as useful introductions to the issues.

Part Six on "Ethical Problems in Field Studies," in William J. Filstead (ed.), *Qualitative Methodology: Firsthand Involvement with the Social World* (1970).

"Sociological Snoopers and Journalistic Moralizers: Retrospective on Ethical Issues," in Laud Humphreys, *Tearoom Trade: Impersonal Sex in Public Places* (1975).

Chapter Seven on "Disguised Participant Observation," in Edward Diener and Rick Crandall, *Ethics in Social and Behavioral Research* (1978).

Chapter XIII on "Deceptive Social Science Research," in Sissela Bok, *Lying: Moral Choice in Public and Private Life* (1978).

Chapter 7 on "Unknowing Participants and Analysis of the Research Dilemma," in Paul Davidson Reynolds, *Ethical Dilemmas and Social Science Research* (1979).

II. THE KNOWN INVESTIGATOR

Writers on naturalistic methodology generally conceive the major entry problems of the known investigator to be *strategic* rather than ethical, implying a rather sharp distinction between open and covert research. For the sake of clarity, this distinction between open and covert research is a useful one. However, it is also essentially artificial. Julius Roth has stated the case most succinctly.

All research is secret in some ways and to some degree—we never tell the subjects "everything". . . . So long as there exists a separation of role between the researchers and those researched upon, the gathering of information will inevitably have some hidden aspects even if one is an openly declared observer. The following are at least some of the reasons for this.

1. The researcher usually does not know everything he is looking for himself when he first starts out and structures his study to some extent as he goes along. Some of the things he finds of interest to study as the research goes on are things which the subjects might have objected to if they had been told about it in the beginning.
2. In many types of study of social behavior, the researcher does not want the subjects' behavior influenced by his knowledge of what the observer is interested in.
3. Even if the subjects of a study are given as precise and detailed an explanation of the purpose and procedure of the study as the investigator is able to give them, the subjects will not understand all the terms of the research in the same way that the investigator does. The terms used have different connotations to them, their experiential contexts differ, and their conceptions of the goals of the study are likely to be different. . . . (Roth, 1970:278–279; see also Fine, 1980; Hilbert, 1980.)

And, Roth might have added, all research is secret to some degree because the people under study do not always remember that the researcher *is* a researcher (Thorne, 1980, 1979).

Bearing in mind, then, that the ethical dilemmas engendered by covert research have not disappeared with the decision to be a known investigator but have merely been muted, let us concentrate on the strategic problem of entry. This differs somewhat depending on whether or not one is already a full participant in the setting.

A. The Participant Researcher Role

The principle of "starting where you are," as we have seen, leads many naturalistic investigators to do research in their own "nests," as it were. If they decide to conduct that research openly, they have the task (as do outside researchers) of making their intentions known, gaining cooperation from the setting participants, and, depending on the character of the setting, perhaps seeking formal permission. The participant researcher, however, has the advantage of already knowing the "cast of characters." The outside researcher must discover whom to ask or tell, whom to ask or tell *first,* whether formal permission is required, whether a letter is necessary, and so forth. To the participant researcher, such knowledge is part of the badge of membership and easily (if not always successfully) put to use.

B. The Outside Researcher Role

The major strategic problem of getting in, then, falls to the outsider seeking admission to a setting for the purpose of observing it or access to individuals for the purpose of interviewing them. Researchers deal with a wide range of topics, settings, and situations, and the types of people who might stand between them and their research are necessarily a varied lot—much too varied for the strategies of getting through or around them to be succinctly codified. The experiences of many fieldworkers over the years, however, suggest that you are more likely to be successful in your quest for access if you enter negotiations armed with *connections, accounts, knowledge* and *courtesy.*

1. **Connections.** There is a great deal of wisdom in the old saying that "it's who you know that counts." Gaining entry to a setting or getting permission to do an interview is greatly expedited if you have "connections." For example, Joan Hoffman, herself a member of a local elite family, attempted to interview elites in her community who were hospital board members.

> Introducing myself as a sociology graduate student, I had very limited success in getting by the gatekeepers of the executive world. Telephone follow-ups to letters sent requesting an interview repeatedly found Mr. X "tied up" or "in conference." When I did manage to get my foot in the door, interviews rarely exceeded a half hour, were continuously interrupted by telephone calls . . . and elicited only "front work" . . ., the public version of what hospital boards were all about. . . . By chance during the interview, my respondent discovered that he knew a member of my family. "Why didn't you say so?" The rest of the interview was dramatically different than all my previous data. (Hoffman, 1980:46.)

> As another example, Sandra Danziger was interested in doctor-patient interaction during pregnancy and childbirth. She found that the difficult task of gaining observational access to these interactions was smoothed by a letter of introduction from her father, a practicing obstetrician/gynecologist (Danziger, 1979:516.)

These examples are by no means exceptional. It seems quite typical for outside researchers to gain access to settings or persons through contacts they have already established. They cast about among their friends, acquaintances, colleagues, and the like for someone who is already favorably regarded by the person or persons with access control. In short, wherever possible, you should try to use *preexisting relations of trust* to remove barriers to entrance.

2. **Accounts.** It is well worth your while to expend time and effort developing a carefully thought-out explanation or account of the proposed research. Whether you are using the method of intensive interviewing or of participant observation, you are asking people to grant access to their lives, their minds, their emotions. They have every reason for wanting to know why they should allow such an intrusion. Judging from the testimony of veteran fieldworkers, the best accounts are brief, straightforward and appropriate to their audience.

▶ Most listeners are not going to be interested in the details of the researcher's "pet" enthusiasm. What they want is a *brief* and direct answer to the question, "Why should I let you _____ ?", not a scholarly treatise. However, you should be prepared to supply more detail if it is asked for. (Often in bureaucratic settings, for example, a written research proposal will be requested.)

▶ While appreciating the truth of Julius Roth's assertion (quoted above) that "we never tell the subjects 'everything'," it is nonetheless advisable to provide an account that is as *straightforward* as you can make it. If you have decided to do "open" research, there is no point in complicating an already complicated situation by starting out with evasions or lies, or with promises (for example, censorship rights) you will not keep. There will be plenty of difficulties in getting along in the field despite the best of intentions and plans. Setting yourself up at the outset for later charges of deceit is simply begging unnecessary trouble.

▶ Finally, accounts should be *appropriate to their audience;* the way the story is told (not the story itself) should be tailored to the people hearing it. What you tell the director of a nursery school and what you tell the children cannot be identical, not if you wish to be straightforward with both the director and the children (on "accounting" to children, see Fine & Glassner, 1979).

Your account is supposed to help you gain initial access to the research site and thus deserves care in its preparation. It would be an error, however, to attach too much importance to it. As Rosalie Wax reminds us:

. . . Most sensible people do not believe what a stranger tells them. In the long run, [the investigator's] hosts will judge and trust him, not because of what he [initially] says about himself or about his research, but by the style in which he lives and acts, by the way he treats them. (R. Wax, 1971:365.)

3. **Knowledge.** One tried-and-true strategy for getting along in the field is to adopt a "learner" or even "incompetent" role. Since you are seeking to learn, it makes sense to act accordingly; the know-it-all or expert is not likely to be "taught." Like all good things, however, this strategy can be pushed too far, and when it is, it becomes a liability. The getting-in stage of research is one point where overplaying the learner can have negative, perhaps fatal, consequences. If you are to avoid being perceived as either frivolous or stupid and dismissed as such, you should have enough knowledge about the setting or persons you wish to study *to appear competent to do so.* How much knowledge will be enough will vary, of course. If you wish to study the "mothering" experience, it may be enough to know that the persons of whom you are requesting interviews are, in fact, females and mothers. On the other hand, if you are studying public figures, your background research may need to be quite extensive.

The fact that research subjects are public figures means more than the opportunity to do some background work before the interview. Well-known people tend to expect this work—and, in fact, a mastery of what is in the public record. They may grow impatient with questions that could be easily answered by a look at public documents or their writings, or they may not take an uninformed researcher seriously. (Spector, 1980:100–101.)

Age and other personal statuses may also affect how much is enough. We suspect, for example, that younger researchers may be granted more leeway in this regard, since their lack of knowledge is compatible with their age. However, in some settings (highly technical ones, for example) younger researchers may need to demonstrate *more* knowledge than would their older counterparts in order to appear competent—youth itself being taken as a negative indicator.

4. Courtesy. Last, and perhaps most importantly, you will enhance your possibilities for gaining entry if courtesy enters the negotiations. Consider the following:

▶ It is courteous to seek interviews by writing and/or phoning the prospective interviewees to request their cooperation and to inquire about a convenient time and place, rather than by showing up unannounced at their homes or offices.

▶ It is courteous to inform interested parties of your research, even if you don't need their immediate cooperation and they are not going to be part of the group studied.

▶ It is courteous to take the task of getting permission from dependent or subordinate populations you wish to study (children or the hospitalized mentally retarded, for example) as seriously as the task of getting permission from their caretakers.

▶ It is courteous to help others know who you are through connections, to provide them with a reasonable account of what you want to do, and to demonstrate enough knowledge to suggest your competence to do it.

III. POLITICAL AND LEGAL BARRIERS

Recent political and legal trends around the world have exacerbated the already highly problematic character of "getting in," rendering some naturalistic studies exceedingly difficult if not impossible. In the main, the difficulties emanate not from the most directly interested parties—the persons to be researched or their immediate caretakers or supervisors—but from the political, legal, or administrative units of the nation state.

For example, third world leaders increasingly perceive western anthropologists as representing cultural, political and/or economic imperialism and therefore deny them access to many third world societies (Glazer, 1972; Sjoberg [ed.], 1967).

As another example, since the 1970s, social research in the United States has been increasingly subject to federal regulation. Based upon the model (which many researchers regard as totally inappropriate) of medical research with human "subjects," local institutional bodies (usually referred to as Institutional Review Boards or IRBs) have administered regulations that involve assessments of risks and benefits, procedures for "subject" protection, and guarantees of informed consent. How much a barrier these regulations have been to naturalistic research seems to have varied from institutional setting to institutional setting and from IRB to IRB. In some universities, all research—even unfunded and undergraduate research—has been subjected to regulations and review; in other settings, only funded research has been affected. Similarly, some IRBs have interpreted informed consent so literally that "covert" research in public places is eliminated as an option; other IRBs have exempted such research from informed consent mechanisms on the grounds of "no risk." And so on, through a confusing array of interpretations and applications.

In early 1981—as a consequence of heavy lobbying by social research interest groups—most social research, especially naturalistic research, was exempted from regulation. Murray Wax and Joan Cassell describe the changes:

Compared to the previous [Department of Health, Education and Welfare] regulations . . . , these are better tailored to social research. Investigations that pose little or no risk and in which informed consent is implicit in the nature of the research interaction (as in a social survey) have been eliminated from compulsory review. There is a clear delineation of the investigative conditions which lead to genuine risk and which so require monitoring; there is recognition that the very procedures for validating informed consent might themselves generate risks by creating records that link participants to questionable activities. (M. Wax & Cassell, 1981:224.)

However, Wax and Cassell go on to warn that

. . . the revision of the regulations does not guarantee alterations in conduct by local . . . IRBs. The new regulations do not prohibit IRBs from continuing to enforce more stringent standards; nor do they prohibit them from insisting upon reviewing projects not funded by the federal government, but rather encourage institutions to broaden the range of their reviews. (M. Wax & Cassell, 1981:224.)

As of the early 1980s, then, whether the new regulations—despite their liberalization—will continue to erect serious barriers to access in naturalistic social investigations remains to be seen. You are thus well advised to acquaint yourself with the ethical and legal issues raised and the difficulties imposed by the old and the new federal regulations. M. Wax and Cassell (1981) and the bibliography contained therein provide a useful introduction.

As a last example, some investigators have recently been subject to defamation and libel suits, or the threat of them, by persons they have studied (for example, Wallis, 1979:Chapter XI), as well as to other sorts of harassment (Beckford, 1983). The chilling effect of this situation may pose yet another barrier, as social researchers question whether they can risk access in the first place.

Despite the undoubted negative consequences of legal and political difficulties surrounding access in recent years, these difficulties have been accompanied by (and have probably contributed to) an intensified concern among naturalists with the ethics of their activity. This, in our view, is a highly positive occurrence. (For further discussion, see the books and articles referenced in Section I.B., above, as well as Barnes, 1979; Cassell & Wax [eds.], 1980; Glazer, 1972; Klockars & O'Connor, 1979; Sjoberg [ed.], 1967; and Weppner [ed.], 1977:Part II.)

IV. THE QUESTION OF ANONYMITY

In social research, what is commonly called the "assurance of anonymity" is the promise that real names of persons, places, and so forth will not be used in the research report and/or that pseudonyms will be substituted. This practice has long been taken for granted in the naturalistic research tradition. Of course, it is understood that anonymity, like secrecy, is a matter of degree. In intensive interview studies, public place observations, or studies of fluid social groupings, individuals may be able to identify quotations from or descriptions of themselves. They are extremely unlikely to be able to identify anyone else. In studies of stable communities or ongoing groups, however, pseudonyms are unlikely to prevent any of the participants from recognizing, or at least making pretty accurate guesses about, "who's who" (Vidich & Bensman, 1968; Whyte, 1955:Appendix). Despite this potential for slippage in the cloak of anonymity, anonymity itself is standard operating procedure for both known and unknown researchers. For known researchers, in fact, the guarantee of anonymity (and thus the protection) of the people being researched is viewed as an essential technique for getting in.

Beyond the matter of protection for the people being studied, there is another consideration that argues for anonymity as a standard practice. At their best, social researchers are not muckrakers, nor investigative reporters (although these are, of course, important societal roles). Their goal, *as researchers*, should be neither moral judgment nor immediate reform, but *understanding*. The absence of names or the use of pseudonyms (if names, per se, are necessary for clarity) helps both the analyst and the reader to focus on the generalizable patterns emerging from the data and to avoid getting deflected into telling or hearing a "juicy" human interest story.

There are, however, some negative voices among this general consensus on the advisability of anonymity. Some researchers have argued that for studies of publicly accountable behavior or of large, powerful organizations, the guarantee of anonymity is inappropriate (Rainwater & Pittman, 1967). Others have suggested that anonymity may, in fact, impede social scientific (especially social historical) knowledge:

The ideal of scientific documentation is that of full disclosure of evidence essential to critical interpretation and ultimately replication. The burden of proof that names are not essential to social science field reports should be on the investigator. (Colvard, 1967:343–344.)

And Malcolm Spector has reported that in research with public figures, who are used to being quoted and may prefer to speak "on the record," the guarantee of anonymity may impede rather than facilitate access to rich data (Spector, 1980:103–105).

Before giving any promise of anonymity, you might wish to review these arguments, as well as (again) the code of ethics of your academic discipline and any current federal and state statutes relative to privacy. For, while we judge these arguments to raise serious questions about the inevitable advisability of anonymity in *all* research situations, we also believe, in contrast to Colvard, that the burden of proof that names *are* essential to social science field reports—or to the larger scientific endeavor—should be on the investigator. When in doubt, the best advice is still: disguise or obscure.

Having, by hook or by crook, finally gotten access to the data, you must work at maintaining your position—you must deal, that is, with the problem of "getting along."

Getting Along

Like life, being "in the field" is never static. As we have suggested, research in the naturalistic tradition is very much an emergent affair. New problems continually arise; new solutions are continually necessary. Cooperative people may turn nasty. Uncooperative people may become superior sources of data. A bad beginning in a setting may unexpectedly prove to be an advantage, or a good beginning may turn sour. Quiescent difficulties may erupt at any time. Expected difficulties may never materialize.

The course of research is no more controllable than the course of a marriage, or the course of a friendship, or the course of a life. On the other hand, the course of research is also no less controllable. As in all activities, knowing a bit about what to expect, learning from the successes and failures of others, anticipating and thus guarding against pitfalls, and so forth should help to reduce the difficulties of the field experience to manageable proportions.

In what follows, we subdivide our discussion of "getting along" into three tasks: the task of getting along *with self;* the task of getting along *with "the folk";* and the task of getting along *with conscience and colleagues.* In the first, we shall be concerned with the emotional stress which investigators may encounter; in the second, with the problem of achieving continual access to rich data; and in the third, with the ongoing ethical dilemmas which must be faced. This is in reality an artificial division but useful for exposition. We ask you, then, to bear in mind that these three tasks are profoundly interrelated.

I. GETTING ALONG WITH SELF: EMOTIONAL STRESSES

Being a researcher can be an emotionally stressful experience. As Rosalie Wax has described it,

the person who cannot abide feeling awkward or out of place, who feels crushed whenever he makes a mistake—embarrassing or otherwise— who is psychologically unable to endure being, and being treated like, a fool not only for a day or week but for months on end, ought to think twice before he decides to become a participant observer. (R. Wax, 1971:370.)

In the introduction to their *Fieldwork Experience*, William Shaffir, Robert Stebbins and Allan Turowetz are not more optimistic:

Fieldwork must certainly rank with the more disagreeable activities that humanity has fashioned for itself. It is usually inconvenient, to say the least, sometimes physically uncomfortable, frequently embarrassing, and, to a degree, always tense. (Shaffir, Stebbins & Turowetz [eds.], 1980:3.)

Wax is thinking particularly of participant observation by a known observer, while Shaffir, Stebbins and Turowetz are speaking more generally, but all are pointing to the unfortunate fact that being an investigator can be personally difficult.

There is obviously no way to catalog every source of emotional or psychological difficulty ever encountered by fieldworkers. Such a cataloging probably would not be very useful anyway, and it would certainly discourage many people from even attempting naturalistic research. (Consider that if humans *really* anticipated all the difficulties they would encounter in any enterprise, very little, if anything, would occur.) In the belief that some forewarning may help you cope, however, we will look at four common situations of emotional distress: deception and the fear of disclosure; loathing and the desire to withdraw; sympathy and the impulse to help; and marginality and the temptation to "go native."

A. Deception and the Fear of Disclosure

The perception that you, the researcher, are deceiving the persons you are studying and the resulting anxiety over possible disclosure of that deception seems to be the emotional stress situation most characteristic of unknown investigators. From published reports, however, it seems clear that known researchers experience this as well. Because the people you are studying openly *cannot* know everything about what you are doing, there is always the fear that a direct and discomforting challenge is just around the corner (Thorne, 1979). For example:

▶ Did X remember that I was a researcher when she told me that? And if not, when she does remember, will she be angry or upset?

▶ Is this person I'm interviewing, who seems to be getting restless, about to ask me more about my research aims than I really want to tell right now?

▶ Is the caretaker of this group I'm studying going to notice that my research interests have shifted since I received permission to do the research, and if he does, will he still approve?

Unknown observers in open and public settings may also suffer from a nagging concern that "someone will find out." Even though the people in such settings are often not upset when they do find out, that knowledge does not necessarily prevent the investigator from worrying. When Lyn Lofland was observing in public waiting rooms, she was always vaguely fearful that someone would challenge her continued and repeated presence. On only one occasion was she approached—in an airport—and even though the official who discovered she was doing research had no objection to her remaining, she was so uncomfortable, she left almost at once and never returned (see also Karp, 1980).

Unknown observers in closed settings have written little about the emotional stress of deception and the fear of disclosure. But from the reports of investigators in milder situations of deception and, more directly, from the evidence of persons in nonresearch "passing" situations (spies, "closet" homosexuals, and so forth), there is evidence that for many the fear of being unmasked (and of the attendant possibilities for humiliation, embarrassment, abuse) is a constant companion. (On the social psychology of "passing" more generally, see Edgerton, 1967; Goffman, 1963; Warren, 1974.)

B. Loathing and the Desire to Withdraw

Very few researchers have confessed to *loathing* the people they study or interview. Presumably, very few do. After all, if your discomfort, distaste, or dislike is too strong, you are going to be spending most of your time hiding your true feelings, leaving very little energy for the data logging/analysis tasks which are the point of the research in the first place. Or you are simply going to leave the setting. (Numerous fieldworkers have noted, however, that you may learn a great deal from persons you dislike; for example, R. Wax, 1971.) Thus, most investigators don't even attempt research with persons whom they know ahead of time they will thoroughly despise.

Nevertheless, we should not too quickly dismiss this emotional possibility. Consider, for example, that you may only discover your distaste after you are committed to a field situation. Or, while some of the persons you are observing/interviewing may be congenial, others may not (Weinberg & Williams, 1972). Or changing situations in the setting may profoundly alter your view of its participants (J. M. Johnson, 1975). Or, in researching a stigmatized population, popular loathing of that group may be directed at you, leaving you feeling, at minimum, ambivalent about the group (Warren, 1977; Weinberg & Williams, 1972).

Perhaps the most forthright confession of loathing is to be found in passages from Bronislaw Malinowski's private journals, published as *A Diary in the Strict Sense of the Term* (1967). Available in print only many years after the famed anthropologist's death, the diary, kept during his researches with the Trobriand Islanders (among other groups), reveals what one reviewer, Patrick Gallagher (1967:23), called "a magnificent lack of rapport...."

Even more embarrassing, he confesses to despising his subjects ("young females, blackened, with shaven heads, one of them . . . with an animal-like brutishly sensual face. I shudder at the thought of copulating with her"), to distrusting them ("They lied, concealed and irritated me. I am always in a world of lies here"), and even to abusing them ("I was enraged and punched him in the jaw once or twice"). (Gallagher, 1967:25.)

Not surprisingly under the circumstances, Malinowski also admits to withdrawing—if not from the field altogether, at least from contact with the "natives."

He also confesses, repeatedly, to chronic dissipation of time in reading "trashy" novels . . . and, as frequently, to preoccupation with sexual daydreams and "lecherous" acts. (Gallagher, 1967:25.)

Anthropologists continue to debate whether these expressions represent Malinowski's more persistent feelings toward the peoples he studied or whether they are the honest, and very human, expressions of episodic rage and loathing under extraordinarily difficult field situations. Whatever the case, Malinowski's incredibly candid revelations of self stand as a strong reminder to and lesson for all naturalistic researchers. Just as there are no guarantees that you will love and want to be with your relatives, there are also no guarantees that you will love and desire to be around the people who populate your researches.

C. Sympathy and the Impulse to Help

People everywhere tend to need *help*, and it is not at all unusual for investigators to provide some forms of mundane assistance to the people they are studying. But sometimes researchers encounter a more difficult situation of *need*, in which the people being observed or interviewed face severe difficulties that would require a full-time commitment to alleviate. Naturalistic researchers (known or unknown) must often struggle with the personally painful question of whether to throw in the towel on doing research and give themselves over entirely to "helping" or to remain in the field as a chronicler of the difficulties (Gans, 1970; Thorne, 1979).

D. Marginality and the Temptation to "Go Native"

If deception and the fear of disclosure is the characteristic stress situation of the unknown observer, then marginality and the temptation to "go native" (to cease all research and fully join the group) is the characteristic stress situation of the known observer (especially participant observers). This is not to say that other researchers do not also experience marginality. Unknown observers may experience it simply out of the knowledge that they have another self (researcher) whom none of their setting companions knows about. And persons doing intensive interviewing may find themselves feeling that it would be far more comfortable to stop the interview and just have an informal and unrecorded conversation. But it seems to be the known participant observer (either as participant researcher or as outside researcher) who most typically experiences discomforting moments of truth about marginality. Barrie Thorne, writing of a time when members of the draft resistance movement she was both involved in and studying were being asked to commit themselves to an act which might result in arrest, quotes from her fieldnotes:

As M. began the invitation, I felt fear in my throat. Fear, shame, guilt—both a desire to join the group that surged forward after M.'s invitation and a (stronger) reluctance since I didn't feel I could risk arrest and realized that the pressures compelling me to go forward were of a group rather than an individually thought-through kind. But that realization didn't seem to minimize the emotion. People began leaving their pews and going forward. Eventually there seemed to be only a few scattered people remaining in the pews. M. commented over the microphone, "There seem to be more up here than down there." I felt all eyes were upon me; I was sure my face was flushed; I found myself fingering my purse, almost in readiness to run up. But I didn't. . . .

The group—more like a community given its size and solidarity—stood in a solid bunch, spilling out over the sides and the front of the chapel, but clearly demarcated from those of us, scattered and far from constituting a group, who remained in the pews. The spatial arrangements dramatized the gap between the committed and the uncommitted. (Thorne, 1979:80.)

While such dramatic moments highlight the difficulty, marginality usually tends to be experienced as a chronic sense of loneliness, anxiety, and perhaps even alienation. There can be a continual and often subtle sense of separation between the observer and the observed that is painful and poignant. It is as if, daily, one were being told: "You are here and you know a lot about us, but you are not really one of us." For a creature as sociable and as desirous of acceptance as homo sapiens, this can be hard indeed.

E. Dealing with the Stresses

In the face of these possibilities for emotional stress, what are you to do? As we said initially, simply knowing that such possibilities may occur lessen their impact. But not inevitably. You may, in fact, conclude that your research is not worth living with deception and the fear of disclosure, and so confess and depart. You may decide that continued association with persons you find loathsome is unbearable. You may come to feel that the needs of the people you are studying are compelling above all other commitments. And you may come to believe that community with the group being researched is far better than colleagueship with other researchers. Some fieldworkers have, in fact, made such decisions and judgments (for example, Guzman, 1969; Powdermaker, 1966:119).

However, for those who would hope to come through these and other emotional difficulties of "being in the field" and still remain commit'ed to the acquisition of social knowledge, the literature of naturalistic methodology would seem to offer a simple word of advice: Keep in contact with fellow researchers and/or friends with whom these problems can be discussed, placed in context, and weighed. Or, if that option is not available, taking a cue from Malinowski, perhaps a diary is in order.

II. GETTING ALONG WITH "THE FOLK": THE PROBLEM OF CONTINUING ACCESS

As we have seen, you yourself as researcher may be an important barrier to rich data. If emotional difficulties prove great, they can deflect energy and time from the primary task of data collection or lead to abandoning the research altogether. Nonetheless, the major problem of access in the field ordinarily involves the researcher's relations with the "folk" in the setting; that is, the people who are being researched are generally the more serious potential barrier to data.

We noted in Chapter 2 that access is one of the most widely discussed topics in the literature of qualitative methodology, and this remains as true in the "getting along" stage as it was in the earlier phases of the research process. We deal here with only certain issues raised in that literature (although we judge them to be the most central ones). If you wish to pursue particular issues more extensively or are interested in topics not covered here, you might consult the books referenced at the end of Chapter 2, Section II, as well as J. M. Johnson (1975) and R. Wax (1971).

When in the field, investigators are concerned to act toward the people being studied so as to maximize the information that is coming to them. Let us consider how this might be done with regard to *stance, style,* and *situations.*

A. Stance: Trust or Suspicion

A dictionary defines *stance* as an "intellectual or emotional attitude." The naturalistic tradition is of two rather different minds on the question of the most appropriate attitude to take toward "the folk." Rosalie Wax speaks for what is certainly the more traditional and possibly the majority view:

I find it difficult to reproach myself or my fellow fieldworkers for our disposition to regard the people we intend to study as good, honorable, and innocent. . . . I know that there are many societies that have developed elaborate and ingenious devices for relieving any stranger of his money and of his general confidence in human nature. I also know that no respondent or stranger has ever treated me as vilely as have some of my fellow social scientists. On the other hand, I know that *one cannot live with human beings in the field or out of it without trusting them. The great feat in most field expeditions, as in life, is to find the areas in which a mutual or reciprocal trust may be developed.* (R. Wax, 1971:372, emphasis added.)

Jack Douglas takes an opposing stance:

The investigative paradigm is based on the assumption that profound conflicts of interest, values, feelings and actions pervade social life. It is taken for granted that many of the people one deals with, perhaps all people to some extent, have good reason to hide from others what they are doing and even to lie to them. *Instead of trusting people and expecting trust in return, one suspects others and expects others to suspect him. Conflict is the reality of life; suspicion is the guiding principle.* (Douglas, 1976:55, emphasis added; see also Hoffman, 1980 on "camouflaging" intent in intensive interviewing situations.)

We have juxtaposed these passages to highlight the contrast between them. But in truth, the authors are not so far apart as their words would suggest. Wax is well aware that the people she is researching often lie, by commission and by omission, sometimes unintentionally and sometimes quite deliberately. Her accounts of *Doing Fieldwork* are filled with instances of such problems. And Douglas, in a later passage of the same book, softens the tone of his earlier assertion:

It is all too easy for anyone . . . to conclude that we see all of society as [conflict-ridden and secretive] and therefore reject all cooperative methods in studying society. This would be completely wrong, as will be clear in our later discussion. . . . But to avoid any such misunderstandings we should emphasize from the beginning that we see society as being mixed and are proposing a mixed strategy of researching it. (Douglas, 1976:56.)

If you look at Wax's and Douglas's positions as opposite ends of a continuum, then most fieldworkers appear to adopt a stance that is somewhere in the middle—trust combined with a heady dose of skepticism; suspicion mixed in with large portions of faith. Which way you lean will depend on what you are researching. In a very factionalized setting where issues of enormous import are being struggled over, you should undoubtedly keep a copy of Douglas's book in hand. But if you are interviewing people who want to talk about the topic at issue and who have no obvious reason to lie, it would unnecessarily complicate things to view your informants as "unfriendly or hostile witnesses."

B. Style: Presentation of Self

Unknown investigators do not need to worry about whether they are behaving in acceptable investigator *style*. They simply behave in a manner appropriate to the role they occupy. Known researchers, however, must determine how to act or present themselves so as to keep the flow of information coming.

Obviously we do not refer here to donning a persona totally at odds with your natural demeanor. We are speaking, rather, of a question such as an employer might ask about her own behavior relative to her employees, or a teacher might ask about himself relative to the children in his classroom. In many sectors of social life, goal achievement revolves in part around self strategies. In naturalistic research, based on the cumulative experience of many fieldworkers, two complementary methods of self-presentation offer a particularly felicitous personal style: absence of threat and acceptable incompetence.

1. Absence of Threat. Granting but ignoring the exceptions, the first counsel one might offer a prospective investigator is to be nonthreatening to the people being researched, or at least to keep any potential threat within reasonable limits. We do not primarily mean *threatening* in any physical sense (although that, too, of course). Rather, we refer to threats to beliefs, self-confidence, and existing social arrangements by means of argument, ridicule, sarcasm, disinterest, and so forth. In most interview and observation situations, the investigator who is supportive, cordial, interested, nonargumentative, courteous, understanding, even sympathetic, will receive a good deal more information than one who acts in an opposite fashion (Charmaz, 1982).

This advice, however, may be considerably more difficult to put into practice than you might think. Consider how frequently in normal interaction many of us are more interested in talking than in listening, in telling than in learning, in convincing than in understanding, and so on. In fact, many researchers find this continual openness to others and suppression of self exhausting—an additional source of emotional and psychological stress (for example, Paul, 1953).

Being nonthreatening also means being sensitive and attentive to matters of appropriate grooming and dress. What is appropriate depends, of course, on the relation between the researcher as a person and the setting itself. Forty-year-old researchers observing adolescents undoubtedly make themselves *and* the young people appear ridiculous if they copy the latter's dress. Conversely, the casual student garb of jeans and shirt is not an appropriate costume for interviews with corporate executives. A guiding principle for appearance is to dress and groom yourself in a manner that shows respect for yourself and for your hosts (see R. Wax, 1971:47–50).

2. Acceptable Incompetence. A naturalistic investigator, almost by definition, is one who does not understand. He or she is "ignorant" and needs to be "taught." This role of watcher and asker of questions is the quintessential *student* role. Now it happens that the idea of the ignorant student who has to be taught is a commonsensical and widespread notion. People almost everywhere feel they know and understand that role. Thus, the investigator who assumes the role of *socially acceptable incompetent* is likely to be accepted. In being viewed as relatively incompetent (although otherwise cordial and easy to get along with), the investigator easily assumes the role of one who is to be taught. Such persons *have* to be told and will not take offense at being instructed about "obvious" things or at being "lectured to." That is, such persons are in a good position to keep the flow of information coming smoothly (for example, Danziger, 1979; R. Wax, 1971).

The advantages of being acceptably incompetent may be limited or nullified, of course, by particular research settings, situations, questions, and relations. We have already noted that acting too incompetent may endanger entry to a research setting in the first place and have quoted

Malcolm Spector on the need to be knowledgeable when interviewing public figures. There are also settings where even conventionally acceptable incompetents are not tolerated, where one may need some special bond and expertise in order to develop intimate familiarity. For example, investigators studying the world of crime who themselves have criminal backgrounds probably have an edge on those who lack that commonality with the researched. (Again, an advantage of starting where you are.)

There are unquestionably many other situations where the role of incompetent would be a hindrance. And certainly, like being nonthreatening, being acceptably incompetent will be experienced by many persons as stressful, especially over the long run. Nonetheless, for those who can tolerate being what a naturalistic researcher, in fact, *is*—a nonthreatening learner—the rewards of information received can be considerable. You might well keep in mind the admission of Agatha Christie's very intelligent and successful detective, Hercule Poirot. When asked why he, a Belgian by birth, sometimes spoke good and at other times broken English, even after many years of residence in England, he replied,

It is true that I can speak the exact, the idiomatic English. But, my friend, to speak the broken English is an enormous asset [for a detective]. It leads people to despise you. They say—a foreigner—he can't even speak English properly. It is not my policy to terrify people—instead *I invite their gentle ridicule.* (Christie, 1934:174, emphasis added.)

C. Situations and Solutions: Threats to Access

The naturalistic investigator encounters many *situations* in the field which endanger continuing access to rich data and which therefore require *solutions.* The numbers of these may be as great as the numbers of possible research sites or questions, but we will describe only the four that seem to recur with greatest regularity: factions, trade-offs, closed doors, and insider understandings.

1. **Factions.** Almost any social setting is likely to contain factions, cliques, or quarrels of one or another kind. In fact, some internal distrust and dissent seems almost universal in human groupings. *Unknown* observers must necessarily align themselves, at least to some extent, with whatever faction or clique or side of a quarrel is dictated by the nature of their role. Thus, for them, the problem of factions is somewhat simplified. And the intensive interviewer of persons who have no personal connections with one another is even more exempt. But the known observer in a stable setting and the researcher interviewing socially connected persons (the political leaders of a small community, for example) must cope with the problem of how to maintain neutrality in the midst of divisiveness. Such researchers must at least avoid appearing so excessively loyal to one group that they will be denied access to the other (or thrown out of the setting altogether).

One typical way to protect against these dangers is to align yourself with a single broad group within the setting and to remain relatively aloof from internal debates within that group. Thus, investigtors of educational institutions have most frequently aligned themselves with either teachers or students, but not with both. For example, Becker, Geer, Hughes & Strauss (1961) and Becker, Geer & Hughes (1968) studied medical students and undergraduates, respectively, but *not* medical faculty or college professors. And in both settings, the researchers attempted to make clear their interest in students as a category, not in the smaller divisions within the category.

Of course, in the early days of a fieldwork project, you may unintentionally make what later prove to be unfortunate alignments. Weinberg and Williams's advice, which deals with individuals, applies to the problem of factions as well:

In the early phases of field work, when one feels most alone, it is easiest to associate with those held in disrepute; so one learns to keep on the move and neither spend too much time with those whose company is most pleasureful nor avoid those whom one finds least amicable. (Weinberg & Williams, 1972:172.)

On the other hand, researchers have also quite successfully studied disputes between or among factions, moving—either as interviewers or as observers or both—among the conflicting parties (for example, Bromley & Shupe, 1980, 1979; Heirich, 1971; Joseph, 1983, 1978; Shupe & Bromley, 1980a, 1980b; Spector, 1980, 1977; R. Wax, 1971:Chapters 12–14). As best as can be garnered from their accounts, success in this difficult enterprise seems to be partially a function of:

▶ The perception by the participants that the researcher is truly an outsider to the dispute

▶ The continued perception of the researcher's impartiality relative to the dispute

▶ The researcher's scrupulous honesty about the fact of studying both sides, combined with scrupulous confidentiality regarding the content of each side's private views and strategies (that is, one does not play double agent)

▶ Possession of a great deal of accurate information about what each side knows of the other throughout the life of the conflict

2. Trade-offs. As we indicated in Chapter 3, the investigator is able to conduct research only because the people in the setting either consent to being observed or interviewed or don't know that research is going on. Thus, the issue of trade-offs is a legitimate component of the naturalistic process. Unknown researchers in closed settings are already contributing to their respective settings through their roles in them, of course, and in public place research, researchers are largely irrelevant. But the people who are tolerating a known observer or an interviewer in their midst have every reason to ask: What do I get in return? What's the trade-off?

Among fieldworkers, the most common answer has been and is: mundane assistance of one or another sort. In intensive interviewing, such assistance may be as ephemeral as truly listening to someone talk about something they want to talk about (an infrequent occurrence in social life). But interviewers, like their participant observer colleagues, may also trade off with more direct provisions (Charmaz, 1981; Rubin, 1981): rides, loans, delivered messages, coffee served, advice, opinions, illegal goods held, physical defense offered, lies told, and so on, through the entire range of normal "friendly" relations typical to organized social life. Joseph Kotarba, writing of his trade-offs for being allowed to observe in an acupuncturist-physician's office, outlines a typical experience:

I attribute much of my success in developing rapport with the physician and his staff to what I call the "good boy" approach. . . . I have found it valuable in my research experiences not only to take precautions against making gross mistakes (e.g., interrupting doctor-patient consultations) but to become a *positive* influence in the setting. For example, I made a habit of bringing coffee and doughnuts to the office at least once a week. I occasionally helped move patients from wheelchairs to treatment tables, backed by an open offer to be available whenever needed. I never placed myself above involvement with office gossip or idle talk. In other words, I tried my best to be liked by everyone in the office. (Kotarba, 1980:59.)

Less commonly, the assistance may be in the form of more esoteric goods and services. William F. Whyte, for example, during his participant observation in an Italian neighborhood, found himself voting four times (once in his own name, three times under assumed names) in a single local election (Whyte, 1955:313–317). In the context of actual field situations, you must decide for yourself where to draw the line at helping. Whyte, himself, upon reflecting, rejected the propriety of this helping behavior:

I knew that it was not necessary; at the point where I began to repeat, I could have refused. There were others who did refuse to do it. I had simply got myself involved in the swing of the campaign and let myself be carried along. I had to learn that, in order to be accepted by the people in a district, you do not have to do everything just as they do it. In fact, in a district where there are different groupings with different standards of behavior, it may be a matter of very serious consequence to conform to the standards of one particular group.

I also had to learn that the field worker cannot afford to think only of learning to live with others in the field. He has to continue living with himself. If the participant observer finds himself engaging in behavior that he has learned to think of as immoral, then he is likely to begin to wonder what sort of person he is after all. Unless the fieldworker can carry with him a reasonably consistent picture of himself, he is likely to run into difficulties. (Whyte, 1955:316–317).

A line, then, may and should appropriately be drawn. But unless you wish to be seen as odd, cold, and withdrawn, and perhaps completely shut out from the research setting, you cannot forego the helper role altogether—it is your trade-off for access. (On "exchange" and access, see Gray, 1980.)

3. **Closed Doors.** Even when you have achieved entry to a setting or successfully begun a series of interviews, you are still in no way guaranteed that all aspects of the setting you wish to observe or everyone you wish to interview

will be available. In the face of such "closed doors," experienced fieldworkers frequently make use of *allies*. These may be some of the same persons who helped them "get in" (see Chapter 3, Section II.B.1.), or they may be persons you have met during the course of the research itself who have indicated a desire or willingness to assist.

Sandra Danziger, for example, in an attempt to observe doctor-patient interaction during pregnancy and childbirth, gained limited access to maternity wards but had difficulty getting permission from physicians to enter the more "inside" observational sites she desired. To achieve this, she sought the counsel and assistance of the head nurses in the units—a strategy which proved successful (Danziger, 1979:516–517). Joan Eakin Hoffman, having completed her interviews with hospital board members known personally to her, enlisted the help of these prior interviewees to secure interviews with those she did not know (Hoffman, 1980:47).

Perhaps the most famous ally within the naturalistic tradition of sociology is William F. Whyte's "Doc." Whyte had been "fiddling" (the only appropriate word) around Cornerville (his pseudonym for the Italian neighborhood he was attempting to study) for some time and getting nowhere. Finally, he went to a local settlement house.

In a sense, my study began on the evening of February 4, 1937, when the social worker called me in to meet Doc. . . . "I want to see all that I can. I want to get as complete a picture of the community as possible," [Whyte said. Doc replied:] "Well, any nights you want to see anything, I'll take you around. I can take you to the joints—gambling joints—I can take you around to the street corners. Just remember that you're my friend. That's all they need to know. I know these places, and if you tell them you're my friend, nobody will bother you. You just tell me what you want to see and we'll arrange it." (Whyte, 1955:291.)

But insider-allies like Doc can do more than open doors to other people or parts of the setting. They can also open doors to understanding.

4. **Insider Understandings.** We pointed out in Chapter 2 (Section III.B.1.) that while outside researchers have the requisite distance from the setting to ask questions, by definition they lack the closeness necessary to understanding—that is, to understanding the setting in the way the participants do. We suggested that persons in such situations should therefore seek mechanisms for reducing the distance. Allies are one such mechanism. When allies are important guides to insider understandings, they are generally referred to as **informants** or **key informants.** (In intensive interviewing, all interviewees may be thought of as informants; especially articulate ones are sometimes thought of as key informants.) The understandings of these helpers may, of course, be erroneous or misleading, and the wise investigator is never too gullible. As a general rule, reliance on multiple informants (as is always the case in intensive interviewing) is probably preferable to reliance on only one. Whatever the potential dangers in their use, however, it is unlikely that very many richly empirical and deeply understanding studies could have been achieved by outside researchers without the assistance of

articulate, wise, knowledgeable and helpful informants (for example, Berreman, 1962). If you are an outside researcher, then, the cultivation of informants is virtually imperative.

III. GETTING ALONG WITH CONSCIENCE AND COLLEAGUES: ONGOING ETHICAL CONCERNS

All of the personal and strategic problems we have talked about so far in this chapter may also be or become ethical problems. These problems may arise from a researcher's conscience, colleagues, or both. For example:

▶ Is it ethical to talk to people when they don't know you will be recording their words?

▶ Is it ethical to get information for your own purposes from people you hate?

▶ Is it ethical to see a severe need for help and not respond to it directly?

▶ Is it ethical to be in a setting or situation but not commit yourself wholeheartedly to it?

▶ Is it ethical to develop a calculated stance toward other humans, that is, to be strategic in your relations?

▶ Is it ethical to take sides or to avoid taking sides in a factionalized situation?

▶ Is it ethical to "pay" people with trade-offs for access to their lives and minds?

▶ Is it ethical to "use" people as allies or informants in order to gain entree to other persons or to elusive understandings?

And so on through the catalog of every conceivable fieldwork situation. Much attention has been lavished on questions such as these in recent years, both by fieldworkers themselves agonizing over their behavior and relationships and by specialists in ethics more generally. (References to key writings are listed in Chapter 3, Sections I.B. and III.)

Without in any way denigrating these efforts or belittling the honestly expressed moral anguish of some researchers, it seems to us that too much can be made of the fieldwork setting as involving special and particular ethical problems. In our view, the fieldwork situation is no more (although certainly no less) difficult ethically than everyday life. Particularly when it involves voluntary agreements and relations between researcher and researched and when the situation is one of essentially equal power, its ethical dilemmas come close to those faced daily by morally sensitive individuals:

▶ If I don't tell my husband *everything* about my thoughts, or even about my deeds, am I lying, and is my relationship thus somehow unethical?

▶ If, since I don't want to alienate my spouse and I need her as a babysitter, I don't reveal to my mother-in-law that I dislike her intensely, am I being immoral?

▶ I know about the starvation in Somalia. If I do not give up my job and try to do something directly, have I failed as a moral person?

- I've been through twelve "scenes" in the past six years—what sort of person am I?
- If I try to "dress for power" and I am learning to be assertive, does my strategic view of interaction make me inauthentic?
- I'm staying out of the battle between two of my colleagues at work. Should I?
- I sometimes use flattery to try to get my students to be more interested. Is that improper?
- My father helped me to get my first job and told me a lot about the world I'd be entering. Should I have let him do that?

And so on through the catalog of every conceivable situation in everyday life.

These daily ethical dilemmas are no more readily resolved than the similar dilemmas of field research. But then, why should there be a difference? Fieldwork is not detached from ongoing social life, and the continuing ethical dilemmas of social life seem an inexorable part of the human condition.

IV. POSTSCRIPT: PERSONAL ACCOUNTS OF THE FIELD EXPERIENCE

These necessarily abstracted and perhaps too ordered statements on "getting along" cannot really convey the full flavor of the field experience. For this, we would recommend reading one or more personal accounts, such as in any of the following:

Gerald Berreman, *Behind Many Masks* (1962).

Andres Beteille & T. N. Madan (eds.), *Encounter and Experience: Personal Accounts of Fieldwork* (1975).

Morris Freilich (ed.), *Marginal Natives at Work: Anthropologists in the Field* (1977).

Peggy Golde (ed.), *Women in the Field: Anthropological Experiences* (1970).

Glenn Jacobs (ed.), *The Participant Observer: Encounters with Social Reality* (1970).

John Johnson, *Doing Field Research* (1975).

Elliot Liebow, *Tally's Corner* (1967).

Bronislaw Malinowski, *A Diary in the Strict Sense of the Term* (1967).

Hortense Powdermaker, *Stranger and Friend: The Way of an Anthropologist* (1966).

William B. Shaffir, Robert A. Stebbins and Allan Turowetz (eds.), *Fieldwork Experience: Qualitative Approaches to Social Research* (1980).

David Sudnow, *Passing On: The Social Organization of Dying* (1967).

Barrie Thorne, "Political Activist as Participant Observer" (1979).

Rosalie H. Wax, *Doing Fieldwork: Warnings and Advice* (1971).

William F. Whyte, *Streetcorner Society* (1955).

Jacqueline Wiseman, *Stations of the Lost: The Treatment of Skid Row Alcoholics* (1970).

This and the preceding two chapters may have led you to the view that fieldwork is "adventure." It is certainly that, as almost any veteran will testify—endlessly. But it is something else as well, or it is nothing at all: *hard work*—hard, boring, disciplined, tedious work.

We now turn to the most essential aspect of field research—*data logging*. Data logging is the reason we try to get in and get along in the field in the first place. If it is omitted, fieldwork is indeed relegated to mere personal adventure.

Logging
Data

Throughout the research, a process of **data logging** (that is, of careful recording) is carried on in various forms. Field notes and interview write-ups are the most basic of these, but logging may also include mapping, census taking, photographing, sound recording, document collection, and so forth.

The model is that of *logging,* very much in the way our naturalist counterparts in biology have long been accustomed carefully to record observations on the actions and noises of the animals they research. The logging model is especially appropriate because it suggests a receptive, almost passive, approach to amassing data. The task of naturalistic researchers is not so much to "procure" data for recording as it is to *register* the social events unfolding or the words being spoken before them. The researcher does not only (or mainly) wait for "significant" (sociologically or otherwise) events to occur or words to be said and then write them down. An enormous amount of information about the settings under observation or the interview in process can be apprehended in apparently trivial happenings or utterances, and these are indispensible grist for the logging mill. Understandably, then, the complaint of the novice investigator (or the boast of the professional) that he or she "didn't make any notes because nothing important happened" is viewed in this tradition as either naive or arrogant, or both. As Rosalie Wax warns us:

The fieldworker may also think twice about following the example of those would-be ethnographers who assert or boast that they take few field notes or no notes at all. The fact is that most of the people who say that they are able to get along without taking notes do not write anything worth reading. (R. Wax, 1971:141.)

In methodological discussions (especially relative to participant observation), data logging is frequently justified as a "memory device" for the research. It allows you to recall the extraordinarily complex range of stimuli with which you have been bombarded. Such a justification, certainly, is resistant to contradiction. But it seems to us to miss the point. And the point is that *the logging record is the data*. Stated obversely, the data are not the researcher's memories (which notes, interview write-ups, films and so forth merely assist); the data consist of whatever is logged.

It is for this reason that the recording task is the crucial aspect of the naturalistic analysis of social life. And it is here, perhaps more than in any other aspect of the process, that the researcher requires discipline. "Getting in" and "getting along" may involve difficult and painful ethical, personal, and professional choices; they also generate a certain excitement. Data logging, in contrast, is often simply *boring*. As we warned in Chapter 1, if the researcher lacks any personal emotional attachment to the concerns of the research, project quality (even completion) may be jeopardized. And tenacious data logging is certainly one of the key sites of jeopardy.

In this chapter, we begin with a general discussion of the logging task, dealing with matters that pertain both to participant observation and to intensive interviewing. We then consider separately the different forms which the log takes in these two research modes: the interview write-up in intensive interviewing and field notes in participant observation.

I. THE LOGGING TASK

As we have just indicated, the format of data logging in exclusively interview and exclusively observation studies is rather different (although many interviewers also take field notes and many observers also do interviews). Nevertheless, there are many aspects of the logging task which are pertinent to both modes. We shall consider five of these: data sources; researcher roles and access to data; problems of error and bias; protecting anonymity; and duplicating and typing the log.

A. Data Sources

In the naturalistic tradition, the prime sources of data are the *words and actions* of the people you are interviewing or observing. These are recorded mainly via written notes but also, on occasion (depending on appropriateness and resources), via photographs, films, audio tapes and/or video tapes. *Supplementary data* sources—documents, for example—may also be tapped.

1. **Words and Actions.** In both intensive interviewing and participant observation studies, you "get at" your prime sources of data—words and actions—through a combination of *looking, listening,* and *asking*. Which of these three activities is dominant will vary from situation to situation, from one time period to another, and from one mode of research to another. If you are an unknown investigator in a public/open setting, looking and listening will probably dominate, asking being possible only in limited situations (for

example, Karp, 1980, 1973). Unknown observers in closed settings may also have to rely heavily on listening and looking, since too much asking appears out of character for the setting role. If you are involved in intensive interviewing, on the other hand, asking and listening come to the fore, although you are, of course, simultaneously (if not predominantly) observing the interview in progress.

It is probably known observers, then, who have the greatest freedom (and also the greatest necessity) to utilize all three activities. At times, they may merely watch what is going on. At other times they may both watch and listen, or combine looking and listening with asking. Known observers are expected to carry on conversations with people in the setting; this not only serves the task of "getting along," but also (in the form of questioning) will be informational in nature. Asking may elicit information not available from mere passive looking and listening or, at least, may speed up the information collection process. Thus, known participant observers will spend a good deal of their time in the field asking questions such as these:

Who is he?
What does he do?
What do you think she meant by that?
What are they supposed to do?
Why did she do that?
Why is that done?
What happens after _____ ?
What would happen if _____ ?
What do you think about _____ ?
Who is responsible if _____ ?

As a form of activity, such asking is certainly a normal feature of everyday life. The naturalistic investigator is simply using this fact for research purposes—although perhaps asking questions much more frequently than ordinary participants in the setting would do. Questioning of this kind is often called "casual interviewing"—and it is a key part of participant observation. The observer (and the intensive interviewer) may also utilize a more indirect means of asking questions—what David Snow, Louis Zurcher and Gideon Sjoberg have called "interviewing by comment" (1981). This is an attempt to elicit information verbally by making a statement rather than by asking a direct question. And as we suggested above, participant observers may also engage in intensive interviewing with people in the setting. These interviews, however, tend not to arise out of consideration of a general topic—as in traditional intensive interviewing—but out of specific queries that have accumulated in the field.

None of these activities are esoteric. People in everyday social life carry on precisely this kind of interweaving of looking, listening and asking. Naturalistic research differs only in that these actions are more self-conscious, directed, and intentional.

2. **Supplementary Data.** Depending on the question or questions being asked, on the character of the setting, on the form of the research, and so on, amassing data through supplementary sources may also be undertaken.

Investigators frequently collect documents that are generated by the setting or that have to do with questions or topics of interest. Census taking may be useful, and—where physical setting or settings are pertinent—so may map making. Materials on the historical aspects of a people, setting, issue, and so forth will help place the data in context. Relevant newspaper and magazine clippings may expand your understanding of the present. In short, conscientious naturalistic investigators scan not only the immediate data site for words and actions but are sensitive as well to the possible value of a wide range of supplementary information which may come their way (see for example Webb et al., 1981).

B. Researcher Roles and Access to Data

As we have seen in the earlier stages of the research process, differing researcher roles and situations engender differing problems and advantages. This is no less true with regard to data logging.

1. **Unknown Investigators.** In public and open settings, the unknown observer experiences few blockages to data access. In many such locations—waiting settings, parks, restaurants, coffee houses, and so forth—note taking is facilitated by the typical self-engrossed activity of lone persons within them. That is, you can simply spend your time writing (or map making or census taking or whatever) without appearing "strange." (The use of cameras, tape recorders, and so forth may be more difficult.) Of course, as we noted above, unknown observers must rely primarily on what they see and hear, since much asking activity would "blow the cover." Hopefully, however, they have correctly evaluated their data site, and the kinds of data they are logging are appropriate to their interests.

The unknown observer in a closed setting has particularly good access to insider understandings (for which the known observer—especially the outside researcher—often must rely on informants, as discussed in Chapter 4, Section II.C.4.). You can become intimately familiar with the particular role you are playing simply by playing it, and you are likely to become intimate with at least some of the other participants in the setting with whom problems and experiences are being shared. On the other hand, there are limitations to data access built into occupying an existing role. When you actually perform a role that is necessary to and already a part of the setting, you must use a good portion of your time performing that role. This reduces freedom to wander about and observe the activities of other roles. And since no one knows about your "researcher self," actions which express that self, such as questioning and open or frequent note taking, must also be curtailed. The range of matters into which you can openly inquire is restricted. If you move beyond asking about things that are role-appropriate, suspicion may be aroused. And people may become suspicious if you jot down notes openly or withdraw too frequently for the purpose of surreptitious note taking.

2. **Known Investigators.** Known investigators—whether doing intensive interviewing or participant observation—enjoy the tremendous advantage of being able to move about, observe, and/or question in a relatively unrestricted way. Of course, known observers who are also full participants in a

setting share some of the time-space restrictions of their unknown counterparts. But like known outside observers and intensive interviewers, they do not have to cover up their investigative activities. Only common standards of decorum, tact, courtesy, and circumspection—that is, only the necessity of getting along with the participants—need interfere with their "snooping" and "prying." And note taking is generally not problematic. Interviewers are usually expected by the people they are interviewing to be taking notes. In fact, their failure to do so may communicate lack of seriousness or inattention. And while it can be situationally inappropriate or strategically unwise for known observers to take notes in the immediate presence of the people being researched, known observers are also considerably freer to structure their own time so as to withdraw intermittently for note taking purposes (Danziger, 1979; Thorne, 1979).

3. **Teams.** For data logging purposes, *team research* can be quite advantageous. Two or more observers or interviewers can simultaneously be looking, listening, and/or asking in different places and with different people, generating a potentially broader and richer data log in a shorter period of time. If analysis is to be facilitated, however, all members of the team must be as familiar with the data being logged by their teammates as with their own. As the sheer quantity of data increases, this can become burdensome, if not impossible. Teams may also intensify the problems of "getting along" simply because more people in the field can generate more errors (see for example Shaffir, Marshall & Haas, 1980). Nonetheless, if data quantity and familiarity problems can be solved and if social relations aspects are adequately coordinated, the logging advantages of team research certainly recommend it as a model for naturalistic investigators.

C. Problems of Error and Bias

We indicated in Chapter 2 that naturalistic investigation, with its preferences for direct apprehension of the social world, has somewhat fewer problems with validity than do research traditions which rely on indirect perception. Nonetheless, the fact remains that every piece of information received by the naturalistic researcher *must still raise a question regarding its truth*—regarding the degree to which it is an accurate depiction of physical or verbal behavior or belief. We know from our everyday experience that disagreements about the facts of an event, for example, are quite common. A good part of the work of courts of law is devoted to sorting out more or less plausible but opposing depictions of "the facts." Similarly, disputes about the facts abound in historical research and among operators of military, industrial, and other systems of intelligence. And, it would seem that everyday life, law, history, and intelligence systems teach us that there is no easy way to determine what are "the facts."

Therefore, you, the investigator, like people in everyday life and in more specialized areas, are constantly faced with the question of "what really is the case?" You are faced with this question at two levels. First, regarding your own perceptions: Have I seen or heard this accurately? Second, regarding other people's reports: Is this reporter providing me with an accurate account?

While there is no royal road to truth, there are nonetheless some basic questions or tests that can be used to evaluate your own perception and the perceptions of other people:

▶ *Directness of the report.* Is this account based on direct perception, or does it come second-, third-, or fourthhand? If the latter, is it therefore to be treated with caution *as fact*, even if it is accurate as image?

▶ *Spatial location of the reporter.* Even if firsthand, what was my (or my reporter's) spatial location such that this perception might be accurate in some respects but still skewed or partial?

▶ *Social locational skewing of reported opinion.* With regard to reports of opinion, what might there be about the relation between myself and the reporter that might lead her or him to lie, distort, omit, falsely elaborate, or otherwise be less than accurate?

▶ *Self-serving error and bias concerning reports.* From what I know on other grounds about my own or the reporter's commitments, values, and announced biases, are there reasons to be suspicious of the content of this report? Does it fit all too conveniently with what I want to believe, or what the reporter might want to believe, about people and events? That is, is it *self-serving* and therefore to be regarded with caution?

▶ *Previous plain error in reports.* From what is known about my or the reporter's previous perceptions, am I an accurate observer/listener? Is the reporter? Have I or the reporter made errors in the past, even though these are not self-serving errors?

▶ *Internal consistency of the report.* Is this report consistent within itself? Are there spatial-temporal facts stated at one point that contradict spatial-temporal assertions at other points? Were the events of this report possible within the time and space constraints given in the report or known about on other grounds? Do the people involved unaccountably contradict themselves within this report?

▶ *External consistency; agreement among independent reports.* Is this account consistent with other accounts of the same events or experiences? Have I assembled enough independent accounts, subjected them to the above questions, and then compared them for degree of agreement? On points of remaining disagreement, have I made sufficient effort to speak with more participants in the event or persons involved in the experience—persons who are otherwise qualified reporters—in order to arrive at a truthful account?

Of course, reports can pass all these tests and still be false. Against that possibility, we offer the maxim that truthful observation/listening depends heavily upon the sincere good faith, open-mindedness and thoroughness of the observer. In the end, too, the readers of your analysis will also subject it to these same kinds of questions and thus decide what degree of trust to place in it.

Peculiarly, despite considerable professional and philosophical concern about error and bias in naturalistic studies, those topics rarely arise in connection with accomplished works. They appear rarely, even, as unpublished allegations along the grapevine of professional social science. Perhaps constant general worry about potential error and bias protects the naturalistic investigator from their actual occurrence. (See further R. Wax, 1971:140–141 on diligent and thorough note taking as a corrective to investigator bias.)

D. Protecting Anonymity

In most naturalistic investigations, the question of providing anonymity to the people studied (discussed in Chapter 3, Section IV.) does not usually arise until the writing-up stage is reached (see Chapters 10 and 11). That is, it is ordinarily only when the fruits of your research have been written as analysis that you become concerned to disguise identities and locations (if disguise is what you intend). However, there are some sorts of sensitive research that push this concern with confidentiality backward in time to the point of data logging. If you are studying persons engaged in illegal or politically suspect activity, for example, or persons involved in activities kept secret from their associates, or well-known figures who are speaking openly only with the assurance that it is "off the record," and so forth, you may want to take considerable precaution with the data log itself. Carol Warren's handling of her research log on "closet" gay men is exemplary:

. . . Tape recorded interviews were stored without identifying tags (although voices could be identified), and were erased after transcription and use. Field notes were kept in unlocked storage; however, pseudonyms were used throughout the recording of field notes, and a master list of names matched to pseudonyms [kept in locked storage] was discarded following the write up of the material. (Warren, 1977:96.)

E. Duplicating and Typing the Log

For reasons that will become clear in Chapter 9 (and having to do with manipulating data in order to generate analysis), it is essential that the data log—whether in the form of recorded interviews or field notes—be *duplicated,* so that you have at least two or three copies of each page of interview transcription or field notes. You can do this in a variety of ways: carbon paper or carbon sets for the initial recording; photoduplicating; recording on spirit masters or stencils for "run-off"; or, if you have access to the newer technologies, logging directly into a word processor (Seidal & Clark, 1982a, 1982b).

As should be apparent, we also strongly advise that the data log be *typed* (and typed with wide margins—see Chapter 9). Researchers who prepare their notes or transcribe their interviews by hand are adding another level of tedium to an already tedious task and are quite likely, as a consequence, to settle for incomplete, shallow interview write-ups and sketchy field notes. Additionally, the manipulation of the log in the analysis phase is greatly facilitated by the sort of clarity and legibility achieved through typing. Prospective fieldworkers who can't type—who can't even "hunt and peck" with reasonable speed—should simply *learn* to do so before entering the field. Naturalist research relies primarily on social relations and analytic skills, but if its one requisite technological skill—typing—is absent, these skills may easily be negated. (The alternative—secretarial assistance—is a rare occurrence but will be discussed below.)

As we have seen, the data logging tasks in intensive interviewing and participant observation are similar in many ways. But there are also several important differences. It is important, therefore, that we now consider each mode separately.

II. DATA LOGGING IN INTENSIVE INTERVIEWING

In intensive interviewing, the data are initially logged via an instrument known as an "interview guide." In this section, we will first discuss the preparation of such a guide, then go on to the matter of actually doing the interview with the guide, and finally consider the production of the actual log: the writing up of the interview.

A. Preparing the Interview Guide

The interview guide is considerably less formal or structured than the questionnaire or interview schedule used in survey research or opinion polling, but the care with which it is created is no less crucial. Its production requires serious thought.

1. Puzzlements and Jottings. Logging data by means of intensive interviewing with interview guides reasonably begins with you—the prospective investigator—taking some place, class of persons, experience, abstract topic, or whatever, as problematic—as a source of puzzlement. If you take this puzzlement seriously, that is, if you decide to pursue it as a topic of investigation, and if you judge that interviewing is the most appropriate procedure (see Chapter 2), you then sit down in a quiet place and use what is called "common sense." You ask yourself: Just what about this thing is puzzling to me? Without worry about coherence and the like, you begin to jot down questions about these puzzling matters and, at various times over several days or weeks, continue to do so. Questions may occur at odd moments—while taking a shower, listening to conversations, driving, opening mail, and so forth—and thus you should keep a small notebook in close proximity at all times. In this phase, it is also useful to mention the topic to friends, acquaintances, and associates, who may suggest additional questions or stimulate new dimensions of puzzlement. These too are jotted down.

What are you doing in this stage? You are "teasing out" and recording those things defined as puzzling in the context of the cultural understandings of yourself and your associates. You are preparing to use, as a point of departure for interviewing, what is puzzling relative to that cultural perspective. A not insignificant element of this cultural perspective will, one hopes, be some knowledge of those puzzlements institutionalized in the literature of a relevant social science discipline. In addition, it is entirely proper to locate and to read books and articles on the particular, concrete matter of concern. In reading, you can discover what others who have written about and studied this matter found puzzling and what kinds of questions they have asked. And, too, you can note the kinds of answers they have offered.

At the operating level, it is wise never to put more than one puzzlement or particular kind of question on a single sheet of paper or card (or whatever you like to write on). The effort at this stage is to retain maximum flexibility in organizing. Listing no more than one thought per page extends your capacity to organize and reorganize at will.

2. **Global Sorting and Ordering.** As these puzzlements accumulate, they develop into an incoherent assembly. Hopefully, as you have been going along, you have also been thinking about the kinds of general clusters or topics into which these various puzzlements fall. You should also have recorded ideas on the overall structure or organization of the puzzlements, because eventually you must give these puzzlements or questions a global or comprehensive design. If they have been written on separate pieces of paper or cards, you can thus begin to sort them physically into separate piles of paper or cards on some flat surface. Several sortings and resortings may be necessary in order to establish the number of "piles of paper"—or, more abstractly, *topics*—that seem best to arrange your accumulated concerns. Whatever the several topics, it is not necessary to strive for any kind of sophisticated social scientific sense in formulating them. Indeed, it is preferable for the topics to be quite straightforward and commonsensical, the better to communicate with the people to be interviewed.

The following is an example of global organization, drawn from Lyn Lofland's interview guide for her study of "loss and connection." Note that it does not, except in its lack of "elegance," differ greatly from outlines of other kinds—the outlines of articles, books, or structured interview schedules. Here, as elsewhere in life, straightforward, logical, orderly thought is applied:

1. Who was lost?
2. When?
3. Tell me about the relationship prior to "loss": dyadic career.
4. Tell me about the loss itself.
5. Prior loss experience.
6. Immediate response to the loss: emotional, physical, behavioral.
7. Development/changes through time regarding feelings and actions.
8. Looking at the relationship from current perspective. (L. Lofland, 1982.)

Sometimes sorting at the global level generates a list of topics, areas or questions which come to constitute the entire guide, as for example in Ritchie Lowry's guide for interviews with community leaders:

1. Could you indicate several major changes in Micro City [a pseudonym used by Lowry] in the last decade which you feel are particularly important?
2. In your opinion have these changes been good or bad for the community?
3. In light of these changes what do you predict for Micro City's future?
4. Will these future changes and problems be good or bad?
5. What do you think constitutes an "issue" or problem to us here in Micro City? Can you give some examples?

6. Can you indicate several leaders of the community who in your opinion have contributed most to Micro City in their concern for these changes? Can you identify the general sources of effective leadership in Micro City?

7. What role do you think community organizations, institutions (like the college, PG&E, PT&T), individuals, the mass media, and the general public have played and should play in community issues and problems?

8. What is the best way of handling issues or problems like those you have mentioned in a community like ours?

9. If you had the power to do anything you wanted for the good of this community, what would you do or suggest be done? What changes would you like to see made in the community? (Lowry, 1965:235–236.)

In constructing your global design, try to adopt the perspective of the interviewees and to think about what will make sense and be most acceptable to them. If some topics are of a sensitive character or potentially embarrassing to them or to you, it is often better to address these toward the end of the interview. The hope is that by treating the less sensitive material first, you will build trust and rapport during the course of the interview itself, making it easier subsequently to deal with more tension-laden topics. Sometimes it is wise to begin with relatively neutral "facesheet items" (see Section II.A.5. below) as an innocuous way of getting into the question-and-answer process.

3. **Section Sorting and Ordering.** Once an overall design for the guide has been at least tentatively established, and assuming it does not constitute the entire guide, you can turn to particular piles of puzzlements within the overall design and begin to plan a reasonably commonsensical ordering of concerns and questions. For example, Sarah Matthews's interview guide for her study of old women contains a global section dealing with the question "Who are the people you see most often?" Within that section, the guide then specifies (after obtaining age and relationship information) the following questions to be used about each person mentioned:

a. What does _____ usually call you?

b. What do you do with _____ ?

c. When you are with _____ what do you usually talk about?

d. Do you avoid talking about some things with _____ ?

e. Do you think that _____ avoids talking about some things with you?

f. Are there some things that _____ says or does that make you feel uncomfortable?

g. Have you noticed any difference in the way _____ treats you since you've gotten older?

h. Do you ever take advantage of your age when you are with _____ ?

i. Do you ever do things that you know _____ will disapprove of just to make a point?

j. Are there times when you feel very conscious of your age when you are with _____ ?

k. Are you ever surprised by what _____ expects of you?

l. Are there many things you avoid doing with _____ ?

m. Do you think that _____ tries to do too much for you or makes too many decisions for you? Or not enough?

n. Do you sometimes feel that _____ treats you as if you were a child?

o. Do you ever think that _____ talks to you just to be polite?

p. Do you think of yourself as old when you are with _____ ?

q. Do you think _____ thinks of you as old? (Matthews, 1979:177–179.)

Similarly, global section 6 of Lyn Lofland's interview guide on loss and connection (see above) contains the following questions:

a. What exactly did you do in the first days or week following the loss? Different than normal?

b. What exactly did you feel in the first days or week following the loss? Different than normal?

c. How did others act toward you? How did you feel about their actions?

d. Did the loss seem appropriate, timely, untimely, meaningless, meaningful?

e. Did the loss in any sense seem to free you? How?

f. [If appropriate,] did you attend the funeral or other services? (L. Lofland, 1982).

4. **Probes.** In interview guides, the emphasis is on obtaining narratives or accounts in the person's own terms. You want the character and contour of such accounts to be set by the interviewees or informants. You might have a general idea of the kinds of things that will compose the account but still be interested in what the interviewees provide on their own and the terms in which they do it. As the informants speak, you should be attentive to what is mentioned and also to what is *not mentioned* but which you feel might be important. If something has been mentioned about which you want to know more, you can ask, "You mentioned _____ ; could you tell me more about that?" For things not mentioned, you might ask, "Did _____ happen?" or "Was _____ a consideration?"

Such questions are called **probes.** In interview guides, a series of probes are often connected to a specific question in order to remind the interviewer to probe for items that might not be mentioned spontaneously. One of Sarah Matthews's questions—"Do you have any trouble hearing? seeing?"—contained the following probes:

When are you conscious of this?

With whom?

Do you avoid going places because you cannot hear well? (Matthews, 1979:179.)

And in asking about "relational career," Lyn Lofland's guide contains a reminder to probe for:

How did relationship develop?
What sorts of things done together?
What sorts of things talked about together?
Intensity—time together in a typical week/year
Changes in intensity through time
Emotional tone
Changes in emotional tone
Importance placed by you on the relationship
Changes in importance (L. Lofland, 1982.)

This is not to say that every question must be outfitted with one or more prepared probes. It may happen that you do not, at a given time, have much idea of what to probe for. Many on-the-spot probes are likely to be used spontaneously in order to amplify or clarify an account. And many kinds of questions may not especially require probes (although they can doubtless be invented for any question).

5. **Facesheets and Post-Interview Comment Sheets.** For purposes of identification, bookkeeping, and generally keeping track of the interviews and the social characteristics of interviewees, it is common for interview guides to devote a page or so to gross factual data. Such a page is often the first sheet of the guide and is therefore called the **facesheet.** The following are among the items typically appearing on the facesheet. (Any given facesheet may, however, omit particular items if they are not relevant to the study.)

Interviewee's name (or a code number, if the topic is a sensitive one and names keyed to code numbers are to be kept in a separate place)
The number of the interview (if you choose to keep track of interviews by number rather than name)
Date of interview
Place of interview
Sex
Age
Education
Race or ethnicity
Place of residence
Place of birth
Occupation or other position
Religion

Beyond information of this sort, additional social items will probably be structured according to the purposes of the interview and will therefore vary a good deal from one study to another. Even though the facesheet is typically the first sheet, facesheet questions are not necessarily the first questions asked. Depending upon the topic, the degree of trust, and so forth, it may sometimes be preferable to go directly into the interview itself after giving the introduction. In that case, the facesheet questions are sometimes treated almost like a formal afterthought, a minor duty that you have to perform in interviewing. Whether filled out first or last, you will probably still want the facesheet to be the first sheet of the guide so you can later easily identify the guide itself.

In addition, interviewers sometimes find it useful to append to the guide a post-interview **comment sheet**. This is not material that is shared with the informant. Rather, it is simply a space for the interviewer to use, after you and the informant have parted, to jot down some field notes on the interview itself. Time of day of the interview, its emotional tone, any particular difficulties (methodological or personal) that were encountered, your own feelings during and about the experience, insights and reflections, and so on may all be appropriately included. The jotted notes on such sheets are later incorporated into the interview write-up and become a portion of the data log.

B. Doing the Interview

Much about the social relational aspects of interviewing has already been discussed in Chapter 4. Here we shall deal with the more technical matters of introduction, format, leading questions, interviewer activity during the interview, and the use of separate guides.

1. **Introduction.** Recall from Chapter 3 (Section II.B.2.) that the "getting in" phase of intensive interviewing requires an "account"—an introduction, as it were, to the potential informant. This account indicates the topic or topics to be covered, the probable length of time required, promises of anonymity if appropriate, and so forth. At the time of actually sitting down to the interview, you should repeat much of this material and, if called for, provide additional information. The point at both stages is to acquaint the person honestly and clearly with what you are asking her or him to do. The list of self-instructions in Fred Davis's guide for interviewing handicapped persons provides a stellar example of proper introductory material:

▶ Explain purpose and nature of the study to the respondent, telling how or through whom he came to be selected.

▶ Give assurance that respondent will remain anonymous in any written reports growing out of the study, and that his responses will be treated in strictest confidence.

▶ Indicate that he may find some of the questions farfetched, silly or difficult to answer, the reason being that questions that are appropriate for one person are not always appropriate for another. Since there are no right or wrong answers, he is not to worry about these and do as best he can with them. We are only interested in his opinions and personal experiences.

▶ He is to feel perfectly free to interrupt, ask clarification of the interviewer, criticize a line of questioning, etc.

▶ , Interviewer will tell respondent something about himself—his background, training, and interest in the area of inquiry.

▶ Interviewer is to ask permission to tape record the interview, explaining why he wishes to do this. (F. Davis, 1961.)

This list should be read as a set of points to cover, some when asking for the interview and all when beginning the interview. But it should not be interpreted, mechanically, as a set order of items to be run through in rote fashion. You will probably want to vary the style and order of coverage according to the dictates of the circumstances. The important point is that these are matters of common politeness and involve information that the interviewee has a right to know.

2. **Flexible Format.** As can be seen from the wording and layout of the interview guide examples provided above, a guide is *not* a tightly structured set of questions to be asked verbatim as written, accompanied by an associated range of preworded likely answers. Rather, *it is a list of things to be sure to ask about when talking to the person being interviewed.* For this reason, the interview instrument is called a *guide* rather than a schedule or questionnaire. You want interviewees to speak freely in their own terms about a set of concerns you bring to the interaction, plus whatever else they might introduce. Thus, interviews might more accurately be termed *guided conversations*.

It happens that people vary a good deal as to how freely they speak or how chatty they are. When you encounter less verbal interviewees, it is likely that you will go through the interview guide in the order that you have set up the questions. The interviewee may provide little in response to each question, giving you little place to go save on to the next question.

Fortunately, however, many people are verbal, chatty types. In response to a given question they will raise all manner of leads and puzzlements that may merit pursuit, either at that point or reasonably soon thereafter. (Ideally, you should pursue such a lead at a moment when it is also of concern to the interviewee.) Also, in the course of talking about things the interviewee cares about, some of the questions in other parts of the guide may inadvertently get answered. The interview guide in such cases provides a checklist of sorts, a kind of inventory of things you want to talk about during the interview. You can check them off as they are accomplished.

3. **Leading Questions.** A word of caution about wording questions: Avoid posing questions in such a way that they communicate what you believe to be a preferable answer. Questions so posed are known as **leading questions.** Thus, instead of starting off with "Don't you think that . . . ?", begin with something like "What do you think about . . . ?" Instead of "Is it not likely that . . . ?", use something like "How likely would you say it is that . . . ?"

The following are extracts from two interviews that illustrate not only neutrality in wording of questions but also something of the free-flowing and probing character of intensive interviewing. In the first, Albert J. Reiss is interviewing a young man about his contacts with a homosexual:

When queried about his relationship with this man and why he went with him, Thurman replied: Don't know . . . money and stuff like that I guess.

What do you mean? . . . stuff like that?

Oh, clothes . . . .

He ever bought you any clothes?

Sure, by this one gay . . . .

You mind being blowed?

No.

You like it?

Don't care one way or the other. I don't like it, and I don't not like it.

You like this one gay?

Nope, can't say I like anythin' about him.

How come you do it then?

Well, the money for one thing . . . I need that.

You enjoy it some?

Can't say I do or don't. (Reiss, 1968:377.)

The second example is from an interview by Carl Werthman, speaking with a ghetto youth on how teachers grade students:

How do you know how the teacher is grading you?

You don't know whether the stud is bribing you with a grade, whether he givin' you a bad one cause you don't kiss behind him, or whether he straight. Or maybe he like the gym teacher that give out the grades any which way.

But how do you find out what basis the teacher is using?

Well, you gotta ask around the class. Find out what other kids got. Like when I get my report card? I shoot out and ask my partners what they got. Then I go ask the poopbutts what they got.

Do they always let you look at their report cards?

They can't do nothing but go for it. Like they got to go home sometime. I mean we shoot them with a left and a right if they don't come across. I mean this grade shit is important. You gotta know what's happening.

Why?

Well, shit, how you gonna know what the teacher like? I mean if he straight or not. (Werthman, 1963:47.)

4. **Attending, Thinking, Taking Notes, Taping.** In our view it is imperative that you tape record the interview itself. Since there is no strict order of questioning and since probing is an important part of the process, you must be very alert to what the interviewee is saying. If you have to write everything down at the same time, you are unlikely to be able adequately to attend to the interviewee. Your full attention *must* be focused upon the informant. You must be thinking about probing for further explication or clarification of what is now being said; formulating probes that link current talk with what has already been said; thinking ahead to asking a *new* question that has now arisen and was not accounted for in the guide (plus making a note

so you won't forget the question); and attending to the interviewee in a manner that communicates to her or him that you are indeed listening. All of this is hard enough simply in itself. Add to that the problem of writing it down—even if you take shorthand in an expert fashion—and you can see that the process of note taking in the interview decreases your interviewing capacity. Therefore, if conceivably possible, *tape record.* Then you can interview.

But there are dangers in tape recording, too. Some people have found themselves not listening to the interviewee because they assume they have it all down on tape. The best way to fight against this tendency is to take sparse notes—key sentences, key words, key names, and so forth—in the course of the interview and keep close account of what has already been talked about and what remains to be talked about. This is note taking in its best sense: for the purpose of staying on top of what is going on in the interview. You take notes on what has already gone on, and notes on what should go on—what has now come up that you should ask about before the interview is over. (You also have a basis for reconstructing the interview should—terrible of terribles—the tape recording fail!)

5. **Separate Guides.** Because the interview guide provides a checklist and a memory device—that is, a place for taking small notes during the interview—it is wise to use a fresh copy of the guide for each interview. Various cheap means of reproduction are available for providing such copies. The annotated guide for each separate interview thus becomes a recording and memory device at the time of writing up the interview and during full analysis. For jotting purposes, too, you should be careful not to cram the questions and probes together on a page, but rather space them out, leaving ample room for notes.

C. Writing Up the Interview

Having completed the interview, you can, if you are affluent or have extraordinarily indulgent associates, simply have the tape transcribed verbatim. You can then study the transcript and begin to analyze it. However, a strong caution should be given about such transcriptions: *Do not let the transcripts pile up without studying them as they become available.* You should spend, *at minimum,* at least as much time *immediately* studying and analyzing the interview material as you spent in the interview itself. Ideas for analysis should be set down in the form of memos. Possible requests for a reinterview of the same person or particular topics should be considered. Filing and classification should be performed as you go along, rather than after all the interviews are done. (See Chapter 9 for the rationale behind these admonitions.)

So much for the affluent. More numerous are the do-it-yourself transcribers. Transcribing tapes is a chore. But it also has an enormous virtue. It *requires* you to study each interview. Listening to the tape piece by piece forces you to consider, piece by piece, whether you have accomplished anything in the interview or not. It stimulates *analysis* (or at least this is the proper frame of mind to adopt while doing it). When a distinction, a concept, or an idea occurs to you, write it into the transcription as a note or analysis. For out of these bits and pieces of analysis you will be able to build the larger analysis that will become your research report.

It is generally not necessary to transcribe every word, exclamation, or pause that occurs in an interview. Indeed, there may be entire answers or descriptions given by the interviewee that you will feel need only to be summarized or recorded as *having occurred.* You do not necessarily need a verbatim transcription of everything the interviewee said, as the written record will indicate where to look for it on the tape. If you later want to have a verbatim version of a particular part of the interview, it can easily be located and transcribed.

The writtten record of the interview, then, is an amalgam of the following:

1. Summaries and notes of what the informant said generally at some point
2. Verbatim transcription of responses that seem important at the point of the write-up
3. Ideas—little, tentative pieces of analysis
4. Methodological difficulties or successes
5. Personal emotional experiences

The process of writing up is a crucial one in this kind of research enterprise. You should expect to spend about *twice* as long writing up the interview in this fashion as you spent in conducting it.

One other point: In the course of writing up the interview, new questions and puzzlements are likely to occur. These should be recorded and later considered for incorporation into future interviews as questions or probes. If there are a great many new questions that require interviews, you should consider doing some reinterviews.

Interviews of this kind tend to produce a rather large amount of rich material. Before long, you have assembled a significant data log that needs somehow to be managed. Indeed, the management problem is such that researchers who conduct studies utilizing qualitative interviewing tend to employ rather few interviews. It is our impression that such studies are typically based on only about 20–50 interviews. Given the material management problem, numbers in that range seem quite reasonable. The researcher legitimately sacrifices breadth for depth.

III. FIELD NOTES

What the write-up is to intensive interviewing, field notes are to participant observation: the crucial data log out of which the analysis will emerge.

For better or worse, the human mind forgets massively and quickly. The people under study are no exception. So in order to have any kind of an edge on the participants in articulating and understanding their world, you must have some means to overcome this tendency in yourself. Writing is such a means. Without continually writing down what has gone on, the observer is hardly in a better position to analyze and comprehend the workings of a world than are the members themselves. Writing, in the form of continued notes by which the past is retained in the present, is an absolutely necessary if not sufficient condition for comprehending the objects of observation. Aside from getting along in the setting, the fundamental concrete task of the observer is the taking of field notes. If you are not doing so, you might as well not be in the setting.

A. Mental Notes

Let us assume you are somewhere—meeting with persons, say, or attending an event. The first step in taking field notes is to evoke your culturally commonsensical and shared notion of what constitutes a descriptive report of an event. From reading newspapers, magazines, and the like, you are already familiar with the character of "sheer reportage." It concerns such matters as who and how many were there, the physical character of the place, who said what to whom, who moved about in what way, and a general characterization of an order of events.

The first step in the process of writing field notes is to orient your consciousness to the task of remembering items of these and, as the research develops, other kinds. This act of directing your mind to remember things at a later point may be called making *mental notes*. You are preparing yourself to be able later to put down on paper what you are now seeing.

B. Jotted Notes

If you are writing actual field notes only at the end of a period of observation or at the end of a day—which is a relatively typical practice—you should preserve these mental notes as more than electrical traces in the brain. Such traces have a very high rate of decay. One way in which to preserve them provisionally is with *jotted notes*. Jotted notes are constituted of all the little phrases, quotes, key words, and the like that you put down during the observation and at inconspicuous moments in order to have something physical to refer to when you actually sit down to write your field notes. Jotted notes have the function of jogging your memory at the time of writing field notes.

Many fieldworkers carry small, pocket-sized tablets or notebooks precisely for the purpose of jotting down notes. Any surface will do, however— the cover of a book, a napkin, the back of a pamphlet, and so forth.

1. Memories. In the field, a present observation will often bring back a memory of something that happened on a previous occasion that you forgot to put in your field notes. Include these memories—identified as such—in your jotted notes also.

2. Jotting Inconspicuously. As mentioned above, whether you are a known or an unknown observer, the general rule of thumb is "don't jot conspicuously." Of course, you may also be doing interviewing in the field while observing. In that case, in order to seem competent, you should take notes of the kind described for intensive interviewing. Indeed, the interviewees will *expect* you to take some kind of notes in order to indicate that you are indeed seriously interviewing them! And there may be other occasions when someone expects you to write something down on the spot.

But in ordinary day-to-day observation it seems wisest not to flaunt the fact that you are recording. If you are a known observer, the observed are already well aware of being observed. You need not increase any existing anxieties by continuously and openly writing down what you see and hear. Rather, jot notes at moments of withdrawal and when shielded. (In settings that have "meetings," members will sometimes themselves make notes. Under such conditions you can feel free to go along with the crowd.)

3. **Fuller Jottings.** In addition, and before getting to the full field notes, you might—on the way home, while waiting for a bus, before going to bed—make more elaborate jottings.

C. Full Field Notes

At the end of the day (or of a shorter observation period), you should cloister yourself for the purpose of making *full field notes*. All those mental notes and jottings are *not* field notes until you have converted them to a running log of observations.

1. **Mechanics.** Before we discuss the typical contents of fieldnotes, some "mechanical" aspects need to be described.

As a general rule *write promptly*. Full field notes should be written no later than the morning after an observation day. If you observed only in the morning, then write them up that afternoon. If you observed only in the afternoon, do the notes that evening. The underlying rule is to minimize the time period between observation and writing field notes.

Psychologists have found that forgetting is very slight in the first few hours after a learning experience but accelerates geometrically as time passes. To wait a day or more is to forget a massive amount of material. Happily, it has also been found that memory decays very little during sleep. That is, forgetting has more to do with the acquisition of new experience than with the sheer passage of time. Therefore, it is reasonably safe to sleep on a day's or evening's observations and to write them up the first thing next morning, thus avoiding the necessity of staying up half the night. But if you wait for days, you are likely to remember only the barest outlines of the observation period.

As we have previously emphasized, the writing of field notes takes *personal discipline* and *time*. It is all too easy to put it off for a day or so, especially since the actual writing of the notes may take as long or longer than the observation. Indeed, as a rule of thumb you should plan to spend as much time writing as you spent observing. This is, of course, not invariant. Some observers spend considerably less time on notes and are still able to perform good analysis. Many others have been known to spend considerably more than equal time in writing up their notes. How much time you personally spend depends, too, on the demands of the setting you are observing and the proportion of your total time being devoted to the study.

But one point is inescapable. All the fun of actually being out and about mucking around in some setting must be matched by cloistered rigor in committing to paper (and therefore to future usefulness) what has taken place.

Some observers have access to the luxury of dictating machines and secretaries. And, of course, "talking" your field notes takes much less time than writing them. Such affluents need the same advice here as was given for intensive interviewers: Get the transcriptions as soon as possible and review them thoroughly, making further notes in the process. While dictation saves time, it also keeps you from really having to think about what has happened and from searching out analytic themes. Writing, on the other hand, stimulates thought, or at least so it seems for a great number of people.

2. **Contents.** Of what do field notes consist? Basically, they are a more or less chronological log of what is happening to and in the setting and to and in the observer. More specifically, the types of material described below typically and properly appear in field notes.

▶ For the most part, field notes are a running description of events, people, things heard and overheard, conversations among people, conversations with people. Each new physical setting and person encountered merits a description. You should also record changes in the physical setting or persons. Since you are likely to encounter the same settings and persons again and again, such descriptions need not be repeated, only augmented as changes occur.

Observers often draw maps into their field notes, indicating approximate layouts and the physical placement of persons in scenes, as well as the gross movements of persons through a period of observation. And, since the notes will be chronologically arranged, you should also keep records of the approximate times at which various events occur.

The writing of running descriptions is guided by at least two rules of thumb: (1) Be concrete; and (2) Distinguish verbatim accounts from those that are paraphrased or based on general recall.

Rather than summarizing or employing abstract adjectives and adverbs, attempt to be behavioristic and *concrete*. Attempt to stay at the lowest possible level of inference. Avoid, as much as possible, employing the participants' descriptive and interpretive terms as your own. If Person A thought Person B was happy, joyous, depressed, or whatever, report this as an imputation of Person A. Try to capture Person B's raw behavior, leaving aside for that moment any final judgment as to B's actual state of mind or the "true meaning" of his or her behavior. The participants' beliefs as to the "true meaning" of objects, events and people are thus recorded as being just that—beliefs.

Truman Capote claims to be able to recall verbatim several hours of conversation. Such an ability is strikingly unusual. More typically, people recall some things word for word and many other things only in general. Whether you are giving a verbatim account should be indicated in your field notes. You might consider adopting notations such as those employed by Anselm Strauss et al. in their study of a mental hospital: "Verbal material recorded within quotations signified exact recall; verbal material within apostrophes indicated a lesser degree of certainty or paraphrasing; and verbal material with no markings meant reasonable recall but not quotation" (Strauss, Schatzman, Bucher, Ehrlich & Sabshin, 1964:29; see also Schatzman & Strauss, 1973:Chapter Six).

▶ As observation periods mount up, you may find yourself recalling—often at odd moments—items of information you have not previously entered into the field notes. An occurrence previously seen as insignificant, or simply forgotten, now presents itself as meriting record. Summoning it up as best you can, enter the item's date, content, the context, and so forth into the current day's notes.

▶ If you are working at it at all, analytic ideas and inferences will begin to occur to you; for example, how things are patterned in the setting, how present occurrences are examples of some sociological or other concept, or how things "really seem to work around here." Some of these ideas may seem obvious and trivial; some may seem farfetched and wild; and many may seem in between. *Put all of them into the field notes.* The only proviso is to be sure to mark them as analytic ideas or inferences. (A good way to do this is to enclose them in brackets.)

When you eventually withdraw from the setting and concentrate on your analysis, you should thus have more than raw field material. The period of concerted analysis is greatly facilitated if during the fieldwork itself you are also logging conceptual material, creating a foundation of possible lines of analysis and interpretation. Such material may range from minute pieces of analysis to broad ideas about the master theme or themes of the study.

You are likely to have more of these memos on analytic directions in your notes than you will ever include in the final report. But, by building a foundation of tentative pieces of directions for analysis, the analytic period will be much less traumatic. Analysis will become a matter of selecting from and working out analytic themes that already exist.

▶ In addition to providing a record of the setting and of analytic ideas, field notes are used for recording your impressions and feelings. You have personal opinions of people, emotional responses to being an observer and to the setting itself. You can feel discouraged, joyous, rejected, loved, and so forth. In order to provide some degree of distance, you should also record whatever aspects of your emotional life are involved in the setting. If you feel embarrassed, put down, looked upon with particular favor, if you fall in love, hate someone, have an affair, or whatever, this private diary should be keeping track of such facts. This can serve at least two important functions. (1) In being (at least privately) honest with yourself about your feelings toward objects, events, and people, you may find that some of the participants *also* feel quite similar things and that your private emotional response was more widespread, thus providing a clue for analysis. In feeling, for instance, that some person in the setting is getting "screwed" by a turn of events, and getting privately angry over it, you may also discover later that many other people privately felt the same way. And a fact of this kind may lead to important analytic trails. (2) Periodically, you will review your field notes, and during analysis you will work with them intensively. A concurrent record of your emotional state at various past times can, months later, away from the setting and in a cooler frame of mind, allow you to scrutinize your notes for obvious biases. You become more able to give the benefit of the doubt in cases where you were perhaps too involved or uninvolved in some incident. This running record of your opinions, impressions, emotions, and the like should, of course, be labeled as such in the notes.

▶ Any given day's observations are likely to be incomplete. An account of an incident may lack an adequate description of a given person's behavior or conscious intentions. The incident may only be sketchily known. A well-described incident may lead you to look for further occurrences of events of that kind. In other words, a given day's notes raise a series of observational questions and call for notes for further information. It is reasonable to make these notes as you are writing up your full field notes. You can then review and assemble them as reminders of unobtrusive questions to ask particular people or of things to look for.

3. **Style.** There are several additional stylistic aspects of field notes that relate to both the mechanical and content matters we have discussed.

For one thing, there is the inevitable question of how long and full the notes should be. How many pages should notes run for a given observation period? It happens that observers differ enormously in the detail and length of the field notes they keep. Some seem to be frustrated novelists and have been known to write 40 or more single-spaced pages on a three-hour period of observation. Other observers might write only a few pages. Here there are no set rules. Settings differ enormously, as do observers' verbal compulsions. The kinds of phenomena to which observers are sensitive vary quite widely. At minimum, though, you ought to write up at least a couple of single-spaced typed pages for every hour of observation. It is quite likely that you will want to write much more.

Field notes are typically quite private documents, or at least accessible only to your trusted friends, as in most team observer situations. So, *let them flow.* You need not attempt to employ totally correct grammar, punctuate with propriety, hit the right typewriter keys, say only publicly polite things, be guarded about your feelings, and all the other niceties most people affect for strangers. The object in field notes, rather, is to get information down as correctly as you can and to be as honest with yourself as possible. Since your notes will *never* be public documents, you can *write on.* Let all those mental and jotted notes flow out, typing like the "compulsive" you are hopefully becoming.

Field notes are, after all, behind the scenes. It is at the next stage—concerted analysis—that all of this is processed for propriety.

We have perhaps made field notes sound intimate and revealing and therefore fascinating reading. To a degree they are. But the overwhelming portion consists of running descriptions that are mundane, uneventful, and dull. Indeed, if they were otherwise, people would simply publish their field notes. It is precisely because they are little in and of themselves that it is necessary to do analysis. Therefore, do not start out believing that the field work venture, and field notes in particular, will be an exciting affair. Patience, persistence, drudgery, and dullness occur here, as everywhere else in social life. Still, field note writing can be punctuated by periods of elation and joy over events and over the occurrence of insights, ideas, and understandings.

D. Field Notes as Compulsion

If all this sound unbearably tedious, take heart. Once you have established a regime of jotting regularly and then making disciplined, full notes, it can come to have a demand and a logic of its own. You can come to feel that unless something you remember appears in your full notes, you are in peril of losing it. That is, you can come to experience a *compulsion* to write up everything lest it be lost forever. Upon reaching that level of felt responsibility for logging data, you are fully engaged in fieldwork.

The preceding chapters describe only the first part of the story of doing naturalistic research. The whole point of starting where you are, of getting in and getting along, and, most especially, of logging data, is the performance of social science analysis. To that challenge we now turn.

PART TWO

Focusing Data

 Naturalists in the social sciences are engaged in a strategy of calculated chaos. They intentionally immerse themselves in the logging of data regarding subjects that are of personal concern to them, a process that initially need have little or no specific social scientific orientation. The theory of the naturalist is that a direction will emerge, will be "discovered."

The discovery of social scientific substance is assisted and guided, however, by three kinds of consciousness that form a set of "focusing" aspects. These are:

Thinking units of social settings (Chapter 6)

Asking questions about such units (Chapter 7)

Being interesting in what you say about the units and questions (Chapter 8)

Thinking
Units

The term *social setting* is an appropriate holistic label for describing the social scientific domain. It is not, however, precise enough to be useful in actual analysis. For that purpose we must employ a set of more refined terms, known collectively as **units** of social settings.

Specifically, a unit is a tool to use in scrutinizing your data log. There is no definitive list of such units, but several are traditional, and all are well studied. In this chapter we will describe eleven which we consider to be the most basic and the most useful. In Chapter 9 we will discuss more specifically *how* to use them.

Except for the first unit we will describe ("meanings," which are present at all levels), the units are arranged from the microscopic to the macroscopic in terms of duration and human population. Put differently, the *scale of social organization* is increasing as we move from unit to unit. It is important to recognize, therefore, that each new unit introduced *contains* units discussed prior to it rather than being separate from them.

I. MEANINGS

The most fundamental and ubiquitous aspect of a human social setting is that of **meanings.** These are the linguistic categories that make up the participants' view of reality and with which they define their own and others' actions. Meanings are also referred to by social analysts as *culture, norms, understandings, social reality, definitions of the situation, typifications, ideology, beliefs, world view, perspective,* or *stereotypes.* Terms such as these share a common focus on a humanly constructed set of concepts which are consciously singled out as important aspects of reality. Meanings are *transbehavioral* in the sense that they do more than *describe* behavior—they define, justify, and otherwise *interpret* behavior as well.

A. Variations in Scope

Meanings vary in terms of the breadth or range of situations to which they apply. On the broadest scale are those that are life-encompassing in scope, claiming to encompass virtually any topic that might be brought up. Such broad-ranging schemes are often called "ideologies," "world views," "*weltanschauungs,*" or "philosophies." In writings on social settings where the participants possess such well-developed cognitive schemes, a significant section of the report is often devoted to this aspect in just these terms. In book length reports, an entire chapter or more may be so given over. Often, the task is to extract not just the obvious but also the more latent themes. Thus, in a now classic characterization of the ideology of the American student movement in the 1960s, sociologist Richard Flacks described "the main value themes" of the students under these seven captions:

1. Romanticism
2. Anti-authoritarianism
3. Equalitarianism, populism
4. Anti-dogmatism
5. Moral purity
6. Community
7. Anti-institutionalism (Flacks, 1967:54–57.)

Meanings can also be more discrete or middle-ranged. That is, they can be both attached to more delimited aspects of a person's life and still rather general in their application. In observing inmates of mental hospitals, Kaplan, Boyd, and Bloom noticed that a person so placed in the world seems to be caught in a dilemma:

On the one hand he experiences great pressures to accept the fact of his illness and the therapeutic potential of the hospital. However, by becoming a patient, his self-image is threatened insofar as he recognizes the prevailing negative attitudes toward his illness.

If [mental patients] are to achieve maximum therapeutic benefit from their experience, they must resolve this conflict in a way that permits acceptance of the fact of their patienthood while minimizing the strain occasioned by the perceived disparagement of their status. (Kaplan, Boyd & Bloom, 1968:363.)

According to these observers, people caught in such a bind seem to evolve a number of meanings or strategies that "apparently function to mitigate this stress." Reduced to simplest form, these are:

1. Assert the commonality of illness among the total patient population.
2. Favorably compare their situation with those of less privileged patient groups.

3. Deny the superiority of the staff and extra-institutional population.
4. Emphasize any rewards that might attach to the position of "mental patients."
5. Confine their temporal orientation to the immediate present. (Kaplan, Boyd & Bloom, 1968:363.)

Analysis of meanings often centers on the question of how members define for themselves a given problematic topic. For example, in observing a religious group that strongly believed it was destined to make thousands of new converts and which worked hard to achieve that goal, John Lofland found it failing time after time. The group members also perceived this failure. How, then, did they "define" or explain this chronic gap between aim and actuality? Members of the group seemed to have three basic explanations:

First, the American group was an offshoot of the Korean founding body, which had gone for years without success before beginning to make large numbers of converts. They would remind themselves that they were perhaps only following "the Korean pattern."

Second, they would apply their general "principle of restitution" which held that God and Satan alternated in their influence. Current failure was due to Satan's dominant influence, which would later be counterbalanced by God's good influence on prospects in the making of converts.

Third, members believed that God would deliberately withhold his help from them in order to see how well they could do on their own. Current failure was testing for strength. (J. Lofland, 1977:244–245.)

On an even narrower or "situated" scale, meanings may be attached or applied to only a small part of a person's full round of activities. The pioneering work here is that of Gresham Sykes and David Matza in their formulation of definitions that youth appear to apply to their (occasional) delinquent acts. Calling these "techniques of neutralization," Sykes and Matza outlined what appear to be five "definitions favorable to the violation of law":

1. The denial of one's personal responsibility for the act
2. The denial of anyone's being injured by the act
3. The denial of the victims' right to protection, because they are disreputable persons
4. The denial of the condemners' rights to condemn the perpetrators because they are hypocrites
5. The claim that loyalty to one's friends or other groups supersedes loyalty to legal rules (Sykes & Matza, 1979.)

B. Rules as Meanings

Rules or norms are shared meanings. They differ from other meanings mainly in the positive moral preference attached to them and in the clarity of their formulation. Specific situations may be analyzed in terms of the rules that participants bring to them. In one such analysis, Albert J. Reiss interviewed low-income male youths regarding the shared and positively valued meanings they brought to the circumscribed situation of allowing adult males to perform fellatio upon them. Reiss discerned four major moral rules or definitions of the relationship:

1. A boy must undertake the relationship with a queer solely as a way of making money; sexual gratification cannot be actively sought as a goal in the relationship.
2. The sexual transaction must be limited to mouth-genital contact. No other sexual acts are generally tolerated.
3. Both peers and queers, as participants, should remain affectively neutral during the transaction.
4. Violence must not be used so long as the relationship conforms to the shared set of expectations between queers and peers. (Reiss, 1968:374–381, italics omitted.)

C. Unarticulated Meanings

Some of the most important meanings employed in a setting may be unrecognized as such by the participants. One of the key jobs of the social analyst is to articulate such latent meanings or, to use a current term, latent **typifications.** The inarticulateness of participants and the task of articulation by the analyst are both incisively illustrated in David Sudnow's analysis of what he calls "normal crimes" as a meaning complex in the world of the public defender (P.D.):

I shall call *normal crimes* those occurrences whose typical features, e.g., the ways they usually occur and the characteristics of persons who commit them (as well as the typical victims and typical scenes) are known and attended by the P.D. For any of a series of offense types, the P.D. can provide some form of proverbial characterization. For example, *burglary* is seen as involving regular violators, no weapons, low-priced items, little property damage, lower class establishments, largely Negro defendants, independent operators, and a non-professional orientation to the crime. (Sudnow, 1979:478.)

"Normal crimes," then, is a typification used by the public defender based on a large range of categories, such as the personality, class, race, and age of the defendants; the scenes; the victims' characteristics; and the criminal acts themselves. These categories cohere into batches of "usual" or "routine" kinds of criminal events (as distinct from narrowly construed, statutorily defined criminal acts):

When a P.D. puts questions to the defendant he is less concerned with recording nuances of the instant event (e.g., how many feet from the bar were you when the cops came in, did you break into the back gates or the front door), than with establishing its similarity with "events of this sort." That similarity is established, not by discovering statutorily relevant events of the present case, but by locating the event in a sociologically constructed class of "such cases." (Sudnow, 1979:485–486.)

While the term *normal crime* is not likely to be found in the vocabulary of public defenders, they do use more narrow working terms. P.D.s often refer to "such cases," "crimes such as this," "the same kind of case as the others," as well as to "burglars," "petty thieves," "narcos," and so on. Sudnow invented the term *normal crimes* as a more encompassing designation of this class of meanings.

Characterizing "clients" in this way is particularly common in circumstances where a small number of "servicers" process or otherwise deal with a large number of people. Such situations give rise to simplified typifications or "client typologies" (Mennerick, 1974).

D. Reality Constructionist Stance toward Meanings

Meanings are best "seen" and analyzed when one assumes what is called the "reality constructionist" stance. This stance is composed of several themes, among which are these presumptions:

1. Meanings are not inherent in reality but are imputed to it by humans.
2. Meanings are fragile and precarious and therefore treated gingerly by most people (see, for example, Simmons, 1964) and defended when attacked.
3. Meanings are devices by means of which advantaged people defend and legitimate their privileged circumstances and the less advantaged accommodate themselves to their disadvantaged positions—that is, meanings are self-serving (see Zurcher et al., 1966).
4. Because the situations of living are constantly changing, new and often novel meanings are constantly being generated to cope with the new contingencies.

II. PRACTICES

The smallest behavioral unit of a social setting may be envisioned as a social **practice,** a recurrent category of talk and/or action which the observer focuses on as having analytic significance. The category so isolated is, by definition, an activity the participants regard as unremarkable, as a normal and undramatic feature of ongoing life. It is only the analyst who, by collecting instances of it and dwelling on it, singles it out as something remarkable. We will offer two examples of such inventive "dwelling."

First, while interviewing students who were coping with the open-ended, never-finished task of studying, Stan Bernstein developed the concept of the "fritter"—"a justification a student gives to her or himself for not doing student work in response to felt pressures to work." He discerned four main classes of fritters:

1. Person-based, including "biological necessity" and "rest on your laurels."
2. Social-relations based, including group discussion and group work fritters.
3. Valuative-based, including fritters of "the Higher Good," "experience broadens," and "existential moods."

4. Task-based, including work scheduling (e.g., "time symmetry" and "great divide" fritters), preparation and creativity fritters (e.g., "the first step is the hardest"). (Bernstein, 1978.)

Second, George Gmelch became intrigued with what seemed to him some very odd practices among baseball players. Reflecting on these practices, he categorized them as "rituals," "taboos," and "fetishes":

1. *Rituals* include such activities as tapping the bat on home plate a precise number of times while at bat and taking a "lucky" automobile route to the ball park.
2. Rituals prescribe positive action, whereas *taboos* forbid given actions in the belief their occurrence is unlucky. Never mentioning a no-hitter while one is potentially in progress is a taboo shared by all players. Personal taboos include avoiding a given "unlucky" food before a game.
3. Objects too can be endowed with special practices and become *fetishes*. A pair of shoes, an old baseball cover, even a hairpin may be used, kept, and cherished in the belief that it brings special luck. (Gmelch, 1971.)

Gmelch interprets these seemingly strange practices as anxiety management devices, employed under situations with a high degree of uncertainty. He notes that they are not associated, for example, with the act of fielding the baseball, which is in fact performed successfully 97.5 percent of the time. Instead, rituals, taboos, and fetishes abound with regard to that most central and problematic of acts—batting—which overall players perform successfully only about 25 percent of the time.

Here, as with the other units we will describe, it can be seen that *meanings* also enter into the analysis. Thus, a "fritter" is a type of meaning and not *only* an act or practice found in a social setting. The ubiquitousness of meanings ought not to trouble us, however; it merely points to their fundamental importance in analyzing social life.

III. EPISODES

In contrast to practices, **episodes** are, by definition, *remarkable* and *dramatic* to the participants, and therefore to the analyst as well. Precisely because of this, the ordinary varieties of episodes are frequently studied: divorce, sudden and catastrophic illness, being a victim of a crime, committing a crime, social and natural disasters, crowd disorders, and so forth. Indeed, a significant portion of several social analytic specialties are devoted to the analysis of episodes. We have in mind, especially, the study of the family, deviance, crime, crowd behavior, and social movements.

Episodes differ in the number of people and the length of time they involve. As an example of a study of a relatively individualistic and brief episode, we may refer to Donald Cressey's well-known work on embezzlement (or "trust violation"). Cressey did intensive interviews with imprisoned embezzlers and attempted to formulate the general sequence of the embezzlers' definition of their situation that led to acts of violating a position of financial trust. Through a process of successive revision, Cressey provided what appears to be a generally applicable series of three stages. Trusted persons become trust violators when they:

1. Conceive of themselves as having a financial problem which is non-sharable;
2. Are aware that this problem can be secretly resolved by violation of the position of financial trust;
3. Are able to apply to their own conduct in that situation verbalizations which enable them to adjust their conceptions of themselves as trusted persons with their conceptions of themselves as users of the entrusted funds or property (Cressey, 1971:30.)

Episodes which involve a few more people and extend over months or years are the focus of Fred Davis's study of families with a child stricken by polio. He reports that such small groups must cope with problems the child has with (1) *appearance*, with regard to usual assumptions about people's physical attractiveness, wholeness, and symmetry of body parts; (2) *participation* in usual childhood activities; and (3) *association* with peers (F. Davis, 1972).

Since the stigma of polio is visible, the families cannot employ the strategy of "passing." They use, instead, strategies of "normalization" or "disassociation":

1. Normalization is the effort to make light of the handicap or to deny that it has any importance.
2. Disassociation involves efforts to insulate the child and family as a whole from events and involvements that might force recognition of the handicap as a "difference." Disassociation frequently involves the following:
   a. Resentment and anger toward "normals" accompanied by feelings of self-hatred deriving from the child's inability to live up to the prized normal standards.
   b. Passive acceptance of the child's exclusion from the world of "normals" punctuated periodically by attempts to ingratiate him or herself.
   c. Retreat to a more or less privatized sphere of hopes and fantasies in which the harsh impress of the normal standard is tenuously kept at bay.
   d. An attempt to recast and reformulate personal values, activities, and associations so as to avoid or remove the sting from the often negative, condescending, and depreciating attitudes of "normals." (F. Davis, 1972:103–130.)

Episodes can involve thousands or even millions of people, as they do in "revolutionary" situations (Walton, 1983), crowd disorders, natural disasters, joyous public occasions (J. Lofland, 1982), or even community decision crises (Zablocki, 1980). An analysis of a special subtype of crowd disorder called the "ghetto riot" illustrates one important approach to these types of episodes. Focusing on American ghetto riots in the 1960s, Quar-

antelli and Dynes propounded a three-stage model that is based on changing emotional expression and treatment of property:

> In the initial stage, property tends to be destroyed and accompanied by
> expressions of rage. Rocks and bottles thrown at police and property
> destruction are "symbolic acts of defiance." This continues but subsides
> in the second stage where more calm and sober looting begins. Property
> destruction is more confined to that necessary for successful looting. This
> sets the stage of "redefinition of property rights" and the drawing in of a
> large segment of the ghetto. Looting becomes a "mass activity" and the
> so-called "carnival spirit" emerges. Looting is calm, open, orderly and
> conducted by groups, some of whom are families. (Quarantelli & Dynes,
> 1968:8.)

IV. ENCOUNTERS

An **encounter** is a tiny social system formed when two or more persons
are in one another's immediate physical presence and strive to maintain a
single (ordinarily spoken) focus of mutual involvement. The life-span of an
encounter is only as long as the people remain together. Thus, most encounters endure only a few minutes or at most a few hours. Drug store purchases,
hallway conversations, committee meetings, job interviews, and individual
meetings of college classes are prosaic illustrations of encounters.

Encounters differ from the units discussed above (and from some
which will follow) in that they tend to be bounded **social systems**, that is,
fields of forces set up and maintained by the *relations* among the people
who are present. In the same sense, encounters are similar to some of the
units we will discuss below, especially small groups, relationships, and formal organizations. These units also comprise bounded fields of forces
(although the fields must generally be maintained for a longer period of
time).

One approach to the study of encounters is to seek out a key or defining
feature and then trace it in one or more analytic directions. For example, in
looking at those duties of U.S. deputy marshals which involve encounters
(taking accused persons into custody, delivering convicted people to federal
prisons, serving subpoenas, and so forth), Lachlan McClenahen and John
Lofland were struck by the fact that the central feature of such encounters
is the delivery of bad news. Before and during their encounters, the deputies
were concerned to:

1. Avoid the moral taint of delivering bad news
2. Keep the recipient under emotional control
3. Keep their own emotions under control in the presence of the recipient

These problematic aspects of the situation were managed in three stages:
preparing, delivering, and shoring up after delivery.

1. Preparatory tactics and strategically functional arrangements include:
   (a) distancing by means of anonymity, differences in race/class/edu-

cation identities, and distinctive equipment and settings; and (b) presaging the message.

2. Delivering tactics center on treating the news as "it's just routine."
3. Shoring tactics include (a) manipulating the news by (1) scaling down the badness ("it's not as bad as you think," "it could have been worse"), (2) playing up the positive; (b) mitigating the stress by displays of being constrained by impersonal roles, use of quips, and tactful disattention. (McClenahen and Lofland, 1978.)

An allied approach is to analyze an entire *class* of encounters in its own terms, as did Laurel Walum in her analysis of the "door-opening ceremony" in American society. Walum argued that this class of encounters has traditionally represented a situation of domination generally and of sex domination specifically. Encounters in which men open doors for women define men as creatures of authority, activity, and independence, and women as creatures of subordination, passivity, and dependence. The coming of women's liberation in the 1970s spawned challenge and confusion in these encounters and increased the number of "deference confrontations" (at least on the Ohio State University campus in the early years of that decade, the time and place of Walum's observations).

"What stances do people take to deal with their changed ceremonial world?" Walum asked (1978:135). She found people displaying strategic stances of the following kinds:

1. The confused—males bumbling ahead despite all
2. The tester—males inquiring into the woman's disposition
3. The humanitarian—males attempting equalitarianism
4. The defender—males persisting righteously in the traditional ceremony
5. The rebel—women who aggressively confront in the situation (Walum, 1978.)

V. ROLES

In their clearest form, **roles** are consciously articulated and abstracted categories of social "types of persons." In this sense, a role is both a label which people use to organize their own activity and one that they apply to others as a way of making sense of their activity.

A. Ascribed and Formal Roles

The most obvious instances of roles are, of course, those that are "ascribed." Ascribed roles are more or less inherent or otherwise successfully implanted in a person before, at, or shortly after birth. Such roles are based on, for example, ethnicity, race, nationality, sex, and age. Formal roles are linked to such notions as "position," "office," and "occupation"; they are commonsensically understood in societies with an abundance of formal organizations and "organizational charts."

B. Informal Organizational and Occupational Roles

Within formal roles of an organizational or occupational sort, there commonly exist informal *supplements* to the formal role structure. Thus, in observing naval disbursing officers, Ralph Turner discerned that they are (or were in 1947) in a generic situation of role performance conflict between the ideal of bureaucratic impersonality and the realities of bureaucratic life. Three such realities are that (1) regulations themselves are often in conflict, providing no sure guide to action; (2) a person of higher rank than the disbursing officers can bring pressure on them; and (3) informal ties and groups can make strong "improper" claims on them. The situation is thus quite difficult and is coped with, at the informal role level, along these global lines:

1. The *Regulation* type approximates the true bureaucrat in that he remains impervious to rank, informal structures, and the orders of his superiors. . . .
2. Opposite is the [*Scoffer*] . . . who doubts the potency of the General Accounting Office and . . . will do anything for a friend or superior without debate. . . .
3. On a different axis . . . is the *Sincere* type . . . [who] fails to recognize conflicts between regulations and orders from superiors and is unaware of the importance of informal systems. . . .
4. The commonest type is the *Realist.* Regulations are seen as illogical concatenations of procedure . . . [which] often, when strictly applied, defeat . . . the purpose for which they were constructed. . . . They [can] assume the regulation facade . . . but know how any payment can be made "legally" if the request comes from an important enough source. (Turner, 1947.)

Informal roles may transcend a single organizational context. One form of this transcendence was captured by Alvin Gouldner in his contrast between cosmopolitans and locals in college teaching:

1. *Cosmopolitans:* those low on loyalty to the employing organization, high on commitment to specialized skills, and likely to use an outer reference group orientation [; further divided into:]
   a. The Outsiders
   b. The Empire Builders
2. *Locals:* those high on loyalty to the employing organization, low on commitment to specialized skills, and likely to use an inner reference group orientation [; further divided into:]
   a. The Dedicated
   b. The True Bureaucrat
   c. The Homeguard
   d. The Elders (Gouldner, 1958:446–450.)

Settings involving captivity commonly generate what are known as *argot roles*, roles characterized by the use of labels produced by and reflecting the problems of the setting. Prisons are lush gardens for argot roles. In male prisons, for example, researchers have recorded such slang labels as "the right guy," "wolf," "tough," "gorilla," "hipster," and "ball buster" (Giallombardo, 1966:285). And in a very painstaking and detailed study of inmate-designated roles in a prison for women, Rose Giallombardo discovered a highly elaborate set of labels for "the mode of response exhibited by the inmate to the prison situation and the quality of the inmate's interaction with other inmates and staff" (1966:270):

1. Snitchers, Inmate Cops, Lieutenants
2. Squares, Jive Bitches
3. Rap Buddies, Homeys
4. Connects, Boosters
5. Pinners
6. Penitentiary Turnouts, Lesbians, Femmes, Stud Broads, Tricks, Commissary Hustlers, Chippies, Kick Partners, Cherries, Punks, Turnabouts (Giallombardo, 1966:275–285.)

C. Social Types

Social life is highly fluid, and because of this, an understanding of formal and informal organizational/occupational roles alone may not be sufficient; additional devices for "coding" persons in any position may be needed to help people construct their own actions and to decipher the actions of others. The concept of "social types," as developed by Orrin Klapp, is one important supplementary device of this sort. Social types may be thought of as "concepts of roles that have not been fully codified and rationalized ... [that are] a chart to role-structures otherwise largely invisible and submerged" (1958:674). They are constructs that fall, conceptually, somewhere between individual, idiosyncratic behavior on the one side and formal/informal role behavior on the other. "Between knowing a person's formal status only and knowing him intimately, there is a kind of knowledge that 'fills in' " (1958:674). Social types make possible a "finer discrimination than the formal ... structure recognizes" (1958:674). Consider, for example, such types as:

Underdog	Two-timer
Bigshot	Uncle Tom
Smart operator	Dragon lady
Dude	Crackpot
Good guy	Fanatic
Bully	Simpleton
Liar	Sissy
Fool	Sad sack (Klapp, 1971:12.)
Cheat	

The social type of the "fool" has been of special interest to investigators over the years. Analyses of the fool have focused especially on the *functions* persons playing that role serve in maintaining the groups of which they are a part; thus, they have countered the conventional assumption that fools are merely troublesome (see Chapter 7, Section VI.C.).

D. Social Psychological Types

Pushing the concept of role to its extreme, some investigators have conceived of as types of roles what are usually thought of as personality traits or types. One of the most ambitious efforts of this nature is the work of Murray Davis and Catherine Schmidt, who distinguish between "obnoxious" and "nice" persons in terms of differing *interaction roles* (1977). We can note also the intriguing work of political scientist James Barber, who has developed a social psychological interaction typology of United States presidents. By classifying them in terms of activity versus passivity and happiness and optimism versus sadness and irritability, Barber claims to have found four patterns:

1. The "active-positive" type tends to show confidence, flexibility, and a focus on producing results through rational mastery (for example, Harry Truman).
2. The "active-negative" tends to emphasize ambitious striving, aggressiveness, and a focus on the struggle for power against a hostile environment (for example, Lyndon Johnson, Richard Nixon).
3. "Passive-positive" types come through as receptive, compliant, other-directed persons whose superficial hopefulness masks much inner doubt (for example, William Howard Taft).
4. The "passive-negative" character tends to withdraw from conflict and uncertainty, to think in terms of vague principles of duty and regular procedure (for example, Dwight Eisenhower). (Barber, 1972.)

E. Articulation of Roles

Roles differ (both among themselves and from person to person) as to how clearly they are *articulated,* that is, conveyed by distinctive words in a person's vocabulary. The role examples above were presented in decreasing order of degree of articulation. That is, the later they were discussed, the less obvious and the more subject to dispute they are. Thus, Professor Barber's analysis of U.S. presidents is considered quite controversial. Nonetheless, the mandate of the social analyst is to strive to articulate the less obvious roles that exist in a setting.

F. Role Tactics

The foregoing subsections focus on the global and holistic analysis of roles themselves. It is also possible to study the dynamics of *doing* roles, to analyze role *tactics*. Among the more obvious aspects of such tactics are discovering a role in the first place, assessing it, gaining (or avoiding) entry into it, and even inventing it. Once a role is occupied, there are tactics for rising in it ("making out"), for maintaining a position in it or defending against difficulties encountered ("getting by"), and so on (J. Lofland, 1976:Chapter 9).

David Hamburg and his research team were interested in how people in the formal role of college students "made out." They focused on the strategies new college students use to deal with the unfamiliar situation of new subject matters, heavier workloads, increased requirements for initiative, and new demands for self-regulation. The tactics they documented include:

1. Projecting a clear self-image as an effective doer
2. Mobilizing new combinations of skill
3. Using assets to test new images of growth potential
4. Using upperclassmen as resource persons
5. Identifying with faculty-at-a-distance

They found that students handle disappointments by means of such short-run tactics as:

1. Recentering one's efforts within a long-term purpose
2. Working out alternative sources of gratification, often extracurricular
3. Remodeling prefabricated images of a vocational role
4. Setting intermediate goals in working out long-term plans
5. Referring to the high academic standards by which they were selected
6. Using interpersonal supports (Coelho, Hamburg & Murphey, 1963.)

Relative to social type roles, Orrin Klapp's observations on tactics that seem to be used by "heroes" in achieving that role are pungent. Klapp asked himself how talented but undramatic figures act in order to induce their audiences to think of them as heroes. He answered by specifying four basic kinds of tactics:

1. Aspirant heroes provide "color," which is the judicious use of eccentricity, the avoidance of total propriety and conventionality. This takes such concrete forms as (a) acceptably odd practices (for example, Ronald Reagan eats jelly beans); (b) trademarks (for example, General Patton's pearl-handled revolvers); (c) dramatic acts (for example, Toscanini, on the spur of the moment, conducting *Aida* entirely from memory).
2. They act alone. They avoid an overshadowing, too talented and too ambitious staff. They credit others generously, but hog the main scenes carefully.
3. They are aggressive, but carefully and guardedly so.
4. They promote personal encounter in dramatic moments. (Klapp, 1964.)

VI. RELATIONSHIPS

Two parties who interact with some regularity over a relatively extended period of time, and who view themselves as "connected" to one another, form a social **relationship**. Such pairings vary in myriad ways: the positive or negative character of the emotions prevailing, the degree of interdependence, the amount of trust, the parties' relative amounts of power, the amount each knows about the other, and so forth. Terms used to describe relations that capture certain of these variations include *friend, intimate, bargain-*

ing, marital, cultivated, stranger, adversary, tyrannical, impersonal, and *bureaucratic.*

As an example, Odis Bigus's analysis of American milkmen is a study of relationships that are relatively impersonal and involve a subordinate who needs to "cultivate" a superordinate. Milkmen are precariously dependent on making sales to a public, because the processes of suburbanization, growth of supermarkets, price regulation, and certain other factors have made it increasingly difficult for them to make a living in the home delivery of dairy products. Generically, the milkman's situation is one of extreme dependence on reluctant superordinates, or, as Bigus calls it, of "power asymmetry." Milkmen cope with this situation by cultivating relationships with customers:

1. In acquiring new customers they employ soliciting tactics of "personalizing" and "dealing."
2. Once acquired, a variety of tactics are employed to promote customer trust, including the "sincerity act," "contrived disclosure," and "accentuated honesty."
3. In carrying out their tasks, they nurture pseudofriendship and promote a customer's sense of obligation to themselves. (Bigus, 1978.)

No relationship is always stable; they all have histories of change. An analytic study by Fred Davis focuses on such changes. By observing the relationships developed by people who are physically handicapped in a visible way, he sought to "delineate in transactional terms, the stages through which a sociable relationship" between a "normal" and a visibly handicapped person may typically pass. He found three such stages:

1. *Fictional Acceptance.* Unlike earlier societies . . . in which a visible handicap automatically relegates the person to a caste-like, inferior status . . . in our society the visibly handicapped are customarily accorded . . . the surface acceptance that democratic manners guarantee to nearly all.
2. *"Breaking Through"—Facilitating Normalized Role-Taking.* In moving beyond fictional acceptance, what takes place essentially is a redefinitional process in which the handicapped person projects images, attitudes and concepts of self which encourage the normal to . . . take his role . . . in terms other than those associated with imputations of deviance. . . . As the handicapped person expands the interactional nexus, he simultaneously disavows the deviance latent in his status; concurrently, to the degree to which the normal is led reciprocally to assume the redefining . . . self-attitudes, he comes to . . . view as more like himself . . . those aspects of the other which at first connoted deviance for him.
3. *Institutionalization of the Normalized Relationship.* Having disavowed deviance and induced the other to respond to him as he would to a normal, the problem then becomes one of sustaining the normalized definition in the face of the many small amendments and qualifications that must frequently be made to it. . . . This third, "normal but" . . . stage of the relationship, if it endures, is institutionalized mainly in either one of two ways. In the first, the normal normalizes his percep-

tions to such an extent as to suppress his effective awareness of many of the areas in which the handicapped person's behavior unavoidably deviates from the normal standard. . . . [The second way] is for the normal to surrender some of his normalcy by joining the handicapped person in a marginal, half-alienated, half-tolerant, outsiders' orientation to "the Philistine world of normals." (F. Davis, 1961:120–132.)

In a brilliant monograph titled *Intimate Relations*, Murray Davis addresses all the major stages of that kind of relationship, from meeting, to constructing, to reviving, to dismantling. With regard to the last phase of intimacy, "the vitiated sociological skeleton of their relationship [tends] . . . to be difficult to dismantle" (1973:285). Among the complex tangle of dismantling moves, four important ones are:

1. The party who most wants to terminate forces the other actually to make the break.
2. A "have it out" gets out of hand, leading to sudden overkill.
3. One or both experience "gestalt switch" such that the person whose features were once totally good becomes totally bad.
4. Simple flight. (M. Davis, 1973:Chapter 8.)

VII. GROUPS

A few (up to a dozen or so) people who interact with some regularity over an extended period of time and who conceive of themselves as a social entity (a "we") form a social **group.** Informal leisure and work groups, cliques, networks, and families are prime examples.

A. Hierarchy

Members of groups generally rank one another and possess different degrees of influence over one another. Collectively considered, these personal differences in power, influence, and centrality form a social *hierarchy.* There may be struggles over placement in the social hierarchy, over the hierarchy itself, or between two or more hierarchies in the same setting; nonetheless, there tends to exist a ranking system, even if it is fluid and changing. Such a system, among a street-corner group that William F. Whyte calls "the Nortons," is shown in Figure 6-1. Note that while it is composed of separate individuals, the system requires the members simultaneously to specify the relative positions of several individuals. And being based on a principle of hierarchy, it illustrates the most fundamental and primitive structural meaning of the concept of a group.

B. Cliques

Some types of informal groups weave their way through larger, more formal organizations; they bind their members in invisible but powerful ways. Such groups are commonly called *cliques.* In observing executives in several commercial and industrial firms, Melville Dalton noticed that the webs of infor-

Figure 6-1. Organization of a Street-Corner Group

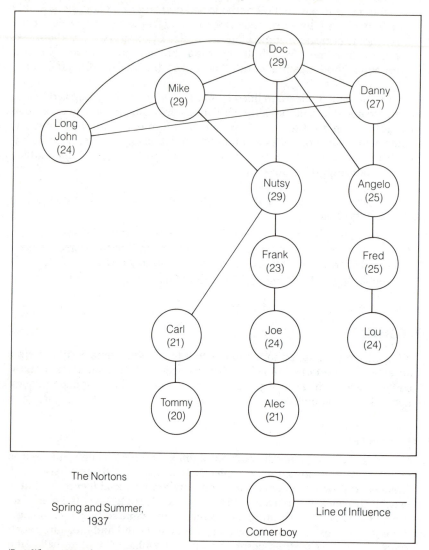

The Nortons

Spring and Summer,
1937

Corner boy ⎯ Line of Influence

(From Whyte, 1955:13, by permission of the University of Chicago Press. Copyright 1943 and 1955 by the University of Chicago Press.)

mal ties among them assumed different forms, which he classified in terms of their relation to the formal structure of the encompassing organization:

1. *Vertical Cliques* usually occur in a single department . . . between a top officer and some of his subordinates. They are vertical in the sense that they are up-and-down alliances between formal unequals.

   a. *Vertical Symbiotic Cliques.* The top officer is concerned to aid and protect his subordinates. . . . The subordinates fully advise him of real or rumored threats to his position. . . . There is a satisfying exchange of services.

    b. *Vertical Parasitic Cliques.* The exchange of services between the lower and higher clique members is unequal. The lower ranked person or persons receive more than they give and may greatly damage the higher officer.

2. *Horizontal Cliques* . . . cut across more than one department and embrace formal equals for the most part.

    a. *Horizontal Defensive Cliques.* It is usually brought on by what its members regard as crises . . . [and] is strong for only the limited time necessary to defeat or adjust to a threat.

    b. *Horizontal Aggressive Cliques.* Their action is a cross-departmental drive to effect changes rather than to resist them, to redefine responsibility, or even directly to shift it.

3. *Random Clique.* As compared with the more functional cliques, this one is random in the sense that its members may come from any part of the personnel, managers and managed, and that they do not anticipate important consequences of their association. (Dalton, 1959:57–65.)

C. Adaptive Significance

Groups have *adaptive significance;* that is, they provide ways for people collectively to cope with their circumstances. Among industrial workers with extraordinarily monotonous jobs, for example, Donald Roy observed group efforts to relieve the pressures of highly repetitive work. Himself employed in such a job (one that involved stamping leather or plastic parts all day), Roy observed that his work group was structured around the adaptive activities of "times" and "themes."

1. *Times* consisted of almost hourly group breaks or interruptions that served to punctuate the monotony. Roy enumerated a variety of times in the daily series: "peach time" (group sharing of a peach), "banana time," "window time," lunchtime, "picking-up time" (someone coming for their latest output), occasional talk, "fish time," "Coke time," and so on.

2. *Themes* consisted of a range of sometimes nonsensical, sometimes serious talk in which the group members engaged. There were a variety of kidding themes, sexual themes, themes about people's problems, and simple "chatter themes." (Roy, 1976.)

VIII. ORGANIZATIONS

Organizations are consciously formed collectivities with formal goals that are pursued in a more or less articulately planned fashion. Some major aspects of the analysis of organizations include the circumstances of their formation, how they recruit and control members, the types and causes of the goal-pursuit strategies they adopt, and the causes of their growth, change, or demise. Analyses of organizations as goal-pursuing entities often focus on their strategies—especially those that are less than formal. Philip Selznick's principle of "cooptation" is one example. He defined *cooptation* as "the process of absorbing new elements into the leadership or policy-defining structure of an organization as a means of averting threats to its stability or existence" (1953). This idea evolved out of Selznick's immersing himself in the day-to-day operations of the Tennessee Valley Authority. He discovered that it was useful to conceive of

this general mechanism . . . [as assuming] two basic forms: formal cooptation, when there is a need to establish the legitimacy of authority or the administrative necessity of the relevant public; and informal cooptation, when there is a need for adjustment to the pressure of specific centers of power within the community. (Selznick, 1953:259.)

From this viewpoint, an infinite variety of acts could be understood as instances of one or another of the two basic types of cooptation, and cooptation itself thus became the major organizing principle in his analysis.

Among efforts to depict generic *types* of organizations, we may refer to Erving Goffman's concept of the "total institution." Observing a mental hospital, Goffman began to contemplate ways in which that establishment resembled organizations not usually thought of as similar to it. As he thought about such other organizations, such as tuberculosis sanatariums, monasteries, boarding schools, and so forth, he began to see his own research setting as an instance of a more general type of setting:

When we review the different institutions in our Western society, we find some that are encompassing to a degree discontinuously greater than the ones next in line. Their encompassing or total character is symbolized by the barrier to social intercourse with the outside and to departure that is often built right into the physical plant, such as locked doors, high walls, barbed wire, cliffs, water, forest, or moors. These establishments I am calling *total institutions*. . . .

A basic social arrangement in modern society is that the individual tends to sleep, play, and work in different places, with different coparticipants under different authorities, and without an overall rational plan. The central feature of total institutions can be described as breakdown of the barriers ordinarily separating these spheres of life. (Goffman, 1961: 4–6.)

Having formulated and explored the general characteristics of this abstract concept, Goffman then went on to trace out and explicate the conclusions and corollaries that seemed to follow from these characteristics. In so doing, he made the minute aspects of social life in the hospital take on a more general meaning and relevance typical to all total institutions.

Attuned to Max Weber's concept of the quintessential "bureaucracy" (1949), Jerry Jacobs came away from a year's employment as a social case worker in a public welfare department with the distinct sense that he had been exposed to something quite different. Studying the contrast between Weber's idea of bureaucracy and what he had actually observed, Jacobs concluded that the disparity was great. To capture adequately what he actually saw go on in some of the organizations ostensibly labeled "bureaucracies," he defined a new type of organization:

It is possible for an organization to conform little or not at all to the conditions of bureaucracy, while maintaining an image of complete adherence to bureaucratic ideals. The existence of such a situation will hereafter be referred to as "symbolic bureaucracy." (Jerry Jacobs, 1979:144.)

Armed with this concept, he then reviewed the data on his organization to assess the degree to which it might be said to be a "symbolic bureaucracy," as distinct from Weber's bureaucracy:

An example of an organization closely approximating an instance of "symbolic bureaucracy" was the department studied by the author. The following discussion will concern itself with whether or not this department functioned within what [have been] . . . considered to be the four essential conditions for bureaucracy, i.e., specialization, hierarchy of authority, system of rules and impersonality. Each of these aspects will be evaluated with respect to the degree of their functional adherence against the degree of their apparent adherence within the department. (Jerry Jacobs, 1979:145.)

IX. SETTLEMENTS

Complexly interrelated sets of encounters, roles, groups, and organizations, existing within a socially defined territory and performing a range of life-sustaining functions, are known as **settlements.** Very large settlements—cities of many thousands or even millions—are considerably beyond the grasp of the naturalistic researcher. But the study of smaller settlements—villages, towns, ghettos, neighborhoods, blocks—is richly represented in naturalist literature. The classic anthropological study, for example, is a descriptive account of an entire, "simpler" society; these societies generally comprise a single village or cluster of villages. Thus, the analytic unit for a good deal of work in anthropology is, in fact, the settlement. (See for example Naroll & Cohen, 1973.)

Within sociology, a number of studies that are considered classics of fieldwork are also studies of settlements. Three of these, interestingly enough, focus on Italian (or mixed-Italian) neighborhoods in large cities: William F. Whyte's *Streetcorner Society: The Social Structure of an Italian Slum* (1955), in Boston's North End; Herbert Gans's *The Urban Villagers: Group and Class in the Life of Italian-Americans* (1962), in the West End; and Gerald Suttles's *The Social Order of the Slum: Ethnicity and Territory in the Inner City* (1968), in Chicago.

As in most naturalistic research, the settlement study is normally conducted by a lone investigator, or at most by a two-person team. As long as the unit is not too large—that is, no larger than a contained neighborhood or a small town—this has proved a satisfactory arrangement. (See for example Gans, 1967; Hochschild, 1978; Jerry Jacobs, 1974; S. Johnson, 1971; Kornblum, 1974; Lyford, 1964; West, 1945; for a review of many such studies, see Bell & Newby, 1972.)

However, the study of larger settlements—medium-sized towns or small cities—requires the use of research teams, sometimes of considerable size. Robert and Helen Lynd's pioneer study of Muncie, Indiana (1929), for example, was made possible by a research team composed of the authors, two additional investigators and a staff secretary; the restudy performed by Caplow et al. (1982) was enormously more elaborate. The data for Arthur Vidich and Joseph Bensman's study of a rural community (1958) was produced by a larger project, the "Cornell Studies in Social Growth," which involved a substantial research team. And the classic "Yankee City" series—five volumes recording several years of study of Newburyport, Massachusetts—was the work of W. Lloyd Warner, a number of other major investigators, and a host of students, mostly undergraduates, from Harvard and Radcliffe. (The series includes Warner & Lunt, 1941, 1942; Warner & Srole, 1945; Warner & Low, 1947; and Warner, 1959.)

Historically, at least within sociology, when the unit of investigation has been at the level of the settlement, researchers have rarely moved beyond detailed description in their reports. The written production might contain small pieces of analysis of less encompassing units (see, for example, William F. Whyte's depiction of street-corner group hierarchy in Section VII, above), but analysis of the settlement as a unit has been largely ignored. At most, investigators have contented themselves with establishing the presence or absence of "community," that is, whether or not the territorial area under study was meaningful to the inhabitants.

More recent work, however, has begun to consider the settlement unit in more complex terms. In Gerald Suttles's study of an inner-city Chicago neighborhood, for example, he attempted to articulate the particular form of social organization exhibited by what he called the "Addams Area." In so doing, he went far beyond the question of presence or absence of community:

The overall pattern is one where age, sex, ethnic and territorial units are fitted together like building blocks to create a larger structure. I have termed this pattern "ordered segmentation" to indicate the two related features: (1) the orderly relationship between groups and (2) the sequential order in which groups combine in instances of conflict and opposition. (Suttles, 1968:10; see also 1972.)

As another example, Albert Hunter, in his study of Chicago neighborhoods, argued that, since community is a multidimensional concept,

rather than asking whether "community" does or does not exist, we should approach the problem by asking whether this or that element of community is present and to what degree. (Hunter, 1974:4.)

He identified the crucial elements as the "ecological community," the "symbolic-cultural community," and the "social structural community," and he developed techniques for determining their degree of presence in a given territory (1974; see also 1975, 1978).

X. SOCIAL WORLDS

Modern means of transportation and communication provide the basis for the rise and proliferation of a nebulous type of social unit, one that contains most if not all of the types described above but is not reducible to any of them. The term **social world** is often used to capture these sprawling, shapeless entities, examples of which include the sports world, the California political world, the worlds of sociology, stamp collecting, and Wall Street.

Drawing on the work of David Unruh, a social world may be said (1) to encompass a large but indefinitely known population; (2) to have vague boundaries that can be crossed simply by choosing to stay abreast of events in that world (through the relevant communications media); (3) to have no or weak central authority; (4) to have a high rate of social change; and (5) to contain predominantly informal social roles—although in some instances, roles may be quite formal (Unruh, 1983).

One important method of analyzing social worlds is in terms of the social roles that seem most dominant. Unruh, for example, has compared the prevalence of stranger, tourist, regular, and insider roles in various social worlds (Unruh, 1980, 1979a).

XI. LIFESTYLES

Last, in recent years, some social scientists have begun to try to understand what are called **lifestyles,** that is, global adjustments to life by large numbers of similarly situated persons. Lifestyle is the broadest unit we will discuss here (though not yet as broad as units of social class, subculture, and society). Benjamin Zablocki and Rosabeth Kanter (1976) have distinguished lifestyles in terms of those that are dominated by a person's location in an economic system and those that are not. Economically dominated lifestyles can in turn be divided into three types:

1. Property-dominated, as in the "elite ranks of the upper class"
2. Occupation-dominated, as in those occupational pursuits that virtually absorb their practitioners
3. Poverty-dominated, as in American urban ghettos

Probably due to greater ease of access, the third type has been perhaps the most studied. Elliot Liebow's analysis of Black streetcorner men, for example, is organized around the five main areas of the men's lives, expressed in the chapter titles as:

1. Men and Jobs
2. Fathers without Children
3. Husbands and Wives
4. Lovers and Exploiters
5. Friends and Networks (Liebow, 1967.)

And in another study of a Black American ghetto settlement, Ulf Hannerz distinguished "four main lifestyles . . . the mainstreamers, swingers, street families and streetcorner men" (Hannerz, 1969:37).

But, as Zablocki and Kanter have argued, lifestyle is not always reducible to economic status (1976:271–294). Values and tastes, among other factors, enter in and stimulate a vast number of diverse lifestyles: gay liberationists, born-again Christians, punks, surfers, nudists, hermits, hoboes, and urban guerillas, to name but a few.

XII. USING UNITS IN NATURALISTIC INQUIRY

In any given inquiry, you are not confined to analyzing a single unit. One may be selected as the central construct around which the analysis is organized, but some or even many of the others inevitably enter in as supporting and supplemental foci.

It may be observed that naturalists tend to focus on the smaller, more "microscopic" units—those that are literally easier to see. Thus, we have not discussed such common "macrosocial" units as social class and society, because they are not easily observable or often used by naturalists, *except* insofar as they can be apprehended by means of smaller units. Certainly the units we have discussed here can be, and in fact are, used to capture more macroscopic units.

The preference for smaller units is part of the epistemological bias of the naturalist. Naturalists tend to believe that the larger the unit, the less viewable it is in a literal sense, the more likely the investigator is to impose her or his own biases on it. And, they tend to believe that the comparative and composite analysis of smaller-scale units is a more valid basis for generalizing "up" to larger-scale units, such as social classes and entire societies.

Asking
Questions

 Units of social life are entities about which one asks *questions.*
Whether the entity is an encounter, a lifestyle, or whatever, in
the beginning is the question (compare Adler, 1940:183–184).

Social analysts commonly pose seven basic questions about
units of social life. These questions should be thought about
conjointly with the units of social organization just outlined in
Chapter 6. In order to facilitate such conjoint thinking, we have
presented the units and questions as a matrix in Figure 7-1;
this figure can be consulted as we go along.

I. WHAT IS THE UNIT'S TYPE?

Perhaps the most creative and important (but often unappre-
ciated) moment in social analysis is the act of posing and
answering the question, "What *is* this thing (or things) I see
before me?" At this point, you already know what unit(s) you
are dealing with. Thus, the answer sought is not "It's an
encounter," or "It's an organization," but rather what specific
type of encounter or organization it is.

A. Single Types

Many of the most important advances in social analysis are
simply artful depictions of a single type of practice, relationship, group, or other social unit. Consider, for example, Erving
Goffman's isolation of the concept of the "total institution" (see
Chapter 6, Section VIII.). As we saw, he developed this organizational type after considering the features of the particular
organization he was studying (a mental hospital). By asking
himself what were the *general* features of that hospital, he evolved
the idea of the "total institution."

Figure 7-1. Units and Questions Conjoined

QUESTIONS

UNITS	1. What type is it?	2. What is its structure?	3. How frequent is it?	4. What are its causes?	5. What are its processes?	6. What are its consequences?	7. What are people's strategies?
1. Meanings							
2. Practices							
3. Episodes							
4. Encounters							
5. Roles							
6. Relationships							
7. Groups							
8. Organizations							
9. Settlements							
10. Worlds							
11. Lifestyles							

Philip Selznick's scrutiny of the Communist party and his characterization of it as a "combat party" display the same logic. Selznick observes that, analytically,

the major concern is to identify the system, to state what the "nature of the beast" is. The task is to construct a conceptual model of a functioning institutional system. But this is also an exercise in typology. We view the structure we are studying as an instance of a class of objects whose general features are to be explored. The class may have only one member but it is the kind of thing we are dealing with that interests us. We ask, What kind of a social system is the Communist party? We answer by developing a model of the "combat party," including its strategies. (Selznick, 1960:xiv.)

B. Multiple Types

This logic is, of course, easily extended to conceiving of numerous types of units. Especially if you are observing more than one concrete setting, the variance that naturally exists among the units you will encounter is likely to make multiple "typing" not only a possibility but a necessity. For example, in the course of her research on bar behavior, Sherri Cavan performed observation and interviewing in some 100 San Francisco drinking places. It became apparent to her that bar patrons distinguished rather strongly among bars in terms of their uses. She then developed and articulated "four general types of public drinking places," based on this concept of "use" (1966:15):

1. *The Convenience Bar.* The first is official or manifest use; the public drinking place as a setting to obtain a drink, as a setting that may be used as a kind of social convenience.
2. *The Nightspot.* The second [use] is that of amusement; public drinking places may be used primarily as a setting for entertainment.
3. *The Marketplace Bar.* . . . Public drinking places may be used for the exchange of various types of commodities, as if they were a kind of marketplace.
4. *The Home Territory Bar.* [Bars] . . . may . . . be used as though they were private places, similar to one's residence or club, and in this way one may speak of the "home territory." (Cavan, 1966:15; see also Chapters 7–10.)

Again, looking back through Chapter 6, we see multiple types used in many studies, including:

Types of informal roles among naval disbursing officers, as developed by Ralph Turner (1947) and summarized in Section V.B.

Types of cliques in organizations, as reported by Melville Dalton (1959) and summarized in Section VII.B.

Types of lifestyles, as propounded by Ben Zablocki and Rosabeth Kanter (1976) and summarized in Section XI.

Types of meaning — ind.

C. Rules of Typing

Classification or type schemes are guided by two basic rules of procedure and outcome. First, you should choose the content of the classification/type in such a way that each case can be placed into only one category thereof. This is called the *rule of mutual exclusiveness* of categories. Second, the categories you devise should make it possible to classify all (or almost all) of the relevant cases. This is called the *rule of exhaustiveness*. Thus, if Cavan's four categories of bars (above) had served to classify only, let us say, 25 of the 100 bars she observed, we, as analysts, would feel that her scheme was in serious need of revision. Still, as a practical matter, in most research there will be at least a few cases that defy categorization. These residual cases you can simply put to one side and label "other" or "mixed."

D. Typologizing

On occasion, the units under study seem to possess some complex but systematic interrelation. In such a case, you can often discover what the interrelation is by specifying a small number of relevant variable factors whose *conjoint* variations accurately incorporate the patterns you have already discerned (and usually point out still others you have not yet fully contemplated). This process of charting the possibilities that result from the conjunction of two or more variables is known as **typologizing.**

For example, in his study of a proselytizing religious group, John Lofland found that the members' strategies for attempting to contact prospective converts seemed to revolve around:

1. Whether . . . to impart information and make new contact in a face-to-face manner or to employ mediated means such as radio and newspapers
2. Whether . . . to make clear initially that the group believed in a new Christ and the imminent end of the world or to withhold revelation of these beliefs
3. Whether . . . to attempt contact in religious places (for example, churches) or secular places (for example, street corners) (J. Lofland, 1977:Chapters 5–6.)

A typology of these three dichotomous variables shows eight basic patterns or possibilities (Figure 7-2). Typologizing thus provides a certain degree of systematic coherence in the analysis. It can also serve to call attention to existing but still unnoticed patterns, or to the absence of a logically possible pattern (thus raising the question of why it is absent).

We must caution you, however, that typology construction can easily become a sterile exercise. Unless you perform it within the context of full and extensive knowledge of, and sensitivity to, the actual setting, it will reveal little or nothing. Arbitrary box building is not a substitute for a close feel for the actual circumstances. Typologizing is simply a tool to aid in systematic understanding.

Figure 7-2. Example of a Typology: Types of Proselytizing Strategies (From J. Lofland, 1977:66.)

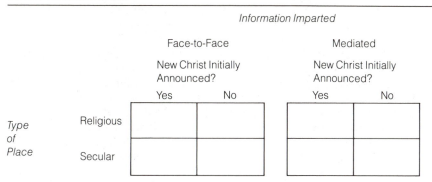

		Information Imparted			
		Face-to-Face		Mediated	
		New Christ Initially Announced?		New Christ Initially Announced?	
		Yes	No	Yes	No
Type of Place	Religious				
	Secular				

II. WHAT IS THE UNIT'S STRUCTURE?

Deriving detailed, refined, and systematic answers to the question, "What type of unit is it?" leads you to the next question: "What is its structure?" Aside from the single feature or the few features that differentiate it from other social units, what are its more intricate and precise characteristics? Of what more complicated and exhaustive properties and traits is it composed?

The idea of a structure is easiest to grasp with social units at the "group" level or larger. Turning back to our discussion of the group as a unit-level (Chapter 6, Section VII.), look again at Figure 6-1, William Whyte's depiction of the structure of a street-corner group. The logic Whyte illustrates in that diagram is the logic underlying many analyses, at all unit levels, that attempt to answer the question, "What is the unit's structure?" Metaphorically, the task of depicting structure is like drawing a picture of a building: First you provide an overall outline of it, and then you fill in the major internal parts. Literally, of course, social structures are not as concrete and well defined as physical structures, but the principle is much the same.

An additional strategy for depicting structure is **ideal typing.** As you begin to identify the components of a structure, you may notice that the case or cases at hand display many tendencies that you have not "played out" to their logical extremes. The pattern you actually see is partial, attenuated, or weak in some fashion. But the cases at hand *tend* toward some logical structural pattern that you, as analyst, can envision. Such a realization makes it possible for you to use the cases under study to define a potential "pure" or "ideal" type or types. Max Weber, an important user of this practice in social science, stated it thus:

[An ideal type] . . . is not a description of reality but it aims to give unambiguous means of expression to such a description. We construct the concept "city economy" [for example] not as an average of the economic structures actually existing in all the cities observed but as an ideal-type . . . formed by the one-sided accentuation of . . . a great many diffuse, discrete, more or less present and occasionally absent concrete individual phenomena. . . . In its conceptual purity, this mental construct. . . cannot be found empirically anywhere in reality. . . . Research faces the task of determining, in each individual case, the extent to which this ideal-construct approximates to or diverges from reality. (Weber, 1949:90–93.)

Put differently, an ideal type is a logical extreme, an ideal form, a hypothetical case, a pure case, or an ideal construct (Lopreato & Alston, 1970:95).

One recent and highly creative use of ideal typing is Joyce Rothchild-Whitt's formulation of contrasts between bureaucratic and collectivist-democratic organizations (1979). Observing six collectivist work organizations in a Southern California city, she was struck with their tendency toward structuring themselves quite differently from more "ordinary" work organizations. Drawing on existing theories of formal organizations, she specified eight areas or dimensions of organizational functioning (as shown in the left-hand column of Figure 7-3). Then, she contrasted an extant ideal type formulation of features of bureaucratic organizations with the ideal features she derived for collectivist-democratic organizations. These contrasts are shown in the middle and right-hand columns of her chart.

As a practical strategy, it is helpful to develop ideal types in *pairs* of *polar* (that is, logically or theoretically opposed) extremes. This is well illustrated in Rothchild-Whitt's counterposing of bureaucratic and collectivist-democratic organizations. Such a pairing makes it clear that practically all empirical instances range along the continuum between the given extremes.

Let us now take a brief look at one common ideal-typing procedure. The first step is simply to list all conceivably distinctive and relevant features

Figure 7-3. Example of Ideal Typing: Two Types of Organization

Dimensions	Bureaucratic Organization	Collectivist-Democratic Organization
1. Authority	1. Authority resides in individuals by virtue of incumbency in office and/or expertise; hierarchal organization of offices. Compliance is to universal fixed rules as these are implemented by office incumbents.	1. Authority resides in the collectivity as a whole; delegated, if at all, only temporarily and subject to recall. Compliance is to the consensus of the collective which is always fluid and open to negotiation.
2. Rules	2. Formalization of fixed and universalistic rules; calculability and appeal of decisions on the basis of correspondence to the formal, written law.	2. Minimal stipulated rules; primacy of ad hoc, individuated decisions; some calculability possible on the basis of knowing the substantive ethics involved in the situation.

Figure 7-3 *(Continued)*

3. Social Control	3. Organizational behavior is subject to social control, primarily through direct supervision or standardized rules and sanctions, tertiarily through the selection of homogeneous personnel especially at top levels.	3. Social controls are primarily based on personalistic or moralistic appeals and the selection of homogeneous personnel.
4. Social Relations	4. Ideal of impersonality. Relations are to be role-based, segmental and instrumental.	4. Ideal of community. Relations are to be wholistic, personal, of value in themselves.
5. Recruitment and Advancement	5.a. Employment based on specialized training and formal certification. 5.b. Employment constitutes a career; advancement based on seniority or achievement.	5.a. Employment based on friends, social-political values, personality attributes, and informally assessed knowledge and skills. 5.b. Concept of career advancement not meaningful; no hierarchy of positions.
6. Incentive Structure	6. Remunerative incentives are primary.	6. Normative and solidarity incentives are primary; material incentives are secondary.
7. Social Stratification	7. Isomorphic distribution of prestige, privilege, and power; i.e., differential rewards by office; hierarchy justifies inequality.	7. Egalitarian; reward differentials, if any, are strictly limited by the collectivity.
8. Differentiation	8.a. Maximal division of labor: dichotomy between intellectual work and manual work and between administrative tasks and performance tasks. 8.b. Maximal specialization of jobs and functions; segmental roles. Technical expertise is exclusively held: ideal of the specialist-expert.	8.a. Minimal division of labor: administration is combined with performance tasks; division between intellectual and manual work is reduced. 8.b. Generalization of jobs and functions; wholistic roles. Demystification of expertise: ideal of the amateur factotum.

From Rothchild-Whitt, 1979:519. Reprinted by permission.

of the social unit at hand. Then scrutinize this long and disjointed list with an eye toward trimming it down and determining which elements ar₃ logically related to which others. Group together those features that appear to be interrelated. To put it another way, the unit or units under study present themselves as incoherent aggregations of infinite aspects. The task of the analyst is to "disaggregate" them so as to achieve a coherent identification and ordering.

The hope, of course, is that by providing new concepts and their components (for example, the idea of the "collectivist-democratic organization" and its eight specific features), the range of ordered experience will be widened and our understanding of it enhanced.

III. WHAT IS THE UNIT'S FREQUENCY?

It is sometimes useful and important to count how often a social unit, or an aspect of it, occurs and to develop summarizing statistics in such forms as percentages and means. There are, in fact, some quite elaborate procedures for counting and analyzing many kinds of social phenomena, procedures codified under such rubrics as "descriptive and inferential statistics," "sampling," "survey research," and "systematic observation techniques."

Even though they can be useful, such counting procedures are beyond the scope of this manual. There are many guides available that provide instruction in these procedures; thus, to devote attention to them here would be redundant and would only blur our focus on qualitative analysis. Persons interested in questions of frequency may find it useful to consult, among other works, Babbie (1979) and H. W. Smith (1975) and the sources cited therein.

IV. WHAT ARE THE UNIT'S CAUSES?

"What are the causes of X?" is perhaps the most frequently asked question in social science. It may be phrased in a variety of ways, such as:

What are the conditions under which it appears?
What facilitates its occurrence?
What are circumstances in which it is likely to occur?
In the presence of what conditions is it likely to be an outcome?
Upon what factors does variation in it depend?
Under what conditions is it present and under what conditions is it absent?

A. Requirements of Causal Inference

As with questions of frequency, qualitative field studies are not designed to provide definitive answers to causal questions. This fact may be best understood by briefly outlining what is required in order to say "A causes B" with any reasonable degree of confidence.

First, for whatever you may want to find the causes of, you must have not only instances of its occurrence but also of its nonoccurrence (or absence or attenuation). That is, you must begin with a *variation* in the "dependent variable." The variation need not necessarily be as strong as that between occurrence and nonoccurrence; it can be something on the order of "more present/less present" or "stronger/weaker." In a naturalistic study, this range of necessary variation simply may not occur. There may be instances, say, of "present" or "stronger" but no instances of "absent" or "weaker." And without such variation, obviously, there is nothing to compare.

Second, you must have some reliable and consistent way to determine or *measure* presence/absence, stronger/weaker, over a set of units which display the variation. But quantification procedures are very time-consuming to devise and quite often too obtrusive to perform in a setting. (The inappropriateness of performing paper and pencil tests, systematic check lists, or other such procedures may be a sufficient reason not even to attempt them. See, however, Webb et al., 1981.)

Third, you must consider this measured variation in the dependent variable *conjointly* with some other measured variation that is provisionally thought to cause it in some sense. The simplest possibility is depicted in Figure 7-4, showing a dependent and an independent variable considered in perfect covariation. In order to show that the independent variable is a cause of the dependent variable, the measured instances of both must tend to fall into Cells 1 and 4, or Cells 2 and 3, rather than be distributed evenly across all four cells.

The quest for causes involves, then, showing measured covariation in variables in which, fourth, the presumed cause *precedes* the effect in time.

But there is a fifth complication. There is always the question of whether, despite covariation and proper time order, you can ever be really *certain* a particular independent variable is the cause (or is among the important causes) of the dependent variable. This is the classic problem of "correlation not proving causation." Some other unknown factor, or some known but unmeasured factor, may be the cause or among the causes.

Very elaborate procedures have been developed to meet these requirements for demonstrating causality (procedures that are often quite difficult to implement in field situations). Also, there are procedures designed to meet a number of other requirements we have not mentioned. Collectively,

Figure 7-4. Perfect Covariation of Two Variables

		Independent Variable	
		Present (or stronger, etc.)	Absent (or weaker, etc.)
Dependent Variable	Present (or stronger, etc.)	1 100%	2 0%
	Absent (or weaker, etc.)	3 0%	4 100%

these procedures are often termed "quantitative social research," and many manuals on how to "do" them are available. Among others, we would refer you again to Babbie (1979) and H. W. Smith (1975), plus the readings cited in these books.

B. The Moral

The moral is this: The techniques and technology of qualitative studies are not the same as those of quantitative studies. Using the procedures in this guide alone, you are unlikely to acquire measured and controlled variations in dependent and independent variables and therefore unlikely to have available the systematic quantitative data necessary to determine causation.

Beyond questions of technique and technology are, however, matters of the *frame of mind* associated with each. If you get into a strongly quantitative frame of mind, you are likely to have your attention drawn away from the major qualitative features of the setting itself. You can easily trap yourself into exclusive concern with very small problems simply because these problems are subject to quantification. The point has been put well by Erving Goffman in describing his fieldwork in a mental hospital:

Desiring to obtain ethnographic detail regarding selected aspects of patient social life, I did not employ usual kinds of measurements and controls. I assumed that the role and time required to gather statistical evidence for a few statements would preclude my gathering data on the tissue and fabric of patient life. (Goffman, 1961:x.)

C. Causation and Conjecture

We do not, however, wish to rule out all discussion of causes. Even if the search for them is not your primary task, it can still be a tentative, qualified subsidiary task. You will be continually confronted with many variations that present themselves as simultaneously occurring contrasts (in which two or more elements coexist at more or less the same time), as serial contrasts (in which the same element changes over time), or in other ways. You may thus be prompted to ask what makes these variations come about.

It is perfectly appropriate to be curious about causes, as long as you recognize that whatever account or explanation you devise is *conjecture*. (More formally, such conjectures are called *hypotheses* or *theories*.) You can certainly devote a portion of your report to conjectured causes of variations. But be certain to label them as such. And, since these will merely be stated and likely left untested, it behooves you not to allow causal conjecture portions of the report to become a large or dominant part of the total study. The studies mentioned in Chapter 6, for example, generally contain sections devoted to causal theories, but they do not stand or fall on these auxiliary causal accounts. Whatever eventually might be found to account for the variations and patterns they document, the variations and patterns themselves are likely to stand as findings.

For the above reasons, also, phrase your conjecture in a *qualified* way. Because you are, in fact, unlikely to have systematic knowledge of the association of variations, it is wise to present your conjectures in a way that indicates humility. This necessitates the appropriate use of qualifying phrases such as:

"It is possible that. . . ."
"It seems to be the case that. . . ."
"Although the data are not systematic, it appears that. . . ."

In other words, be honest about the factual standing of your causal assertions.

D. The Importance of Auxiliary Causal Accounts

Auxiliary conjectures in a qualitative report are not only permissible; they play important and indispensable roles in social science. There are three reasons for this. First, because quantitative researchers and theorists are typically at a distance from and ignorant of the phenomena they study, they often turn to qualitative studies to gain a sense of what the phenomena are like and of what variables they ought to look for. In order to find substance for quantitative technology in particular, researchers often study qualitative reports. This is as it should be. The qualitative researcher has gotten close to people somewhere in the world. A fully correct and definitive depiction of causal accounts may not have been developed, but the conjectures raised by the variations and patterns recorded may provide a foundation for quantitative research.

Second, researchers who do not comprehend participants' own causal theories are apt to make profound errors not only in ascribing causes but also in characterization (for example, in answering the question "What is it?"). This is especially likely where there is great social distance (because of differences in age, sex, ethnicity, geography, and so forth) between the analyst and the participant. Specifically, there is a pronounced tendency to define ill-understood behavior as bizarre, sick, or irrational, when on closer inspection such definitions turn out to be quite unwarranted (Snow & Machalek, 1982).

(It ought, moreover, to be obvious that the researcher is not the only person who notices variations and puzzles over their causes. Members of social settings do also, or at least the more verbal, intelligent, and sophisticated of them do. They develop their own hypotheses or theories to account for variations. Often these are quite perceptive and persuasive, perhaps to the point of rendering much further study—and especially quantitative study—a waste of everyone's time and money. Carl Sundholm, for example, observed a series of courtroom trials and asked himself what the conditions were in which prosecutors sought trials by jury. Becoming a regular presence in certain courtrooms and gaining the trust of prosecuting attorneys, he began questioning them about the factors they took into account in making that decision. It turned out that this was a serious and well-reflected-on decision for prosecuting attorneys. They were quite articulate about the relevant factors, and in all likelihood, their accounts of what "cause" them to seek a jury trial are quite correct—or correct enough. [See Sundholm, 1978:37ff.])

Third, under many circumstances of limited time, money, and topic importance, the causal theories which the qualitative analyst presents may be sufficient to the task. Elaborate quantitative research may in any event contribute only small increments of precision to a thorough qualitative analysis. A sense of proportion or perspective is required in applying social research technology. Often it is unjustifiable to send out a quantitative battleship to answer questions that can be dealt with quite adequately by qualitative gunboats.

E. Forms of Causal Accounts

Causal accounts vary in their structure and complexity. We will here describe three forms (with a preference expressed for the third).

1. Single Cause. The most rudimentary account is that which refers to a single factor or cause as explaining some variation. The problem with such an account is not so much that the single factor referred to is unlikely to be associated with the variation, but rather that there are bound to be others. At least, 50 years or more of quantitative social research has yet to turn up any very strong associations between a variation and only one factor. This fact can be taken as a safe guide in developing your own conjectures.

2. List of Causes. You are likely to achieve greater accuracy by developing a series of independent variables that account for a variation, as did Carl Sundholm in the example just above. However, even though such lists may prove "accurate" (if at some point subjected to quantitative tests), you need not be satisfied with them.

3. Cumulating Causes. Rather, you can go on and attempt to specify the manner in which factors must accumulate through time and in a certain sequence in order to cause a particular variation. That is, a more sophisticated causal account focuses upon *process* in the eventuation of outcomes, rather than providing simple, *static* depictions. The concern is with successions of dependencies through time—with ways in which prior conditions may or may not develop into succeeding conditions of a given outcome. Attention is focused upon ways in which alternatives may or may not be present— upon ways in which, and the degree to which, action may be constrained. Thought is oriented to the cumulation of factors: Each factor is a condition of an outcome but not sufficient for it; each factor makes an outcome possible or more probable but not yet determined.

F. Situational versus Dispositional Causes

To a social analyst, the appropriate content of variables to stress in causal accounts is *situational* or *social organizational*. This seemingly obvious point is actually quite difficult to grasp. Beginning social analysts, especially, tend to have a culturally endowed penchant for interpreting individual and organizational behavior as being the consequence of supernatural, physical, chemical, and/or psychological factors.

The pioneering work in the social/situational realm of causes was Emile Durkheim's *Suicide* (1951; originally published in 1897). At the time of his research, suicide was not viewed as something that could be socially caused.

It was Durkheim's genius to establish decisively that it could be and is. Since then, a legion of researchers have documented the fruitfulness of looking first (if not foremost and only) to *current* arrangements, social circumstances, or situations in accounting for meanings, practices, and so forth. The social situationalist approach is thus *now*-oriented. Holding aside "personality" or whatever remote and dispositional notions, you ask yourself what combination of *current* arrangements would conduce almost *anyone* to act in the particular ways observed.

Consider such applications of the situational emphasis as these:

Homosexual encounters are crucially a function of the availability of conducive territories and interaction skills rather than of mere homosexual motivation. (Mileski & Black, 1972.)

Voyeurism has been observed to be a shared, group activity of normal people rather than only a private and psychological aberration. (Feigelman, 1974.)

Waitresses' expressions of distress, such as crying, can be a function of how work is organized rather than of a "waitress" or "female" personality. (Whyte, 1948.)

The structure of power in organizations, rather than inherent gender characteristics, determines women's conduct in large organizations. (Kanter, 1977.)

Stated more broadly, the social researcher seeks the explanation of variations in behavior in situations and social organization rather than in physics, biology, psychology, or other nonsocial realms.

V. WHAT ARE THE UNIT'S PROCESSES?

A dictionary defines the term **process** as "the action of continuously going along through each of a succession of acts, events or developmental stages," and as a ". . . continuing operation or development marked by a series of gradual changes that succeed one another in a relatively fixed way."

Four related concepts provide further help in thinking about processes:

A *stage* is ". . . a period or step in a process, activity or development," or "one of several periods whose beginning and end are usually marked by some important change of structure in . . . development and growth. . . ."

A *step* is ". . . a stage in a gradual, regular or orderly process."

A *period* is a "time often of indefinite length but of distinctive or specified character," or ". . . a division of time in which something is completed and ready to commence and go on in the same order."

A *phase* is a ". . . stage or interval in a development or cycle: a particular appearance or stage of a regularly recurring cycle of changes."

For the purposes of this guide, these four terms are synonyms. We have listed and defined each in order to clarify the idea of processes by highlighting the variety of words with which you can describe their elements.

It is helpful to divide processes themselves into three basic forms: cycles, spirals, and sequences.

A. Cycles

A **cycle** is a "... recurrent sequence of events which occur in such order that the last precedes the recurrence of the first in a new series." It is a "... course of operations or events returning upon itself and restoring the original state," or a "series of changes leading back to the starting point."

All settings do, of course, tend explicitly to be organized in terms of cycles based upon the calendar: seasons, months, days, and so forth. Often such cycles are so well known—so commonsensical to an author's projected audience—that they are not even reported. We may, in the long run, find the neglect of such reportings to have been a serious error. Future audiences with quite different cycles may puzzle over how we, in this period of history, did in fact break up our time and cycle it. Indeed, with the impending extinction of so many ways of life, a description of how cycles are set is already becoming indispensable. The people and settings on which many researchers have reported can often no longer be directly observed. (See, for example, Horace Miner's description of the "yearly round" in St. Denis, a French-Canadian parish [1939:141–168].)

In addition to standard calendar-based cycles, there are revolving regularities of a more unplanned, unrecognized, and less scheduled nature. Thus, in observing some three years in the history of a small, "end-of-the-world" religion, John Lofland perceived that the group went through four cycles of collective hope and despair over the problem of making converts. The group was committed to the goal of making many thousands of converts. In stark contrast to this goal was the fact that very few people could even be interested, and fewer still converted. Each of the four observed cycles of hope and despair during the three years of research had the following characteristics:

1. Some event occurred, or some plan was devised, that provided a collective sense of hope that many converts would soon be made.
2. Action was organized around the event or plan.
3. This action eventually failed, in their own estimation.
4. The failure led to a collective sense of despair of ever attaining the goal.
5. The group then came full circle back to a new event or plan. (J. Lofland, 1977:Chapter 12.)

Such analyses can be further combined with an effort to specify generally the meanings, practices, episodes, and so forth upon which the cycles are predicated. Thus, in this example, four kinds of activities and definitions provided the impetus necessary to initiate the first stage of a new cycle:

New hope was generated when the entire believership decamped and migrated en masse (a rather common strategy in religious history).

New hope was generated by announcing to the believers the imminent but unspecified arrival on the scene of their messiah.

New hope was generated by defining the present time as one for preparatory planning; thus organizing was saved for a later time when, aided by the things done now, goals could really be achieved.

New hope was generated by geographical dispersion of believers on missionary quests. A sense of expansion and potency was derived from new places and people, if not from larger membership. (Adapted from J. Lofland, 1977:Chapter 12).

It is reasonable to mention here what we might call the "master cycle" in the maintenance of all social arrangements. Termed the *self-confirming* or *self-fulfilling prophecy*, in abstract form it goes:

1. People in a social setting believe that X is a fact (for example, women are less capable of leadership than men).
2. People therefore act as if X were true.
3. In so acting, they structure the real world in ways that bring evidence of X as a fact into actual existence (for example, fewer women are in leadership positions).
4. The results of the structuring work in Step 3 are then interpreted as evidence of the validity of the initial belief (Step 1).
5. As a result, the cycle closes, and X is believed to be a fact.

B. Spirals

Some processes do not show the degree of relative stability seen in cycles. Instead, they display a **spiral** pattern, a "continuously spreading and accelerating increase or decrease." One of the more familiar forms of this phenomenon is seen in the tension or conflict between social units that are hostile to one another—especially relatively large units, such as settlements, tribes, neighborhoods, and total societies. There are even special terms for this type of spiral: *escalation* and *deescalation*.

Edwin Lemert's analysis of a spiraling interaction process that led to a person's being labeled and hospitalized as "paranoid" provides a classic illustration of the spiraling process within a smaller social unit. In his "Paranoia and the Dynamics of Exclusion," he describes these stages of the spiral:

1. The person ("X") who is disposed to participate in subsequent stages already displays one or another kind of interpersonal difficulty with his work associates, in particular a tendency to disregard primary group loyalties, to violate confidences, and to assume privileges not accorded to him or her.
2. X's associates tend for a time to perceive X as a variant normal, but one or more events cause a reorganization of the associates' views; they now see X as "unreliable," "untrustworthy," "dangerous," or someone with whom others "do not wish to be involved."
3. Associates begin to engage in patronizing, evasive, and spurious interaction with the person; X is avoided and excluded from interaction.
4. X perceives the associates' new attitudes; this strengthens X's initial

tendencies to disregard confidences and so forth (Step 1) and promotes X's demands to know what is happening.

5. The associates deal with the increasing difficulties posed by X by strengthening their own patronizing, avoidance, and exclusion (Step 2). They begin, moreover, to *conspire* among themselves in developing means to deal with X.

6. X senses this conspiracy, but it, and all other difficulties, tend to be *denied* by the associates. The flow of information to X declines more and more, and the discrepancy between expressed ideas and true feelings among the associates widens, thereby increasing X's ambiguity as to the nature of situations and of the associates.

7. Steps 4–6 repeat themselves, creating greater and greater tension. X and the associates each respond to the difficulties posed by the other, in a process that spirals and feeds upon itself, a process that is *mutually* constructed.

8. Finally, if all the associates' efforts to discharge or transfer X fail, they will attempt to force X to undergo an extended sick leave, psychiatric treatment, or, in the extreme case, commitment to a mental hospital. (Summarized from Lemert, 1972:246–264.)

C. Sequences

The most common rendering of a process is as a time-ordered series of steps or phases. The first and last steps are not "connected," as in cycles, nor is there an accelerated movement to a "stronger" or "weaker" level of operation, as in spirals.

In actually studying processes qualitatively, investigators trace processes from one of three types of starting points.

1. Trace-Back Starting Points. Perhaps the most common starting point is an outcome. For example, a person has embezzled money, used a certain drug, or converted to a strange religion; a crowd has rioted; an organization has disbanded; a community has adopted a growth limit law—all of these occurrences can be seen as outcomes.

If you ask, "What are its causes?", you have posed a quantitative question and must proceed accordingly (as in Section IV.A. above). If, on the other hand, you ask, "How did this build up, how did it happen?" and begin to trace back through the histories of various cases of that outcome, you are proposing a study of qualitative process. Your aim is, inductively, to scrutinize relevant cases in order to glean a process or processes from them. A classic study employing this procedure is criminologist Donald Cressey's account of embezzlement or, more accurately, trust violation (1971; see summary in Chapter 6, Section III.).

In a trace-back analysis, the researcher attempts to discern any typical stages through which the actors and/or action pass in a process that culminates (or does not culminate) in a particular outcome. In the context of religious conversion, Rodney Stark and John Lofland found it useful to divide the sequential process of becoming a millenarian cultist into seven stages. Although they called these the sequential "causes of conversion," their model may also be regarded as a descriptive, qualitative history of the process of conversion. For conversion, a person must:

1. Experience enduring, acutely felt tensions
2. Within a religious problem-solving perspective
3. Which leads him to define himself as a religious seeker
4. Encountering the [religious cult] at a turning point in his life
5. Wherein an affective bond is formed (or pre-exists) with one or more converts
6. Where extra-cult attachments are absent or neutralized
7. And where, if he is to become a deployable agent, he is exposed to intensive interaction (J. Lofland, 1977; J. Lofland & Stark, 1965:874.)

2. **Trace-forward Starting Points.** Alternatively, you may be concerned with what happens *after* a decisive event, as in, for example, veterans returning from wars, people being told they are dying, newlyweds adapting to marriage, or communities being hit by a disaster and faced with problems of recovery. One of the most well-known (and controversial) qualitative trace-forward analyses is Elisabeth Kübler-Ross's five-stage model of persons dealing with the knowledge of their own terminal illness:

1. Initial denial: "It can't be me."
2. Anger: "Why me?"
3. Bargaining: "Just let me have that."
4. Depression: "I give up."
5. Acceptance: "I am ready." (Kübler-Ross, 1969.)

3. **Trace-Through Starting Points.** A third starting point is to consider the history of the process as a whole. This method has obvious advantages in situations lacking a dramatic episode from which to trace forward or backward. The most well-known trace-through models are the various depictions of the early stages of human development (as summarized in Bush and Simmons, 1981) and the stages of their development in adulthood (see for example Levinson, 1978).

We conclude our discussion of process analysis by indicating that its special contribution is its power to report the details of social change. It enables us to observe "through what play of forces, in what sequences of stages and with what existential consequences for the persons involved" social life moves (F. Davis, 1972:ix). Julius Roth described this power nicely in his review of a quantitative survey analysis of consumer defaults on loans:

A one-shot interview survey of a population sample provides one with measures of variables to be correlated. At best, it provides frequencies or proportions of cases with given characteristics or in which given things happen. . . . But surely what a consumer protection advocate is most interested in is not so much the percentage of "types of harassment" used by each type of creditor, but rather, the step by step process by which creditors enforce payment and the kinds of counteraction available to consumers to protect their interests. And for the student of some branches of sociology, the most interesting issues are not the percentage breakdowns, but the interrelated actions of creditors and consumers in a context of laws and administrative and legal agencies. For such an analysis, the most relevant data come from detailed studies of appropriate cases. (Roth, 1977:115.)

We should also point out that qualitative process questions and quantitative causal questions *supplement* and *complement* one another. Or as Mirra Komarovsky has put it, a qualitative process study

. . . is often directed to the following problem: assuming phenomena A and B to be associated, can we discern the sequences of stages, the network of links which connects the two? By contrast, [a causal account] poses the problem: why B rather than not-B? Under what conditions, that is, will B appear or fail to appear? For example, [Willard] Waller [1938] criticized the usual [causal] analysis. He traced alienation in marriage as a process moving "in a cyclical fashion to its denouement in divorce." In so doing, Waller does throw a new light on the way in which some marriages come to divorce but he does not face the problem of why others remain stable. On the other hand, the early correlation studies demonstrated the differential associations between regions, size of family, or economic conditions and divorce, but they failed to specify the links involved in these associations. (Komarovsky, 1957:12–13.)

VI. WHAT ARE THE UNIT'S CONSEQUENCES?

The question of consequences may be viewed as the second half of the causal question. That is, we now view the dependent variable as an independent variable and attempt to look at *its* dependent variable consequences.

A. Requirements of Consequential Inference

Since consequence is merely cause "pushed forward," the five requirements of causal inference (Section IV.A.) also apply here. That is, you must have (1) a variation that you can (2) measure (3) in covariation with another relevant variable, in (4) the appropriate time order, and (5) you must control for spurious associations. As we have noted, these conditions are hard to meet in qualitative field studies. But, like causal conjectures, consequential inferences are still legitimate, as long as they are done with qualification and humility (Sections IV.B. and C.).

B. Consequences of What, for What?

Consequential accounts typically depict the relationships among specific units of analysis. A practical approach to consequences is to determine the specific level of social unit at which the variable occurred whose consequences you want to trace. Then, think through the likely effects at each of the unit levels. In order to facilitate such an approach, Figure 7-5 depicts a typology cross-classifying the units explained in Chapter 6. Looking at the left side of Figure 7-5, locate the unit that corresponds to your variable. Then, carefully trace across the horizontal cells, asking yourself what the occurrence (or nonoccurrence) of this variable means for specific aspects of each unit.

This is not to suggest that an analysis of consequences should be a mechanical listing of effects at each level. Your actual analysis (if you elect to deal with effects at all) must take into account such constraints as the amount of relevant data you have (see Chapter 5) and how interesting the things you have to say about them are (see Chapter 8). Indeed, accomplished consequential analyses ordinarily focus at only one or a few levels of social unit.

C. Examples

One traditional type of consequential analysis focuses on a particular meaning or practice and demonstrates its effects. A classic example is Jack Levin's *The Functions of Prejudice* (1975). In this study, Levin classifies the conse-

Figure 7-5. Consequences of What for What?

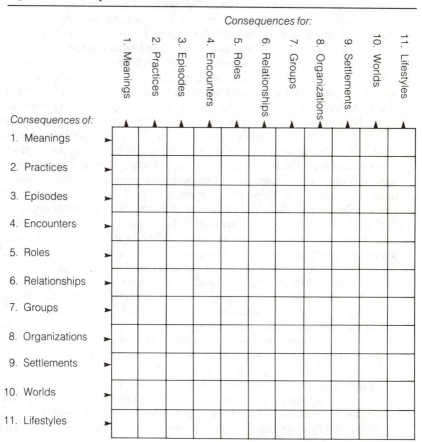

Consequences for:

Consequences of:	1. Meanings	2. Practices	3. Episodes	4. Encounters	5. Roles	6. Relationships	7. Groups	8. Organizations	9. Settlements	10. Worlds	11. Lifestyles
1. Meanings											
2. Practices											
3. Episodes											
4. Encounters											
5. Roles											
6. Relationships											
7. Groups											
8. Organizations											
9. Settlements											
10. Worlds											
11. Lifestyles											

quences of prejudice according to their effects on the majority and minority groups involved. The first three of the six effects on the majority group are heavily psychological, but the second three relate to large-scale units of social organization:

1. Displacement of aggression
2. Protection of self-esteem
3. Reduction of uncertainty
4. Maintenance of occupational status
5. Performance of unpleasant or low-paying jobs
6. Maintenance of power (Levin, 1975:104.)

Effects on the minority group show a similar division between psychological and social effects:

1. Reduction of competition
2. Maintenance of solidarity
3. Reduction of uncertainty (Levin, 1975:104.)

Relating these effects to our Figure 7-5, we see that Levin has taken a relatively microscopic unit (prejudice as a type of meaning or practice) and linked it to more large-scale units (as well as to more psychological levels).

The consequences of "deviant" roles have been of particular interest to social scientists, and this interest has taken an ironic twist. In conventional wisdom, deviant roles are seen as having only destructive and unwanted effects. Several social analysts, however, have argued the reverse. In one such study, deviant informal or social roles found among policemen were identified. These were the "doorman" (or "ass-kisser," a person excessively concerned to impress superiors), the "mouth man" (a person given to indiscrete gossip and "being in the know"), and the "wheel man" (an officer given to reckless driving of a patrol car). In many respects, there was general disapproval of all three roles and of those performing them. The researchers noted, however, that these role players also performed certain necessary and unpleasant tasks in the department. Were these deviants not already available, others would have had to do this "dirty work." More specifically, the mouth man was also maneuvered into tasks of carrying bad news to superiors; the doorman was used strategically to spread information others wanted put abroad; the wheel man was deployed to take risks in situations others quite rationally avoided (Reed, Burnette & Troiden, 1977).

The authors generalized that "deviants make it possible for others to maintain a personal and collective image of moral righteousness in spite of the normative limitations which they face.... [Thus] it is for ... quite concrete, practical purposes that groups often need their deviants" (1977:574). Indeed, many have argued that because of several "functional needs" of social organization, all groups *induce* people to play deviant roles.

Consequential analyses have been performed at many other unit levels. One example is Robert Merton's well-known argument that corrupt political machines in American cities have functioned to provide additional routes of social mobility for talented persons in disadvantaged ethnic minorities.

Political machines thereby make a contribution to the political and social stability of the entire society by keeping down the level of minority dissatisfaction (1968:126–136). And, asking why poverty persists in spite of widespread condemnation, Herbert Gans has delineated fifteen "functions" or benefits the affluent derive from poverty which thus help to explain why it does not go away. Among these functions: the poor do dirty work no one else will; they subsidize a variety of activities for the affluent; they create many jobs for servicing and controlling them; they are a dumping ground for damaged goods, preventing total loss (1972:275–289).

D. Consequences and System Needs: Functionalism

One special form of consequential analysis assumes that the unit of analysis is a social system, an integrated whole that is striving to maintain itself in whatever its current state. Analysts, therefore, look for the contribution that various parts of the system make to maintaining the larger whole. One classic formulation has put it this way:

The *function* of any recurrent activity, such as the punishment of a crime or a funeral ceremony, is the part it plays in the social life as a whole and therefore the contribution it makes to the maintenance of the structural continuity.

By the definition here offered "function" is the contribution which a partial activity makes to the total activity of which it is a part. The function of a particular social usage is the contribution it makes to the total social life as the functioning of the total social system. (Radcliffe-Brown, 1935:396, 397.)

Thus, in the study of deviant roles among policemen summarized above, the specifically functional aspect is that the performance of certain unpleasant tasks is necessary for the maintenance of the police department. The deviant roles documented (or their equivalents, if these particular ones had not developed in the department) are therefore *functionally necessary* roles.

As an analyst, you may or may not feel you are justified in adopting this strong a form of consequential analysis. Often you can do consequential analysis without positing the existence of a social system with "functional needs." Moreover, consequential analysis need not focus only on effects that *maintain* a social arrangement. You can as easily focus on consequences that *bring change* to the arrangement.

E. Other Versions of the Consequence Question

In order to encourage playfulness of mind, we here report several other ways of asking the question of consequences. Here are two variations on the functionalist approach:

What *functions* are served by the existence of this practice that would not be served in its absence?

What *role* does this practice, pattern, or variation play in the maintenance of this setting in its present form?

And here are three nonfunctionalist wordings:

What are the typical *results* of this phenomenon in this setting?
What *ends* are served by the existence of this pattern?
What are the *products* of this variation in the standing pattern?

F. Consequences Distinguished from Intentions

Because a social activity has certain consequences or functions does not necessarily mean that such consequences or functions are intended by the participants. Intention—conscious or unconscious—may or may not be involved.

Thomas Kochman described various verbal practices among ghetto blacks and suggested these functions or consequences of the practices:

. . . Through rapping, sounding and running it down, the black in the ghetto establishes his personality; through shucking, gripping, and copping a plea, he shows his respect for power; through jiving and signifying he stirs up excitement. With all of the above, he hopes to manipulate and control people and situations to give himself a winning edge. (Kochman, 1969:34.)

Kochman here has attributed intention to the participants. He may or may not have been correct in doing so. What is more important is that the functions he asserted can be evaluated independently of whether or not the participants *intended* their practices to have these consequences.

VII. WHAT ARE PEOPLE'S STRATEGIES?

We have just discussed six questions the analyst asks of social units. These questions may be seen as variations on a single point of view. Here, we will identify this viewpoint and contrast it with a different approach to the analysis of social life.

A. Passivist versus Activist Images

We may label the point of view that the six foregoing questions all illustrate, the **passivist** conception of humans and of social life. In this approach, as Herbert Blumer has put it, humans are treated as more or less neutral media through which social forces operate and out of which social forms and organizations are composed (1969). Types, structures, frequencies, causes, processes, and consequences all have their own reality in which humans are incidental aspects or ciphers in the workings of social organization.

There is nothing wrong with this passivist image of humans in and of itself. Social life and organization *do* have their own reality. But the six aspects of the passivist approach, taken collectively, are incomplete. For there is another side, an additional reality to which we must attend. This is the **activist** approach, in which we view humans as creative and probing creatures who are coping, dealing, designating, dodging, maneuvering, scheming, striving, struggling, and so forth—that is, who are actively influencing their social settings. In the activist view, the focus is on how people construct their actions in various situations, on how their activity is pieced together, thought about, tried out, and worked out.

The logical relationship between the passivist and activist view of human life may be likened to the familiar perceptual puzzles in which a drawing "looked at" in two different ways appears to represent two different objects. (See Figure 7-6, which may be seen as either a vase or two human heads in profile facing one another.) The contrast may also be thought of as the difference between regarding a human being as a *product* of social forces and a *source* of social force. In both these images, whether the drawing/person "is" one or the other is not the appropriate question. It is *both*. Whether it is *seen* as the one or the other depends on your point of view.

B. Activist Questions

Once you understand this passivist-activist contrast, the procedural question for doing actual research then becomes how to develop an analysis that implements the activist image.

Just as you use the six questions above to focus your data, in the activist approach, the central question you use is "What are people's strategies?" And, as with the previous questions, this one needs some elaboration to be used well. As an approach to the data, it becomes *two* questions:

1. What is the *situation* being dealt with?
2. What *strategies* are being employed in dealing with that situation?

Figure 7-6. A Perceptual Analogy to the Activist-Passivist Contrast

People do not just act blindly; they construct their actions to deal with situations—with circumstances composed of people, opportunities, and constraints, as these are defined by the actors in them. The activist analyst is concerned, therefore, with deciphering and depicting exactly what sort of situation the participants are facing.

Actual reports tend, in fact, to be organized into two main sections, one of which analyzes the situation and the other of which reports strategies. Many of the studies we have summarized in the preceding chapter and in this chapter exemplify such a situation/strategy analysis. In Chapter 6, for example, illustrations from the discussions of the first six units include the following:

Section I. A., on *meanings:* Mental patients deal with their stigmatized *situation* by devising certain *strategic* definitions of the situation. (Kaplan, Boyd & Bloom, 1968.)

Section II., on *practices:* Students cope with their *situation* by means of "fritter" *strategies.* (Bernstein, 1978.)

Section III., on *episodes:* Parents handle the problematic *situation* of having a polio-stricken child by *strategies* of normalization and disassociation. (F. Davis, 1972.)

Section IV. on *encounters:* The stressful *situation* of delivering bad news leads to the development of several *strategies* for each stage of the delivery. (McClenahen and Lofland, 1978.)

Section V. on *roles:* In the *situation* of a talented but undramatic person, certain *strategies* are available for becoming a hero. (Klapp, 1964.)

Section VI. on *relationships:* The milkman in a declining *situation* develops *strategies* of customer cultivation. (Bigus, 1978.)

These examples highlight the constructed character of relatively microscopic situations and strategies, but more large-scale ones also deserve attention. For example, Gerald Suttles's depiction of "ordered segmentation" in a Chicago slum (summarized in Chapter 6, Section IX.) is a report on a "large" strategy (1968). That is, ordered segmentation as a settlement form is a strategy evolved by many, many people over long periods of time. Because it is a shared, long-term way of coping, it is easy to lose sight of the fact that it is a *constructed* strategy—as are all other large-scale social arrangements.

We tend to lose appreciation of this fact because of the peculiar human propensity for *objectivation,* as Berger and Luckman have termed it (1967:60ff). Humans themselves devise strategic social arrangements but then lose sight of that fact over time, because the "structure" presents itself as an "object" (thus the term *objectivation*). The strategy question is one way to "deobjectify" social arrangements (and, as we will explain further in the next chapter, *demystify* them). By deobjectivation we come to realize that no social arrangement simply "is." Rather, arrangements are incessantly *fabricated.* This can be seen by decomposing them into their strategic components.

Moreover, by asking "what are people's strategies?", you can achieve a better *causal* understanding of many social events. For example, in some social organizations people "speak in tongues" and display "otherworldly," "saved," or "sanctified" behavior that is seen by some insiders as supernaturally caused and by some analysts as psychologically pathological in origin. In contrast to both of these perspectives, the activist asks if the tongue-speakers and their associates engage in activity designed to *produce* such behavior. We find, in fact, that they do so act—that tongue-speakers and their coaches engage in an enormously complex, detailed, and subtle process designed socially and normatively to evoke speaking in tongues (Harrison, 1974). The supernatural and pathological causal accounts are not ruled out, of course. But they are placed in a context of *construction*, of strategic accomplishment.

In conclusion, by pursuing people's strategies, the activist makes the social realm human again by demonstrating human intention and authorship.

VIII. COMBINING UNITS AND QUESTIONS

We end this chapter by repeating the guiding point with which we began: Your evolving analysis is *focused*, through reflection, both on appropriate *units* of analysis (outlined in Chapter 6) and appropriate *questions* (described in this chapter) about the units selected. Figure 7-1, at the beginning of this chapter, summarizes the intersection of these two kinds of concerns. The cells in this typology make up, in effect, a list of 42 basic areas of possible questions. *Within* one or more of these areas, you can evolve a specific analysis.

Chapters 6 and 7 have dealt with two of the three important aspects of focusing analyses. The third, developing a *specific* analysis, raises the question, "Which specific analysis among the alternatives is the most *interesting*?" Answering this question is our concern in Chapter 8.

Being Interesting

8 Utilizing the procedures described in the foregoing chapters (or in the following three chapters) will not, alone, assure that you will produce a report that anyone finds *interesting*, meaningful, or exciting. It is a discouraging but powerful truth that few social analyses are received with enthusiasm. Most tend to be met with disappointment and boredom.

The problem for the analyst, then, is to develop answers to questions that will appeal to an appropriate audience.

I. AUDIENCE PERSPECTIVES: TECHNOCRATIC VERSUS TRANSCENDENT

A first step in this task is to recognize that, even within the special realm of social analysis, audiences are diverse. That is, you must consider whom you wish to interest. While doubtlessly oversimplified and stereotyped, it is useful to distinguish two broad types of audiences for social analyses—types that occur both inside and outside the circles of professional social scientists. The two audiences (and the analysts who write for them) differ most fundamentally in the view they take of the nature of the relation between the analysis itself and the social life/organization being researched.

On the one hand, there is what we might term the **technocratic** view. Here, the aims, assumptions, and perspectives of the people being studied (and/or of the people sponsoring the research) are taken as the appropriate aims, assumptions, and perspectives of the researcher (and thus of the analysis). We use the particular term *technocratic* because, among other reasons, you, as researcher, are presenting yourself as the expert answerer of the questions posed by those studied, or by the sponsors of the research. You form questions and work out generalizations that fit into and further the perspectives of these persons.

The technocratic perspective is more than simply a narrow view of the relation among the social analyst, those researched, and the sponsors. It is also a full-blown construction of reality. In it, the disposition is to develop and phrase questions and answers as matters of relative technical efficacy and efficiency. The argument that collective social choices are always and intimately political, value, and moral choices is shunted aside. Whatever the social world under scrutiny, you should present it as a stable structure of social givens, a solid backdrop against which humans move with certainty (except concerning quite narrow questions of technique).

But there is a quite different view you can take of the relation between researcher, researched, research sponsors. Simply stated, instead of *taking on* the perspective of the researched or research sponsors, you *use* that perspective as the topic of analysis. Terming this **transcendent** view, in its most general form, the "culture of critical discourse (CCD)," Alvin Gouldner has observed that it is "... centered on [the act of] justification.... There is nothing that speakers ... refuse to discuss or make problematic (1979:28). Its essence is *reflexivity*, that is,

the obligation to examine what had hitherto been taken for granted, to transform "givens" into "problems," resources into topics: to examine the life we lead, rather than just enjoy or suffer it. It is therefore not only the present but also the anti-present, the *critique* of the present and the assumptions it uses, that the culture of critical discourse must also challenge. In other words: the culture of critical discourse must put its hands around its own throat, and see how long it can squeeze. CCD always moves on to auto-critique, and to the critique of *that* auto-critique. There is an unending regress in it, a potential revolution in permanence; it embodies that unceasing restlessness and "lawlessness" that the ancient Greeks first called *anomos* and that Hegel had called the "bad infinity." (Gouldner, 1979:59–60.)

This transcendent view, or refusal to take the assumptions of others (or of oneself) for granted, has also been termed (among other labels) the *visionary, critical, ironic, bracketing,* or *humanistic* perspective on social analysis (for example, Berger, 1963, 1971; Gusfield, 1981; Brown, 1977). As a perspective in the modern world, it embodies a cosmopolitanism in which "truth is democratized" by bringing "all ... claims under ... scrutiny" (Gouldner, 1979:59). It renders any "existing world ... an object of scrutiny, not acceptance[, as only] one among many possibilities" (Gusfield, 1981:192). There is, as a consequence, a "diminution of the legitimacy" of elites and, indeed, of the technocratic world view itself. For the transcendent view

presents a world that is political rather than a world of technical necessity. If choice is possible, if new and alternative modes of acting are possible and imaginable, then the existent situation hides the conflicts and alternatives that can be imagined. (Gusfield, 1981:193.)

The transcending perspective is, thus, a means by which

> to penetrate the veil of the apolitical. . . . It makes us aware of the sheer difficulty of avoiding choice between alternatives, of having to engage in the world of politics and moralities, [of having] to take a stand without the benefits of a clear and commanding social vision. (Gusfield, 1981:195.)

A. Need for the Transcendent Perspective

But what is the value of such transcendence? One answer goes like this: In complexly differentiated societies, ordinary people playing out their ordinary lives are enmeshed in devising and enacting ideas and activities that are responsive to their immediate needs. Immersed in acting, they have little time, training, or disposition for collecting information on the multiple facets of their situations. They are not in a good position to assemble such information, to reflect on its meaning, to envision larger contexts in which it might variously be interpreted, or to contemplate feasible and conceivable alternatives to their situations. Additionally, the alliances, accommodations, ruses, mutings, euphemizations, and other necessary avoidances of ordinary life lead people to miss seeing many aspects of their situations, and to develop legitimizing and accommodating meanings for what they do see.

In other words, the requirements of acting weaken or nullify the capacity and honesty to reflect on the actions. Transcendent social analysis facilitates the breakup of collective self-deceptions, the ideological "logjams" to which all social life is inherently prone. Indeed, as the situations in which people are intimately involved grow ever more specialized and arcane, and are submerged in increasingly larger (even planetary) scales of social organization, *situationally induced irrationality* becomes more and more common and its consequences more fateful for all of us. Correspondingly, transcendent analysis comes to be of greater and greater import.

Put differently, the transcendent perspective strives to achieve deobjectivation and demystification. As mentioned in Chapter 7, humans are the authors of all social arrangements. After they are created, however, such arrangements come, perceptually and psychologically, to have an existence of their own, to seem "wholly other" and "out there" (Berger & Luckmann, 1967:61).

This objectivation of social arrangements is perhaps the most fundamental form of *mystification*—the practice of shrouding social performance in an ambience of mystery, of fostering the impression that a social "show" is not fully knowable and that the performers must have very special knowledge and powers (Goffman, 1959:67–70).

Transcendent analysis insists on the human authorship of all social arrangements—on demystifying them. Like Toto in *The Wizard of Oz*, transcendentalists strive to pull away the curtains that hide the petty mechanisms of impressive social action.

B. Qualifications

For clarity's sake, we have sketched the contrast between technocratic and transcendent perspectives in overly sharp terms. Qualifications and demurs are now in order. First, you should view the distinction as one between specific instances of social analysis rather than between particular analysts.

While some researchers may *tend* toward the technocratic or the transcendent, many do both kinds of work throughout their lives. Moreover, some start out with a tendency toward transcendence and then become technocratic. Others do the reverse. Actual researchers, then, are not so easily classified.

Second, any judgment as to which perspective an analysis displays must be considered radically contextual. An analysis judged to be transcendent when first performed can become, because of its wide acceptance, technocratic. Among the most famous instances are Karl Marx's analysis of capitalism and Sigmund Freud's depiction of human psychology. Both have, over the years, moved in their respective circles from mind-boggling transcendence to stale, technocratic orthodoxy.

Third, the transcendent process of bringing assumptions and choices to consciousness is inherently neither conservative nor radical in its political meaning. It *is* inherently subversive of established patterns of thought, but it is subversive of *all* patterns of thought and action. As Peter Berger has pithily expressed it: "Fomenters of revolution have as good reason to be suspicious of [the transcendent perspective] as policemen have" (1971:13). Indeed, some of the most enthusiastically technocratic people are to be found among activists, people who differ from establishment technocrats only in terms of the aims and perspectives they assume and *not* in terms of their fundamental approach. To quote Peter Berger again; "My principal objection to most of my radicalized colleagues is not that they are engaged in the business of 'bringing to consciousness' [using the transcendent perspective] but that they are not doing enough of it" (1971:5). Rather than being easily classifiable as "leftwing" or "rightwing," the transcendent perspective engages in a "consistent, unswerving application of critical intelligence—to the status quo, yes, and to any challengers of the status quo" (Berger, 1971:5). Indeed, if you are a member of a radical group (right, left, *or* center), the most important contribution you might well make is an "ongoing critique" of your own movement (Berger, 1971:5).

The distinction between technocratic and transcendent viewpoints provides us with an initial point of advice about being interesting: Think about your audience. If you have selected a technocratic audience, you may be well advised to avoid qualitative or naturalistic research, as it tends to lead toward use of the transcending perspective. Quantitative research, on the other hand, leads toward a technocratic perspective. It involves a specialized set of devices that make the resulting analysis interesting to its audience and has a well-developed rhetoric of presentation (see Gusfield, 1981:Chapter 4). Our aim in the following sections is to specify equivalent "interest-arousing" procedures for the transcendent perspective.

II. SURFACE DEVICES

We may divide such relevant devices into two categories: those we believe to be broader and more fundamental and those we consider simpler, though often powerful and quite justifiable. We will first consider the latter, which we will refer to as *surface devices.*

Let us first consider the fact that social settings differ in the degree to which they are socially defined as strange, ideologically or behaviorally exotic, prurient, violent, and so on. Some settings may exhibit several of these features and thus may elicit human interest by their mere description. It is, indeed, not without reason that social science fieldworkers have tended to study "strange" settings out of proportion to their numbers in society. One graduate training center in sociology has, in fact, built a virtual research program around the exotic sexual practices that flourish in its geographical region. It has fielded a small corps of graduate students to observe nude beaches, massage parlors, homosexual establishments, and so forth.

Second, to be the *first* report on a setting is to provoke interest because of the sheer novelty of the items reported. A few reports, we may observe, are able to trade on both the first and second devices (and others) at the same time. See for example Laud Humphreys's pioneering work on homosexual encounters in public restrooms (1975).

Third, there is a range of rhetorical devices with which reports can be opened, imbued, and closed and which serve to arouse at least some interest in some audiences. Perhaps the most dramatic of such *forms of appeal* (a term used by Ray Cuzzort & Edith King, 1978) is the *appeal to impending catastrophe.* Here the writer claims that an audience ought to pay attention because "death, mayhem, doom and destruction are imminent" (Cuzzort & King, 1978:3). Therefore, read my report and avoid them! Less drastic but common is the *appeal to injustice*, the promise that exploitation will be unmasked, villains identified and pilloried, and the way to justice shown. Of greater interest to the technocratically inclined is the *promise of practicality* or "How-to-Do-It" (Cuzzort & King, 1978:8), in which some clear and proximate problem is isolated and a solution promised as a part of the report. (Among yet other variations on rhetorical devices, we may refer to Ray Cuzzort & Edith King's discussions of "I-Know-Something-about-Somebody-Who-Is-Somebody" and "We-Have-Been-Led-Astray" [1978]. The former often combines the "first data" technique with an appeal to injustice, a practice anthropologist Laura Nader has termed "studying up" [1977], that is, studying the powerful and rich rather than the powerless and poor.)

III. DEEPER DEVICES

If we conceive of the "transcending perspective" in more active terms, we may say that both surface and deeper devices have as their central theme the claim that "things are not (or are not only) what they seem to be." The surface devices just described are some of the easier ways in which to work out that theme. We will now examine four broader and more difficult devices.

A. The Metaphoric

A dictionary defines the word *metaphor* as "a figure of speech in which one kind of object or phrase literally denoting one kind of object or idea is used in place of another to suggest a likeness or analogy between them (as in, the ship plows the sea)." More broadly, metaphor involves "seeing something from the viewpoint of something else" (Brown, 1977:78). In social analysis, the simplest formula is "X *as* Y," as in Murray Melbin's creative analysis of "Night as Frontier" (1978), a study in which features of the literal concept of "frontier" are applied to "the night." Melbin argues that "time, like space, can be occupied and is treated so by humans. . . . Nighttime social life in urban areas resembles social life in former land frontiers" (Melbin, 1978:3).

One of the most creative of contemporary social scientists, Erving Goffman, has made a career out of metaphoric redefinitions; for example, he has conceptualized:

The problem of failure in social life in terms of the classic confidence game, in which everyone is a mark, operator, or cooler (Goffman, 1962.)

Contact among strangers as a theatrical situation of "performers" and "impression management" (Goffman, 1959.)

Mental patients as having careers (Goffman, 1961:Chapter 2.)

Psychiatry as an instance of the "tinkering trades," or as a mere service occupation subject to the same venal tendencies (Goffman, 1961:Chapter 4; see also J. Lofland, 1980, on "perspective by incongruity" in Goffman's work.)

As you can see, Goffman's special twist on the metaphor device is his preference for using those that violate existing conceptions of social propriety. While he has been a champion in the use of the "violating metaphor," he is hardly unique in this respect. Many other interesting studies have also used it, as in referring to medical school students as "boys in white" (Becker et al., 1961). This contrasts sharply with the technocratic worship embodied in the title of a competing study of medical students: *The Student-Physician* (Merton, Reader & Kendall, 1957; see also Gouldner, 1962).

The point of metaphor is not simply and mechanically to translate one realm into another, but rather to "provide a new way to understand that which we already know [and to reconstitute] . . . new domains of perception" (Brown, 1977:98). As a guide in analytic work, then, the device of metaphor counsels a playful turn of mind, as in these examples provided by Roger Brown:

The Catholic Church is the General Motors of religion.

Heart surgeons run a boutique practice.

Hilton Hotels are factories for sleep. (Brown, 1977.)

B. The Generic

The degree to which the operations just described are metaphoric is, by definition, the degree to which a usage violates understandings of "what is an instance of what." The metaphor is a relatively strong or striking violation of such received understandings.

What may be termed the *generic device* is a less radical violation, one that moves more clearly within accepted traditions of social analysis. With this device, the data at hand are still construed as instances of broader and more general categories, but the categories themselves conform more closely to standard social scientific conceptions.

Three studies summarized in previous chapters illustrate this process of "upward categorization."

The ongoing, daily relationship between milkmen and their customers is framed as an instance of a *cultivated relationship*. (Bigus, 1978.)

The activities of a welfare office are framed as an instance of *symbolic bureaucracy*. (Jerry Jacobs, 1979.)

The stages through which the relationship between a handicapped person and a physically normal person may move are framed as an instance of *deviance disavowal*. (F. Davis, 1961)

In each of these studies, the analyst has asked, "Of what more abstract and social analytic category are these data an instance?" The goal is to translate the specific materials under study into instances of widely relevant and basic human types, processes, or whatever. The generic device transforms obscure social doings into relatively common and basic human concerns. The situation under study is lifted out of its historically specific details and placed among the array of matters that interest (at best) everyone. We try— to use a metaphor (!)—to see the universe in a grain of sand. Or, as Louis Coser put it:

Though there is but little concrete similarity between the behavior displayed at the court of Louis XIV and that displayed in the main offices of an American corporation, a study of the forms of subordination and superordination in each may reveal underlying patterns common to both. On a concrete and descriptive level, there would seem little connection between, say, the early psychoanalytic movement in Vienna and the Trotskyist movement, but attention to typical forms of interaction among the members of these groups reveals that both are importantly shaped by the fact that they have the structural features of the sect. (Coser, 1965:7).

Analysts do not deny the uniqueness of events. But they do search for transsocial organizational patterns of type, structure, cause, function, process, strategy, and so forth:

If one looks at history through the peculiar lenses of the [social analyst], one need not be concern[ed] with the uniqueness of these events but, rather, with their underlying uniformities. The [social analyst] does not contribute to knowledge about the individual actions of a King John, or a King Louis, or a King Henry. But [he or she] can illuminate the ways in which all of them were constrained in their actions by the institution of kingship. The [social analyst] is not concerned with King *John*, but rather, with *King* John. (Coser, 1965:7.)

The generic device becomes most interesting when the case at hand is particularly relevant to a general consideration. Not all data are automatically usable for just *any* generic concern. While given data can be conceived and may be relevant and useful in several generic ways, they are likely to be *more useful* for some concerns than for others.

It is important, then, to be familiar with existing social analytic puzzles and to be alert to which of these puzzles are most amenable to your data. Among recent examples of successful linkages, we may refer to the work of Gary Fine and his associates. They did fieldwork on the seemingly inauspicious topic of Little League baseball—a topic with few obvious generic uses. But they returned from the field with many interesting reports, one of the most intriguing arising from viewing each team as a "culture-creating" entity that elaborated its own "ideoculture." They used their data to help them see culture as a process rather than a hollow concept; that is, they made culture interesting again (Fine, 1979).

C. The Ironic

The term *irony* is ordinarily defined as "a state of affairs or events that is the reverse of what was or was to be expected: a result opposite to and as if in mockery of the appropriate result." It can be applied in social analysis by being attentive to causes, consequences, and other aspects of social units that are paradoxical, unintended, and/or unrecognized by participants.

Irony is most often used with regard to questions of function or consequence (see Chapter 7, Section VI.). In such cases, it requires the ability to distinguish between **manifest** and **latent** functions, that is, to look beyond the recognized and intended (or *manifest*) functions to the unrecognized and unintended (or *latent*) functions. The champion practitioner of sociological irony, Robert Merton, has claimed that "it is precisely at the point where the research attention of sociologists has shifted from the plane of manifest to the plane of latent functions that they have made their *distinctive* and major contribution" (1968:120). And he has powerfully illustrated this assertion with his own examples (as summarized by Arthur Stinchcombe):

Good comes from evil, complexity from simplicity, crime from morality; saints stink while whores smell good; trade unions and strikes lead to industrial peace under a rule of law and a collective contract; law and order candidates are fond of burglary. Merton clearly loves irony. He is most pleased to find motives of advancing knowledge creating priority conflicts among scientists and hardly interested in the fact that such motives also advance knowledge. He likes to find political bosses helping people while good government types turn a cold shoulder. He likes to find Sorokin offering statistics on ideas to attack the empiricist bent of modern culture and to urge an idealistic logico-meaningful analysis of ideas. He likes to range Engels and functionalists down parallel columns to show them to be really the same. The immediate subjective feeling that one has learned something from reading Merton is probably mainly due to the taste for irony. (Stinchcombe, 1975:28.)

Merton has been outstanding, but he has hardly been alone. What is known as the "functionalist perspective" is suffused with irony. Functionalists have been known to propound, among other things, the notions that "increased prostitution may reduce the sexual irregularities of respectable women" (Kingsley Davis, quoted in Schneider, 1975:325) and that incompetent group members may help their groups more than harm them. (See Chapter 7, Section VI.; Brown, 1977:Chapter 5.)

Conceived more broadly, irony involves documenting a contrast between a surface or official understanding of a social arrangement and additional, *also real*, but muted or hidden social facts. Because social life is replete with discrepancies between formal plans and actual conduct, between the official, visible, and public and the unofficial, invisible, and private, social researchers are obviously able to make such contrasts the objects of analysis. Peter Berger has referred to the transcending perspective's emphasis on such contrasts as the "debunking motif" in sociological consciousness. It is a:

> built-in procedure for looking for levels of reality other than those given in the official interpretations of society [, a mandate to] look beyond the immediately given and publicly approved interpretations . . . [in order to] observe the machinery that went into the construction of the scene. The [social analyst thus] "looks behind" the facades of social structure. (Berger, 1979:9–10.)

D. The New Form

A rather more modest (but nonetheless important and creative) device is to discern new variations on established types of social units and on answers to the questions described in the previous chapter. Even though "new forms" can be associated with any of these seven questions, in practice they tend to be answers to Questions I and II: "What is the unit's type?" and "What is the unit's structure?" Erving Goffman's notion of the "total institution" (discussed in Chapter 6, Section VIII., and Chapter 7, Section I.), for example, was a new form at one time.

Among new forms of answers to other questions, you may refer back to these analyses (also from Chapter 7):

Question IV: "What Are the Unit's Causes?" One analysis demonstrates that voyeurism sometimes may be a collective activity of normal persons, casting doubt, therefore, on the notion that it is always pathological. (Feigelman, 1974.)

Question V: "What Are the Unit's Processes?" Defining someone as a paranoid involves a complex, self-feeding sequence of interaction in which the person's "normal" associates actually conspire against the person they fear. (Lemert, 1972:246–264.)

Question VI: "What Are the Unit's Consequences?" Deviant social behavior among persons in organizations serves needed but publicly unacknowledged functions that someone else would otherwise have to perform. (Reed, Burnette & Troiden, 1977).

Question VII: "What Are People's Strategies?" People cope with situations involving open, never-ending tasks by means of myriad "fritter" devices. (Bernstein, 1978.)

Creative discernment of new forms requires more familiarity with existing social analyses than do the devices discussed previously. Consider, for example, answering such questions as these in new form terms:

What new kind of socialization is this?
What new sort of family type is this?
What innovative manner of organizational process is this?

You *can* answer these questions without being familiar with previous work on the subject. You run a high risk, however, of simply rediscovering what is already quite well understood.

The churnings of the modern world are constantly throwing up new and significant variations on everything. Discernment of them is entirely in order; in fact, the few people who are especially gifted at this perform an enormous social service. Some of the best analyses of new forms in recent years have been performed by Tom Wolfe. Wolfe has discovered and defined such modern phenomena as "radical chic," "mau-mauing the flak catchers," "funky chic," and "the me decade" (1970, 1976). Perhaps more than most social analysts, Wolfe should be a model for conceptualizing new forms.

IV. OTHER ASPECTS OF BEING INTERESTING

In concluding this chapter, we will mention three other important matters. First, because all social analysis plays off what is ordinarily believed or felt to be known, an analysis is interesting only insofar as it departs from what is already seen as "obvious." And because what is seen as obvious is itself changing, what is or will be regarded as interesting is also changing (M. Davis, 1971). It is no longer interesting to "discover" total institutions, informal groups, symbolic bureaucracies, socialization, or a large number of other phenomena that are now widely accepted among knowledgeable audiences. There is, therefore, no immutable set of interesting questions or answers. Practically, this means you would be well advised to search published materials and sound out knowledgeable associates in terms of what is and is not currently "common knowledge."

Second, the perspective provided in this chapter helps explain the propensity we find among social analysts to coin new words and to imbue old words with new meanings. Sometimes such practices are mere "jargonizing," but often, analysts are reaching for a transcendent reality and using linguistic alterations and innovations as a vehicle. It must be admitted that such attempts may produce barbarous language and be generally unsuccessful. But the devices employed in the quest for a goal ought not to be confused with or allowed to discredit the goal itself. Carefully and gracefully done, there is much to be said for new coinages, as the works of Tom Wolfe (mentioned above) forcefully illustrate. Let us not, therefore, disparage "jargon" in and of itself, only graceless jargon! For, as we noted at the start of this chapter, the goal is revitalized and rethought vision, and linguistic innovations are an integral aspect of the quest.

Last, we want to stress that using these devices is not and should not be a lifeless and dull task. Animated by penetrating *substance*, it can produce aesthetic experiences of a highly positive and exciting nature. There can be "the experience [of] a thrill at a beautiful idea" (Stinchcombe, 1975:32) that goes very much to the heart of the transcendent vision. In achieving that vision, the social analyst is the person who, so to speak, "shouts 'theater' in the middle of a crowded fire" (Brown, 1977:183).

PART THREE

Analyzing
Data

Your gathered and more or less focused data must now be worked into understandable and written form. This third, analysis phase may itself be divided into two kinds of tasks:

First, the data need to be manipulated in some concrete and physical ways that are described in Chapter 9.

Second, the results of these physical manipulations must be rendered into an orderly and precise report of your research. Suggestions on how best to do this are given in Chapter 10.

Developing Analysis

Researchers sometimes imagine data collection to be one phase of their work and analysis another. This relation is depicted graphically in the left half of Figure 9-1. Such a division of effort will most likely lead to a failure to perform any sort of decent analysis (*or* data collection). A more productive scheme is shown in the right half of Figure 9-1. In this format, analysis and data collection run concurrently for most of the time expended on the project, and the final stage of analysis (after data collection has ceased) becomes a period for bringing final order to previously developed ideas. Contrast this with the former situation, wherein the researcher, after data collection has ceased, has to *begin* to make some kind of coherent sense out of the mass of running descriptions, documents, and so on. Excellent work can, of course, still be produced. We only suggest that it is more difficult to do so.

It is one thing to counsel the overlap of data collection and analysis. It is another to indicate exactly how this can be achieved. The production of analytic ideas summons up your creative abilities, aided by your sociological and other background and (we would hope) by the considerations described in Part Two.

I. FILING/CODING

Moving to the more concrete aspects of the process, let us examine some quite physical and mechanical procedures that can stimulate analysis during the period of data collection.

A. Establishing Files

First and perhaps foremost is the establishment of some kind of filing system. One common scheme consists of file folders combined with "hanging files," which have overhanging metal "ears" that sit on metal rails in a file drawer.

Figure 9-1. Unproductive and Productive Temporal Relations between Data Collection and Analysis

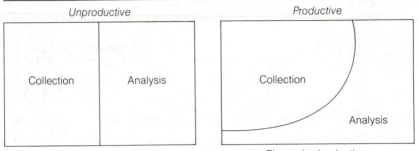

The maintenance of a filing system is actually a physical manifestation of a more abstract process: that of building codes, or **coding.** But because filing is a very common form of coding, and because discussions of coding without reference to the physical aspects of it tend to be arid and difficult to follow, we will stress the actual activity of filing.

We elect to describe filing, moreover, because of its relatively low cost. As mentioned in Chapter 5, one convenient but expensive way to store field notes or interview write-ups is in the memory banks of a word processor. At this stage, you could also code and file the data in a word processor. The enormous flexibility it can achieve makes its use a very attractive possibility, and if one is available to you, by all means use it (Seidel & Clark, 1982a, 1982b). Another possibility is to employ boxes, such as those in which more expensive bond paper is sold, and to establish shelves of them containing material on various topics. And a variety of other systems are available.

Assuming that you are filing (using ordinary file folders and hanging files), several file folders can be placed in a single hanging file. In this way, you can achieve reasonable flexibility in grouping and regrouping data into categories of observations and in ordering and reordering these categories. The aim is to get the material out of the chronological narrative form of your field notes or interview write-ups and into a storage system where you can easily order and retrieve it. It is here that the advice we gave in Chapter 5 (Section I.E.) to make *multiple copies* of your notes assumes supreme importance. The more copies of a particular observation/interview segment or analytic idea you have, the more categories it can easily be filed under (McCall & Simmons, 1969:76). And even if you lack sufficient copies, cross-referencing notes can be made.

B. Types of Files

Although we have been speaking of files as crucial stimulants to the analytic process, we want to emphasize that this is not their only function. Nor are analytic files the only kind you should keep, at least initially.

1. **Mundane Files.** You should also use files simply to keep track of people, places, organizations, documents, and so forth. Mundane files are organized very much like those in any business enterprise, with information grouped

under the most obvious categories, the better to locate it again. Thus, if you are doing participant observation, you will almost certainly want to have a folder on each person—or each "key" person—under observation. The material that you accumulate on the most obvious aspects of social units can help—through review—to bring out crucial points you had not considered about those units. Similarly, such material may reveal patterns not previously contemplated.

Even a study of a highly limited setting with very few people can produce a very complex set of facts, activities, and so forth. You will need aids to keep even the simpler matters straight. Mundane files facilitate your ability to locate a record of something that happened, let us say, several months in the past. You could easily spend hours trying to retrieve it from your chronological notes or your analytic files, but a mundane file lets you find it immediately.

2. Analytic Files. Mundane files are likely to provide a stark contrast to the (physically separate) analytic files. Any given piece of information can easily be imbued with multiple and diverse analytic significance. While this piece of information intentionally has only one or a very few locations in your mundane files, it can, and should, have a variety of locations in your analytic files. When a given episode, situation, or whatever suggests several ideas or matters of significance, write each up in a brief (or extended) fashion, put them (along with a copy of the relevant data) into separate, labeled file folders, and enter these folders into your fuller set of analytic files. Additional pieces of information may then be added to each of these folders if they suggest the same kind of idea or significance.

Early on in this process of building analytic files, you need not be terribly concerned about whether a given category is viable in the long run or will ultimately make any kind of sense. The aim, rather, is to set up as many separate items/files as you are prompted to and feel reasonably excited about. The task of finally reckoning with your analytic impulses comes later, during the period of concerted analysis.

The content categories (literally, the file folder headings) of your analytic files are categories such as those summarized in Chapter 6. Those categories are, however, only examples. You should feel free not only to adopt some of them but also to strike off into other directions. Even a simple idea that at the moment fits together with nothing else is likely to be worthy of its own folder in your analytic files.

The important point is that analytic files are an *emergent* coding scheme by which you are extracting from and ordering the chaotic flux of reality.

3. Fieldwork Files. In addition to mundane and analytic files, you should also have a folder in which material on the process of doing the research itself is accumulated. It is a relatively standard practice to include in the report an account of how you conducted the research. By having a file on this topic already built up, you will find it easier to write such an account later.

C. Periodicity in Filing/Coding

The requirements of interviewing and observation, as well as other facets of your life, will presumably govern the frequency with which you engage in filing or coding. You might prefer to do it every day, once a week, or even once a month, depending on the rate of your interviewing and observation and the accumulation of material that needs to be managed. You might also vary the frequency with which you do different types of filing. Simply to keep track of a large amount of material, you might want to do mundane filing more frequently. You can spare yourself the necessity of daily analytic filing by placing analytic ideas in the running notes. The ideas are thus preserved for later storage in a distinctive place or for signalling in a distinctively coded way.

D. Scissors, Circling, and Filing/Coding

At a very concrete level, all of this means that eventually you will be disassembling copies of your notes and splitting them up into various categories. If you have a limited number of copies, you can literally take scissors to your notes, cutting them into small bits of paper and placing them into file folders. If you have many copies of the notes, you can simply circle or otherwise mark relevant portions of pages before placing them into the files. If copies are especially scarce, you can enter cross-referencing notes in various files.

E. What to File/Code

There inevitably arises the dismaying question of how much material should be filed, especially analytically. Some pieces of information will seem to have no analytic interest or significance whatsoever. Or a given piece of information may be the fiftieth instance of a given category and may by this point seem terribly redundant.

We can offer no firm solution to this problem, save to counsel a middle course. If you find analytic significance in only a very small part of the materials and therefore file or code little, that fact itself ought to be made a central problem of the study. If you spend an enormous amount of time filing practically everything in sight, you might ask yourself whether you have transformed a means into an end, with consequent negative effects upon the *real* end, which is to write an excellent analysis.

Like anything done in excess, too soon, or compulsively, filing can be a vice. It is likely that you will want to do only mundane filing at the beginning of the study. You will want, however, to write down analytic ideas as they occur. But since there is a record of them, and since such ideas shift frequently, it may be of little use to enshrine each and every one in a file folder of its own. Instead, wait until you have obtained a minimum of stability in your analytic formulations. You will know you have achieved this stability when the same ideas keep occurring in connection with similar pieces of concrete data.

F. Maintaining a Chronological Record

Splitting the materials into mundane, analytic, and fieldwork files will facilitate staying "on top" of what is happening and evolving an analysis. But it also tends to obscure that nebulous quality called "context." In scrutinizing a particular piece of filed material, the question can arise: What else was happening at the time that seemed irrelevant then but now seems important? You want then to be able to look back at the more general context. In order to do so easily, you need an intact chronological record of the past. You should therefore keep a full set of your materials in the order in which you originally collected them.

A chronological set of materials is also useful for locating information that is not readily available in one of the other files. And it is useful simply for reading and reviewing from beginning to end, as a stimulus to thinking about larger patterns and larger units of analysis (as outlined in Chapter 6).

II. MEMOS AND GENERAL DESIGNS

During the observation or interviewing phase, you are trying to make some kind of abstract sense of the reality you are encountering. This "sense making" effort should be carried on in at least two forms.

One of these forms is the *small piece* of analysis or **memo**. Memos are statements on topics that will likely be written up finally as only a few pages of text (or at most a section or chapter, if a book-length report is projected). They come from all those file folders that comprise your analytic files, which themselves derive from the interaction of the raw material with your creative and social scientific sensitivities.

The development of your small pieces of analysis is likely to be quite uneven. You might well develop a few memos relatively early in the data collection process; many others will be quite rudimentary and will need to await the period of concerted analysis for their proper articulation. Still others will never be much more than ideas, with little amplifying and illustrative material, and may perhaps never be developed.

The other preliminary analytic form is the *overall structure* or **general design.** Regarding collectively all your memos (or even batches of small pieces), ask yourself, "Into what general design can these be assembled?" One physical answer to this question is simply to review the totality of your analytic files for existing patterns among the small pieces. Arrange and rearrange them for some kind of expository or sociological coherence.

It is quite likely that more than one possible general design for the projected analysis will become apparent to you. Write up and file away all of them.

III. STIMULATING SURRENDER AND DISCIPLINE

At the stage of generating tentative memos and a general design, the project is beginning to "come together." Here and later both *surrender* and *discipline* are involved. The surrender entails opening yourself up to your personal sensibilities, insights, and proclivities, as these interact with the data. The discipline entails channeling and evolving these personal interactions with the data in terms of relevant units of analysis (Chapter 6), appropriate questions (Chapter 7), and the constraints of what is interesting (Chapter 8).

The exact dynamics of analytic surrender and discipline are ill-understood, mainly because the people who do it are so involved in the actual process that they lose virtually all consciousness of *how* they do it.

But though the process itself cannot be clearly described (and thus routinely emulated), its mechanical *stimulants* are known. Some of these have been described in earlier chapters of this manual (for example, in Chapter 5 on field notes and interviewing) and in earlier sections of this chapter. There are, in addition, several "general precepts," as Moshe Rubinstein labels them, that can be drawn from the study of problem-solving behavior. Rubinstein lists a great many in his book *Patterns of Problem Solving* (1975); here, we will describe a few that seem most relevant to the present context.

▶ The sheer way a question (or answer) is *phrased* or worded can greatly facilitate or deter your thinking. When you are blocked, try using new words and new word orders. For example, instead of speaking of *causes*, you might use the related but different term *facilitants;* instead of the verb *functions*, perhaps *serves* might better capture the matter at hand. In this regard, a good dictionary of synonyms and antonyms is extremely useful. (One of the best is Rodale, 1978.)

▶ A more thorough way to change the way a problem is represented is to make a *model* of it, by means of (1) line drawings of the relations among elements, (2) mathematical notations or their equivalents, or (3) physical objects from which you can construct three-dimensional models.

▶ In Chapter 8, we described an important, standard device to aid in ordinary problem solving: the use of metaphors or, more broadly, *analogies:* What is it *like* and *unlike*?

▶ Constantly *comparing* items under analysis can stimulate ideas: How is this instance of X similar to or different from previous instances? How is X in this setting similar to or different from X in another setting? (Compare Glaser & Strauss, 1967:Chapter 5.)

▶ The process of doing social analysis ought not take place in a social vacuum. You ought to be in face-to-face contact with others of a similar turn of mind who have interests in your project. Aside from, and in addition to, the *morale boosting* function of being with friendly fellow analysts, such associates can, through talk, stimulate your thinking. Talking with others who are knowledgeable and supportive can help to clarify in your own mind what it is that you are trying to get at.

▶ Talk, rightly done, is a two-way process. If talking to others can help, so can *listening* to others. Other people may be able to point out critical features you had not previously noticed, even though such features were "right in front of you." Other people may suggest metaphors, ironies, or comparisons that had not occurred to you. You need, therefore, to be an active listener as well as a talker.

▶ As we have emphasized previously in this chapter and will stress in the next, keep *drawing back* in order to think about the total picture. Descend into detail, to be sure, but balance that descent with self-conscious efforts to perceive a general design or overall structure.

▶ Similarly, you should *withhold judgment* about the final shape of the analysis as long as it is possible, in a practical way, to do so.

Students with special interests in or problems with analyzing may find it informative to read one or more first-person accounts written by naturalistic fieldworkers who have, repeatedly and successfully, developed analyses. Among the more easily accessible, four appear in a single, special issue of the journal *Urban Life:* Fred Davis's "Stories and Sociology" (1974); Jacqueline Wiseman's "The Research Web" (1974); Sherri Cavan's "Seeing Social Structure in a Rural Setting" (1974); and Julius Roth's "Turning Adversity to Account" (1974). Others include C. Wright Mills's article "On Intellectual Craftsmanship" (1959) and the reports reviewed and compiled by Robert G. Burgess (1982:Section Nine).

Writing
Reports

For whatever reasons—lack of resources, deadlines, exhaustion, or saturation—observation or interviewing comes to an end. The accumulation of materials stops. You now have only the intact record; the mundane, analytic, and fieldwork files; and, perhaps, miscellaneous other artifacts. Where do you go from here? Happily, if you have performed the procedures outlined above with at least minimal diligence, you have many places to "go." Now you must decide exactly *where*.

I. WITHDRAWAL, CONTEMPLATION, AND ANALYSIS

Having withdrawn from the field, you should also consider withdrawing in another fashion. You have come to a point where you must make far-reaching decisions about how the materials will fit together, about what memos to include in the larger design of the written report, and about what form this general design will take. Thus, it is now strategically wise to enter a period of *quiet contemplation* of these matters and *provisional writing*. In so doing, you should proceed simultaneously in an inductive and a deductive fashion. That is, you must decide how the small pieces will fit together within the context of an overall structure, as well as what overall structure best fits the small pieces.

II. THE AGONY OF OMITTING

This shuffling of memos and designs may involve a great deal of agony. It may happen that an overall structure that successfully organizes a great deal of material also leaves out some of your most favored pieces of analysis. Alternative structures may result in yet other necessary omissions. Unless you decide to write a relatively disconnected report, you must face the hard truth that no general design is likely to encompass all of the material you have on hand. Decisions to omit some things must be made. This, however, does not mean that such topics are lost forever. They can be dealt with in separate papers or even separate books. You simply decide that for the purposes of *this* report, the inclusion of certain items is not feasible.

But there are loopholes here. Topics which are related but which depart from the overall structure you have chosen can be tenuously accommodated by means of one or another of at least four devices. First, you can tack on a related topic as an appendix. Second, you can insert it at some point (such as at the end of a section or chapter) as a digression and frankly label it as such. Third, you can treat it briefly in a footnote. Fourth, if it is very general, it can appear in a preface, epilogue, or afterword.

The underlying philosophical point, perhaps, is that everything is related to everything else in some fashion. To achieve coherence and organization is a difficult but necessary task. If we are to have any kind of understanding, some sort of order must be imposed on this flux of information. We must recognize that no order fits perfectly; all order is provisional and partial, but nonetheless imperative. With this philosophical view in mind, you must try to bring yourself to accept the fact that you cannot write about everything you have seen (or analyzed) and still write something with overall coherence and structure.

III. THE GENERAL DESIGN

Out of this quiet contemplation and painful process of omission, there should evolve a general design within which the small pieces of analysis seem to fit with some logical progression and unity.

The general design specifies an *interrelated* set of questions, topics, or areas. It makes it possible for someone reading your report for the first time to grasp the basic concepts you are dealing with, and to have a sense that the report is starting somewhere, proceeding through a logical sequence, and then arriving at a natural point of termination. Someone seeing only the general design need not comprehend exactly how you are going to deal with each of the interrelated topics, need not understand the argument or the scheme of detailed treatment within the overall structure. But that viewer should be able to discern the existence of a set of logically interrelated areas. Consider the large number of examples of general designs presented in summary form in Chapter 6. Although none are "understandable" in a detailed sense, the general logic of each is nonetheless clear.

A. Reordering the Analytic Files

Concretely, the general design takes the form of an outline, of the kind with which we are all very familiar. (See the many abbreviated examples of them given in Chapter 6.) Armed with it, you may now proceed to order your analytic files according to its terms, setting aside those that won't fit.

As the analysis proceeds and becomes your sole concern, your mundane and analytic files are likely to merge. You are likely to wind up with a single set of files that are analytically organized.

B. Creating a Serious Outline

Students, as a rule, are used to making up outlines to placate teachers. As a consequence, they have been inadvertently trained not to take outlines seriously and to think that they are easy to construct. The upshot is that many students (and other people) simply do not comprehend the necessity of putting hard work into generating a general design. (And, sadly, it shows up in the incredibly sloppy and incoherent work they produce.) *Don't fool yourself.* It is all too easy to create a skimpy general design that will slide by your teachers. But, in the end, you are the one who will be cheated: Your report simply won't cut the mustard (in particular, it is unlikely to pass the test of "being interesting"). The period of quiet contemplation and thinking through of analytic structures is likely to be the hardest, most demanding period of the entire endeavor. It may be accompanied by moodiness, irritability, despair, or even existential crisis. But take heart—it can also be punctuated by profound moments of sudden insight, by the rushing release and coalescence of ideas, and by intense excitement, such that you find yourself working almost around the clock for days on end, unable to stop. Such experiences are sometimes called "writing highs" and are not entirely unlike other kinds of "highs."

For the purpose of accommodating such intensity, you need to have a degree of release from the extensive daily duties that blunt and dull your involvement in the analysis of the materials. It should be said, too, that such emotions and experiences may accompany the entire period of writing. But more on that later.

IV. WRITING THE ANALYSIS

Having achieved some sense of where you will begin, the topics through which you will move, and where you will end, you can now turn to working up in detail, and in draft form, the text of the analysis.

An immediate consideration is the order in which to work on the component parts. Should you start by writing "Chapter One" and then proceed sequentially to the end? It happens that different people have different approaches to this. You must therefore discover your own personal style. If you have prepared your general design well, you can feel free to start writing almost anywhere you feel most "on top of," closest to, or excited about at the moment.

A. Steady Plodders and Grand Sweepers

Different people also have different approaches to, or styles of, writing in general. On the one hand, there are the "steady plodders," people who write a little each day, methodically and laboriously building up their analysis. Such writers grind out their reports slowly, writing and analyzing in detail as they go along. On the other hand, there are the "grand sweepers," persons who write very little actual text at first, but rather work out the entire report very carefully and in detail in the form of outlines and organized notes. Upon completion of this organization process, they then write the entire report in sequence from beginning to end in one fell swoop. Writing becomes the overriding and single governing principle of their lives for whatever period it takes to put their report into text.

We caution the reader that this latter style is not to be confused with the (not uncommon) student practice of "goofing off" all term and then writing 30-page papers by staying up all night the day before they are due. Incredibly hard labor is invested by grand sweepers before they begin to write. The analytic effort is no different from that of the steady plodder who is analyzing and writing at the same time. The grand sweeper merely segregates the tasks of analysis and writing.

As we have said, in the end you must discover your own style, which may well be neither of these. However, we hope that by describing these two patterns, we have helped you to think about just what your personal style might be.

B. Working Out Component Parts

The process of working out the component parts of a report (chapters, sections, paragraphs, and so forth) is logically equivalent to the process of working out a general design. Both involve categorizing and ordering progressively smaller (that is, shorter and more detailed) units of description and analysis. But whereas before you shuffled sets of file folders (or their equivalents) which constituted the entire set of analytic files, now you shuffle only a particular subset of that set of files (that is, just a few file folders). And at a more detailed level, you shuffle the actual pieces of paper that have accumulated in a given file folder.

All of this shuffling means that in the period of constructing a general design neither the steady plodder nor the grand sweeper knows exactly what form the analysis will take at the chapter, section, or paragraph level. You know only where a topic fits in the larger scheme and what materials seem relevant to that topic. The result is that you will probably undergo the same sort of creative effort, consternation, and excitement at each successive level—chapter, section, and paragraph—as you underwent while devising the general design.

Your plans for a particular chapter or section may change their form when you actually get down to the nitty-gritty of considering all the materials you have on that topic. A new formulation of your memos may become apparent and necessary. New patterns may emerge and old ones disappear or seem less cogent.

You engage in creative organization, then, over and over again as you tackle successively smaller pieces of your report. Because of this ongoing process of problem solving, writers may go through many different moods in connection with their work over the course of writing an analysis. For steady plodders and grand sweepers alike, some parts seem to "write themselves" while others admit to no sense at all. Some may put you on top of the world with their beauty; others seem so bad that they send you into deep depression. Such are the vicissitudes of intellectual work.

C. Paper Shuffling at Small Levels

It is at the more detailed levels of analysis—those involving the construction of a limited number of pages of text—that the preparation of field notes and the sorting into analytic files are finally justified. For it is these assembled and ordered bits of information and ideas that permit you at last to say something. For without those little pieces of paper, you wouldn't be able to do anything. It is in these notes that all your labors live; in their absence, qualitative analysis is dead.

When working with your notes, it may be wise to use a table or other large, empty surface upon which to lay out in piles all your small bits of information. This will make it easier to pore over them, arranging and rearranging, labeling and relabeling. When a new piece of information or a small idea seems relevant to the current set of piles you are working with, take it from its file and add it to the piles on the table. If a pile on the table no longer seems to belong to this arrayed set, put it aside.

Once you have worked out a plan for writing a few pages of text, you should withdraw again for a while to consider this section of your report. You might ask yourself questions such as: Is the idea here clear? Does it have a logical order? Is there an illustration I could use? Which illustration would best stress my point in this paragraph? Is there some small scheme that would fit these piles of materials better? Ought they to be reshuffled again? Should I simply put this set of piles away for now and look at them again tomorrow, or next week, when perhaps it will be more clear to me? Perhaps I should look at how well this projected organization is going to fit in with the next section. Will it dovetail? What is going to be the transition here? How does it fit with the previous section? Maybe I ought to work more on the section that will precede this section. Maybe the preceding section will make this section clearer. Maybe I ought to first work out and write the section coming after this one. On close inspection, does this section seem relevant at all? Would it fit better into another chapter? Maybe I ought to drop it altogether. Maybe I should just paperclip all these piles together and put them back into the file for now and work on _____ instead.

Such are some of the activities and thoughts of an analyst at work.

D. From Piles of Paper to Actually Writing Text

We have been stressing thought, planning, and organization, and it may therefore seem that transforming all this into text is a very straightforward, mechanical task. In many ways it can be. At least you are unlikely to become totally lost.

But something happens when you actually begin to write. It seems, in fact, that you do not truly begin to think until you attempt to lay out your ideas and information into successive sentences. All the elaborate planning you just did now serves mainly as a device that allows you to think in an orderly fashion as you write. For better or worse, when you actually start writing, you begin to get *new* ideas, to see new connections, to remember material you had forgotten. And (again for better or worse) you may begin to find that a section just does not make sense. It will not write. Even more disturbing, you may find that the entire general design could and should (or must) be redone, reconceived, or reordered.

The process of thinking while actually writing means that your outline is not likely to be identical to the completed text. This is as it should be. You are never truly inside a topic—or on top of it—until you face the hard task of explaining it to someone else. It is in the process of externalizing (writing) your outline descriptions, analyses, or arguments that they first become visible to you as things that exist "out there," that are available for scrutiny. And when this happens, you can literally see the weaknesses— points overlooked, possibilities unattended, assertions unsupported or unillustrated. (Thus, "writing blocks" are perhaps better thought of as "thinking blocks.")

There are, of course, degrees to which the writing process actually modifies your intentions and your outlines. Very thoroughly thought-out plans and outlines may need to be modified only slightly. Sloppy outlines (even if well-intended) are likely to look very little like the accomplished report.

An important point, then, is this: Be prepared for and open to novelty, excitement, exhilarating new lines of thought, and (perhaps) some dismay when you start writing, even when writing short, well-planned sections. Don't be frightened by any turn of events. In actually thinking while writing, you will only make the analysis better.

E. Organization as a Block to Writing

Sometimes you will know that something is important and must be written up but have no idea where it should go. This uncertainty may make you hesitant to sit down and work it out in writing. Overcome that hesitation. It is better to have the piece written up and not know what to do with it than to continue to carry it around in your head. While we have strongly emphasized the need to organize what you write, we must point out that you can also become a prisoner of organization. If in doubt, *write*. Once it is written, you may find in later days or weeks that your idea has perfectly logical context. The important point is that you now already have the idea written out and ready to place in its newly discovered context. So, don't worry *too* much about where something goes; *write it down*. It is much easier to rearrange the written material later than to stew endlessly over how something should fit in *prior* to actually writing it up.

V. FEATURES TO SEEK AND AVOID IN COMPLETED REPORTS

The concerns of the last chapter and this one have been the *processes* and *techniques* of developing analysis and writing. We will now shift from methods to desired end states or *features* you might aim for (and pitfalls to avoid) in completed reports. These features are of three types: (1) data and focus; (2) report design and presentation; and (3) data analysis.

A. Data and Focus

The first type of feature you should aim for is already well known to you if you have studied Chapters 2 through 8. In brief, your report should fulfill these requirements with regard to data and focus:

1. The data reflect *intimate familiarity* with the situation or setting (that is, you have performed all the data gathering and logging procedures described in Chapters 2–5).
2. The data address one or more *units* of social analysis (as described in Chapter 6).
3. One or more *questions* are posed about the units (Chapter 7).
4. The analysis strives to be *interesting* (as that term is used in Chapter 8).

We have also indicated some of the pitfalls associated with achieving these aims; two in particular, with regard to being interesting, bear repeating. One of these is the problem of being *too late*. For example, you can no longer "discover" the concept of a "total institution" because Erving Goffman did that some years ago (1961). The same is true of any other concept that has already been introduced, unless you have something new to say about it. You can avoid this pitfall by becoming familiar with the accumulated literature of social analysis regarding your subject matter.

A related pitfall is that of being *too elementary*. Thus, you would be wasting time by preparing a report based on, say, "socialization," "informal groups," or the fact that social factors influence behavior, as such ideas are the stuff of basic textbooks. You avoid this pitfall in the same way you avoid being too late: by reading.

B. Report Design and Presentation

The actual presentation of the general design you have devised for your report should move along the following lines:

1. The opening sentences of the report should pose a *general* question or topic involving (a) a specific, substantive *unit* of social analysis and (b) one or more of the seven formal *questions* outlined in Chapter 7. Here is one such opening:

   America is a service society—so much so that essentially non-service institutions, such as stores, take on service-like characteristics. . . . This emphasis on service has given rise to a preponderance of a particular kind of social activity, which I shall refer to as "cultivating," and to an associated kind of social relationship which I will refer to as a "cultivated relationship." (Bigus, 1978:85.)

2. After you have stated the general topic, introduce the specific data you studied. Continuing with the same report:

   One such relationship—that between milkmen and their customers—will be discussed in this paper. (Bigus, 1978:86.)

3. Give a review of previous works on the general and specific topics, and show how they relate to the current inquiry.
4. Proceed to the main part of the report, which should comprise the largest number of pages.

5. State your conclusions and their implications for future analyses.

6. In a footnote, an early section, or an appendix, describe the actual data collection and analysis processes. (Details on what goes into such a description are given below, in Section VI. of this chapter.)

There are also several pitfalls to avoid in designing your report. One that is not uncommon is *general design vacillation*. This occurs when the writer has developed several different general designs and, having failed to decide among them, switches from one to another in the report. Thus the structure may change from sentence to sentence, paragraph to paragraph, and/or section to section. The writer tries, as the saying goes, to throw in everything but the kitchen sink. The result is confusion, for the writer and reader alike.

A second pitfall is to allow your general design to be only a *moral evaluation*. For example, say you are observing a mental hospital ward and do not like the way you see the patients treated. After collecting instances of mistreatment, you begin your report by denouncing mental hospitals and move on to a catalog of grievances, perhaps organized in a highly inventive way. Conversely, you may very much like what you have observed and hence design your report as a catalog of its virtues and a denouncement of mistaken popular ideas about it. Or you may choose to write about a social unit with the intent of improving its practical functioning. Thus, your report might interlace the description of the unit with suggestions on how given aspects might be improved to make things run more smoothly or to make a better contribution to society.

C. Data Analysis

Finally, we will consider the features to aim for (and pitfalls to avoid) in presenting the analysis of data.

1. **A Balance of Description and Analysis.** Filing/coding, writing memos, and devising a general design are all responses to the concrete data you are collecting. As Barney Glaser put it, the inflow of data produces a psychological "sparking" of ideas (1978). These ideas, which are written, filed, and organized along with the data, form the basis of your *analysis*.

Even though the analysis evolves out of the data, each still depends on the other for meaning and understandability. In the final report, the analysis achieves prominence, but many of the data out of which the analysis has arisen are still retained.

Quantitatively, then, you should strive for some sort of *balance* in the written report between data and analysis. While there is no precise formula to tell you what percentage of each you should include in the report, one rule of thumb is that somewhat more than half the pages should be devoted to data: accounts of episodes, incidents, events, exchanges, remarks, happenings, conversations, actions, and so forth. Somewhat less than half should be analysis: abstract categorizing and discussion of the meaning, application, and implications of the data.

A report may appear "out of balance" in several ways. You may err on the side of *descriptive excess*, that is, have too much description relative to the analysis. The author who includes virtually unedited fieldnotes or interview transcriptions and fails to present a sufficient quantity of analysis has fallen into the pitfall known as the protocol error.

A related pitfall involves presenting data in a way that overemphasizes repetitive activities of a setting—what the people do over and over from hour to hour, day to day, week to week. Such a presentation may be well organized, of course, but alone it simply does not go *far enough* in analyzing the setting. (The activity of *logging* such data should not be disparaged, however. Such cyclical behavior may be important to understanding the setting more deeply. See Chapter 7, Section V.C., on "cycles.")

Taken together, then, these two pitfalls of descriptive excess involve becoming so engrossed in rendering the concrete details of a setting that the connection with analytic concepts and ideas that could help to order, explain, or summarize the details is lost. Such reports resemble simple histories or journalistic descriptions.

Falling out of balance in the other direction is known as the error of *analytic excess.* Here, the author becomes so engrossed in the logic of abstract analysis that he or she fails to report very much of the rich, concrete reality to which the analysis purportedly refers. From such excess the reader can learn a great deal about the author's mind, but very little, concretely, about what is going on in the setting. There is too little description of the many events that occurred, and the participants are almost never quoted.

2. **An Interpenetration of Data and Analysis.** Because the analysis has evolved out of the data, the analysis and the data should be *interpenetrated* in written reports. That is, analytic passages should not run on for very long without the use of descriptive materials, and vice versa. Such *alternation* of description and analysis makes the relation between the two more evident. It also helps to convey a sense of "wholeness."

The failure to achieve this interpenetration of data and analysis is a pitfall which we will call the *segregation error.* For example, a writer might devote the first and last sections of the report to an interesting and well-organized analysis of a social unit and question. The middle parts, on the other hand, are devoted to a low-level, commonsensical description that has little to do with the considerations raised in the analysis. That is, the analysis seems to be tacked onto the data rather than evolved from them. Because the two are not in intimate interplay throughout the report, the relation between them is obscure.

Such failure to interpenetrate or achieve integration stems, often, from a failure to develop the analysis out of or by means of the data. A fitting general design may be developed so late in the research process that the analyst is too tired and bored to follow it in actually analyzing the data. Segregation is thus a consequence of a late effort to appear analytic without actually having been so.

3. **An Appropriately Elaborated Analysis.** The efforts to "balance" and "interpenetrate" data and analysis tend, by their own logic, to result in a third feature, an appropriately *elaborated* analysis. "Appropriate elaboration" refers to the number of major divisions and subdivisions of the general design that form the main body of the report. The rule of thumb commonly encountered

is that analyses in article-length reports ought to have on the order of three to five major divisions and perhaps a similar number of subdivisions within each division.

Two pitfalls associated with this aspect of writing reports are *under-* and *overelaboration*. In the most serious form of underelaboration, there are not only too few analytic divisions in the general design, but they themselves are not clearly defined or otherwise explained. An overelaborated analysis comprises perhaps dozens of divisions and subdivisions, producing the impression that the analyst was more interested in the design than in what was being studied.

Judgments of under- and overelaboration are obviously debatable, and there are no precise criteria for categorizing written reports. One helpful generalization, though, is that the longer the report, the greater the degree of analytic elaboration that is both acceptable and expected.

4. Reasons for Balance, Interpenetration, and Elaboration. Why strive for reports with these features? Because they form a *discipline*, a set of guiding constraints to help you produce a report that is both *true* and *generally relevant*. Since we have already discussed questions of general relevance in Chapter 8, we will here simply say a brief word about truth.

The requirements of developing an analysis from the data and presenting the two in a balanced, interpenetrated, and elaborated way are constraints on an analyst's honesty. Both the data and the analysis should prove more accurate by virtue of each "watching" the other, in a manner of speaking. There are, of course, no foolproof roads to truth in data or analysis, but you should find that this has fewer potholes.

VI. TELLING HOW THE STUDY WAS DONE

It is traditional for qualitative and other types of researchers to devote a portion of their report to an account of the research process itself. In books, this account appears variously in an early chapter (usually the second one) or in an appendix, at the option of the writer. In an article, it may be in an early section or in a long footnote. These accounts vary further in the amount of detail provided. Some run only a few paragraphs, while others go on for many pages. (Some fieldworkers have written entire books on how the study was done; for example, see J. Johnson, 1975.)

While the character and content of this account is not standardized, there are certain basic items of information that you should generally include. We have grouped these into five categories. The following are some ordinary kinds of questions you should ask yourself with regard to each category.

A. Inception and Social Relations

How and why did you decide to undertake interviewing and/or observation of this particular social setting?

If a known observer, how did you secure cooperation from the participants? Was permission to perform the study facilitated by a prior acquaintanceship, your personal features, or your social status? Who, if anyone, sponsored your project, by providing money and/or legitimacy for your work?

If an unknown observer, what role did you occupy in the setting, and how did you come to occupy that role?

What, if any, problems did you encounter in getting along with various participants? If the setting contained marked divisions and conflicts, how did you align yourself relative to them?

How did you deal with any suspicion or distrust on the part of one or more participants?

What, if any, informants did you recruit, and how did you recruit them?

What social blunders did you commit, and how did you deal with them?

If a known observer, what kinds of services did you provide the participants in exchange for allowing your presence?

(In addressing these questions you may want to refer again to Chapters 3 and 4.)

B. Private Feelings

How did you privately feel about this setting and its participants at various periods during the research? Were you highly sympathetic or not? Did you experience a possible seduction or "going native" effect? Did you experience, in general, other of the emotional stresses discussed in Chapter 4?

To what extent did you find it difficult or easy, privately, to be in a setting while observing and analyzing it at the same time?

How did you, or didn't you, protect yourself from compromising emotional involvements?

C. Data Gathering

Approximately how much time, in hours, weeks, months, or years, did you spend actually interviewing or exposed to the setting? How much time did the entire study take?

How did you decide when to observe what, or when and whom to interview?

When and in what manner did you take notes on events or during interviews? To what degree did you trust your memory regarding observations and interviews? Did you employ tape recorders or other devices?

What techniques did you employ in writing up notes or interviews?

What kinds of settings and participants were particularly difficult to observe or interview? Which ones were easily accessible? What social barriers and facilitants to gaining information did you encounter?

D. Data Focusing and Analysis

At what point did you begin to do what sorts of filing and analysis?

What devices did you employ in beginning to do analysis? What was the character of your storage and retrieval system?

What lines of analysis or perspectives did you already have before you began to study the setting, if any? To what degree did these perspectives shift or stay the same during the course of the observation and analysis? How clear and specific an idea did you have, at the outset, of what you wanted to observe?

At what point in observation or analysis had you more or less clearly formulated or worked out the lines of analysis now found in your report? To what degree did observation and analysis overlap?

What important difficulties or facilitants did you experience in doing concerted analysis?

What was your personal, subjective experience of the analysis process?

E. Retrospect

Relative to all the above matters, what would you now, with the wisdom of hindsight, do differently were you to do the study over? What advice would you give to someone else studying this social setting, or any social setting?

One prominent fieldworker has commented that what typically goes into describing how the study was done are "the second worst things that happened." We are inclined to believe that this generalization is correct. What person with an eye on the future, who wishes others to think positively of her or him, is going to relate anything that is morally or professionally discrediting in any important way? This is especially the case since qualitative work tends to be performed by younger persons, who have longer futures to think about and less security about the shape of those futures. We delude ourselves if we expect naturalistic researchers actually to "tell all" in print. Nonetheless, a wide range of very useful and neutral things can and should be committed to public print, the better to advance the art. Perhaps someday someone will find it of interest to perform an assured-anonymity study of what, more intimately, can and does go on in fieldwork.

VII. LATER STAGES OF WRITING

Once you have gotten through these major stages of writing your report, there are some additional matters you should now consider (although they can also be attended to in earlier stages).

A. Text Shuffling: Scissors, Staples, Glue

As you look back at what you have written, you are likely to have second thoughts and new thoughts. Often you will want to do some slight rearranging: An illustration may seem to belong in another section, or an idea may fit better in some other chapter in connection with a different scheme. That is, the actual production of text may involve an additional period of shuffling.

There are a number of practical ways to facilitate this shuffling. In order to move sections or paragraphs around, you may have to cut up the text with a pair of scissors and rearrange the pieces on clean sheets of paper by means of staples, glue, or transparent adhesive tape. One way to reduce the amount of scissoring and mounting is to write no more than a single small unit of descriptive and analytic text on any given page. In this manner, the text itself becomes a flexible set of units.

B. Giving Thought to Your Labels

The construction of an analysis means, in a practical sense, that you need to invent or borrow a set of labels for ideas, processes, patterns, and so on. It generally happens that for any given category, a wide range of alternative names are available. Because of this, you should give careful consideration to the choices.

In general, you should avoid being too esoteric and try to invent few, if any, new words. It is perhaps best to use common, everyday vocabulary when possible or appropriate. A review of some of the labels that have actually been used by social analysts (see Chapter 6) should provide a sense of the inventive use that can be made of quite common language. For example, consider the genius of juxtaposing the quite ordinary words *normal* and *crime* to form a useful and self-explanatory label: "normal crime" (Sudnow, 1979; see also Chapter 6, Section I, on "meanings").

Like it or not, one of the truths of social analysis is that a striking (though not outlandish) set of labels gets more attention than a more mundane set, regardless of how incisive the analysis itself may be.

C. Distancing Yourself from Your Work

It is wise to lay your report aside for a while after having written it: for a few days, a week, months, or even a year or more. We all tend to develop a mental attitude toward a piece of work we are involved in—a particular "locked-in" view of what we are doing. It may well happen that your attitude is a very good and insightful one. Then again, it may not. By backing off from a piece of writing for a while, forgetting and losing your commitment to what you had in mind, you can later come back with a fresh view. You will be in a better frame of mind to decide whether or not the report was really so "hot." If at all possible, distance yourself from the report before you give it to other people. Even if you decide that only the prose needs revision, it will at least be better in that regard.

A similar point applies to bothersome sections—sections that you have trouble organizing or writing properly. While such a difficulty may mean that something is basically wrong with the section, it can also mean that you have not discovered the most cogent way to organize it. Rather than engage in prolonged stewing, turn to some other section for now. When you return to the bothersome part, the fresh start may resolve your previous difficulties.

VIII. GENERAL OBSERVATIONS

Finally, we would like to mention three quite general and interrelated matters regarding the naturalistic perspective as a whole.

A. Social Analysis as a System

You may have noticed the degree to which the ten aspects of the naturalistic perspective we have discussed form a coherent system, in which any selected subset of these parts seems to imply logically the others. Most broadly, the elements of the "gathering" phase seem to cohere, in a reasonably logical fashion, with the elements of the "focusing" and "analyzing" phases.

We must report, nonetheless, that not all social analysts appear to subscribe to this notion of a logically consistent relation among these ten parts. There are at least two major patterns or "schools" of disagreement. The first, the *descriptive ethnographers*, assert that one needs only the first phase, that of gathering. Focusing and analyzing are not required, and reporting is accomplished in an ordinary narrative manner (see for example Cottle, 1973; Schwartz & Jacobs, 1979). The second, the *grounded theorists*, take the opposite view: They regard the focus and the analysis as especially relevant, while the data can be gathered from almost anywhere in almost any fashion (see for example Glaser and Strauss, 1967; Glaser, 1978).

These and other patterns suggest, perhaps, that the ten aspects of the naturalistic approach we have presented may not, indeed, have any inherent logical interrelation. At least, it is plainly not sufficient to produce unanimity. But even if the interrelation is not inherent, there are important reasons for considering these elements as an integral package. Together they form a constraining discipline and a creative experience that begins with a deep and emotional relation to the setting and proceeds by steps to articulate that personal relation in ways that are understandable and useful to wider audiences. To omit or skimp on any part is to weaken the product: to weaken the depth of the *data*, the precision of the *focus* and/or the incisiveness of the *analysis*.

B. The Similarity of All Scholarship

We would also like to note that despite some distinctive features, qualitative research and analysis is, basically, the same as all other research and analysis. The particulars of the source materials may vary, as may the difficulties in gathering material and the content of the analysis itself, but the essential process is identical to other kinds of intellectual endeavor. The elements of this essential similarity include tenacity, commitment, thought, reflection, organization, and flexibility. Happily, all these qualities can be learned. Like all learning, they are acquired through practice and repetition.

C. Technique and Impotence

Rules, guides, procedures and other routines such as those that comprise this manual are all quite fine and necessary. But they can themselves become problems, blinders, fetishes or straitjackets. Therefore, draw upon and use what we say with a cautious, judicious, and selective attitude. Keep your creativity and intellectual playfulness alive. As Peter Berger so succinctly expressed the necessary stance: "In science as in love, concentration on technique is quite likely to lead to impotence" (1963:13).

PART FOUR

Guiding
Consequences

 In the last phase of a naturalistic inquiry, researchers seek to guide and cope with the consequences of the data collection and analytic activities in which they have engaged.

Guiding
Consequences

The impacts of a study are partly beyond the control of the author—but only partly. There are several ways you can guide or even construct consequences, should you so desire.

A researcher cannot wait until the study is completed to attempt to shape its consequences. Some types of consequences will be either closed off or unavoidable as a function of decisions made during the research process. That is, some likely consequences are preordained or predetermined by decisions made before the study is completed. For example, if you elect, during the research, to ignore all principles of "being interesting" (Chapter 8), it is unlikely that you will be able to stimulate a positive response to your report from professional social science audiences. Or, if you report highly discrediting aspects of a group and its members without using pseudonyms and other protective devices (Chapter 3), you are likely to cause that group to be angry.

The general point is that consequences need to be thought out and guided *during* the research process rather than only *after* the report is written. You should try to envision the likely and unlikely effects of your report from the very start. If you have done so, you should be more effective in guiding the report's consequences.

In this chapter, we will examine several areas in which you may both *envision* and *guide* consequences.

I. PERSONAL CONSEQUENCES

One critical area centers on you, the investigator/author. As both a goal and a factual consequence of research, you should emerge from the study with developed and sharpened powers to analyze and synthesize—intellectual skills that are applicable to far more than just social analysis. But it is through actually doing analysis and synthesis that your capacities to discern, organize, and communicate clearly are enlarged.

Successfully completing a project in which such skills are strengthened will likely have a positive impact on your sense of self-esteem, self-regard, and self-confidence. And, more broadly, there is the possibility of having a personal "transcending vision" of the "objectivated" nature of social arrangements (see Chapter 8). Such visionary experience is hard to achieve and precarious to sustain, but it is exhilarating. It provides a taste of a certain kind of freedom and the sense of power that accompanies that taste.

Unfortunately, the personal consequences of a completed research project are not inevitably positive. An author may also experience what might be called an "ethical hangover"—a persistent sense of guilt or unease over what is viewed as a betrayal of the people under study. The closer your emotional relationship to those persons, the more you can feel that in transforming personal knowledge into public knowledge, you have committed a kind of treason (F. Davis, 1970; Heilman, 1980; Thorne, 1979). It is not clear whether there is any way to forestall this experience. In fact, some would argue that it is the "just deserts" of the naturalistic investigator. As one veteran fieldworker has eloquently stated the case:

Even [in field situations] in which the [researcher] openly represents himself to his subjects for what he is (i.e., a person whose interest in them is professional rather than personal), he unavoidably, and properly I would hold, invites unto himself the classic dilemma of compromising involvement in the lives of others. Filling him with gossip, advice, invitations to dinner and solicitations of opinion, they devilishly make it evident that whereas he may regard himself as the *tabula rasa* incarnate upon whom the mysteries of the group are to be writ, they can only see him as someone less detached and less sublime. There then follows for many a fieldworker the unsettling recognition that, within very broad limits, it is precisely when his subjects palpably relate to him in his "out-of-research role" self . . . that the *raison d'être* for his "in-role" self is most nearly realized; they are more themselves, they tell and "give away" more, they supply connections and insights which he would otherwise have never grasped. . . .

It is in large measure due to this ineluctable transmutation of role posture in field situations that, when he later reports, the [researcher] often experiences a certain guilt, a sense of having betrayed, a stench of disreputability about himself. . . . I would hold that it is just and fitting that he be made to squirm so, because in having exploited his non-scientific self . . . for ends other than those immediately apprehended by his subjects, he has in some significant sense violated the collective conscience of the community, if not that of the profession. (F. Davis, 1970:273.)

II. REACTIONS FROM IMMEDIATE ASSOCIATES

When a successfully completed project is made known to others in your more or less immediate world, you are identified as someone who can undertake an intellectual project and work it through to an orderly conclusion. This is no mean achievement. You have thus contributed to the seriousness with which other people take you.

The completed study can, moreover, become a positive and unique "identity tag," a way in which other people answer the question, "Who is that?" You become the person who did the study of _____, or developed the idea of _____, or argues that _____. This is, of course, one of the most basic and common ways in which to "be somebody."

But this "somebody" is not just any kind of somebody. The identity provided by the study is one that offers evidence that you are thoughtful, that you have ideas and are prepared to reason about them, think them through, and write them up. In other words, as an author, you begin seriously to be placed by others in the realm of literate and thinking people.

Written reports may generate more than approbation, however. Especially relative to ethical questions, the publication of a report may subject the author to verbal or published rebukes by colleagues (F. Davis, 1970; Humphreys, 1975; J. Lofland, 1970; Vidich & Bensman, 1968) and other associates, or by the people studied (see below). There is probably no way to avoid this contingency absolutely, but you can reduce its probability, or at least prepare yourself to deal with it when it does occur, by giving serious consideration during the course of your research to all the ethical questions and dilemmas discussed in Chapters 2–5.

III. REACTIONS FROM THE PEOPLE STUDIED

You generally cannot avoid making important ethical decisions about how and what to report back to the people studied. In making these decisions, you must bear in mind that it is very difficult to envision in advance the consequences of your report for them. You may, for example, anticipate that they will welcome the report, since it is laudatory, and then be crushed to find that they do not find it so (for example, see Heilman, 1980). Or you may believe that many of the participants will welcome your suggestions for change, only to find that your efforts are resented as "the meddling of outsiders."

There are many similar possibilities for nasty surprises. The point is that you should think very carefully about *all* the conceivable ramifications of circulating the report among the people you studied and about the *manner* and *form* in which you should do so. Specific situations and relations vary, as do ethical preferences and moral aims. Thus it is impossible for us to propound directives. Instead, we can only urge a pondering of questions of these kinds:

1. Should I even attempt to show the analysis to the people studied?
2. If so, exactly who among them should I show it to? Everyone? Leaders only? Followers only? Informants only?
3. When should this be done? Before or after publication? At a busy or at a slow time in the setting? Before or after an event that is important in the setting?

In mulling over these and other questions, bear these generalizations in mind—generalizations for which we have no statistical evidence but which seem to us characteristic of most situations:

▶ Most people do not seem to care very much about scholarly analyses that are written about them. Many don't get around to reading them even when they are provided. There are harsh reactions and conflicts only in a minority of cases.

▶ Reports dealing with stable communities or ongoing groups are much more likely to generate a response from the participants than studies of more amorphous social situations or fluid groupings.

▶ The use of pseudonyms and a scholarly mode of writing tend to minimize the participants' interest in a report.

▶ The most interested and reactive participants appear to be members of elite groups in relatively small communities (for example, see Vidich & Bensman, 1968).

In others words, scholars often have to go out of their way just to get a reaction out of the people they have studied.

IV. CONSEQUENCES FOR FOES OF THE PEOPLE STUDIED

All groups have their antagonists, or, at the very least, circles of people less than enamored of them. This is especially the case where illegal, quasi-legal, politically "deviant," or commercially valuable activities and information are involved. Therefore, an ethical author needs to think about how people other than those studied might be able to employ the report to harm the people in the study—or others like them (Thorne, 1979; Glazer, 1972; Rainwater & Pittman, 1967). You might, of course, actually *want* the participants to be harmed by the report (liberal authors, for example, may have few qualms about harming members of neo-Nazi groups). You should remember, however, that some professional codes of ethics specifically forbid "doing harm" (for example, anthropology's), and you should certainly take the views of your colleagues as well as any relevant regulations into account.

V. IMPACT ON SOCIAL KNOWLEDGE

If a report is not published, it is unlikely to have any impact on the evolving corpus of social knowledge. If it is published, the consequences can be difficult to forecast. Some reports "catch on" right away and shape thinking about topics for many years. Others drift about in the literature for a considerable period of time, then "take hold" suddenly. And, sad to report, many (probably most) published reports have very little or no impact on the corpus of social knowledge.

As explained in Chapter 8, those reports that do have a serious impact on social analysis tend to employ one or more devices to make them interesting, most conventionally the generic device (Chapter 8, Section III.B.). By pointing toward a generic area, an analysis either fits into an established set of studies or points toward the creation of such a set. A set of studies dealing with a single topic lays the groundwork for a *general statement* on that subject. General statements may be of article or book length. Their central feature is that they collate and codify the findings from many different specific inquiries dealing with a particular subject. By comparing and contrasting a number of analyses, broader implications can be drawn out and ways to forward deeper understanding can be suggested.

If you want your report to become part of such a general statement you should envision and aim for that consequence at the outset of the study. You might even consider constructing your own general statement. As a contractor, so to speak, you would obviously select the materials to use in the project. And, having completed a specific inquiry on the generic topic, you will be in a particularly informed position to perform broader review and synthesis. Illustrations of this process of an author moving from specific inquiries to general statements include:

Robert Emerson's work on delinquent youth (1969, for example) became a component of his general formulation on the nature and functions of "last resorts" (1981b).

Robert Stebbins's studies of amateur musicians (1978, for example) became part of his general treatment of *Amateurs: On the Margin Between Work and Leisure* (1979).

John Lofland's study of conversion to a specific religious cult (1966; 1977) was incorporated into a general treatment of conversion (J. Lofland & Skonovd, 1981) and a theory of deviant identity (J. Lofland, 1969:Parts II and III).

Lyn Lofland's observations of behavior in public places (1972) became a component of a comparative historical treatment of relations among strangers (1973).

Our conception of general treatments is confined to efforts characterized by a certain degree of innovativeness. The most obvious and commonplace type of general treatment, however, is the *textbook*, a vehicle through which an even more basic (if undramatic) impact is presumably made.

VI. CONSEQUENCES FOR THE WIDER WORLD

Once in a while, a social analytic report has a decided impact on wider social and political arrangements. Often such works are general statements (other than textbooks) that were themselves built totally or largely on specific inquiries and would not have been possible without them. In such a way, specific inquiries may have an effect on the wider world. Examples of some general statements that have had such an impact include Edwin Lemert on human deviance (1951), Erving Goffman on total institutions (1961) and stigma (1963), and John Irwin on crime (1970).

A few specific inquiries have by themselves had direct effect on larger social and political arrangements. We refer in particular to studies of urban ghetto life, such as those by Herbert Gans (1962), Gerald Suttles (1968), and Elliot Liebow (1967).

The complexities of social trends and the play of social forces are such that, in the end, it is impossible to predict or even guide consequences with much certainty. In view of such indeterminancy, you must do what you think best. In other words, we have come full circle and back to where we began: The most certain thing you can do is to "start where you are" and, armed with ethical sensitivity and the discipline of the craft, have faith in what you are doing, irrespective of the presumed consequences.

References

Adler, Mortimer J.
    1940   *How to Read a Book: The Art of Getting a Liberal Education.* New York: Simon and Schuster.

Allon, Natalie
    1979   "The Interrelationship of Process and Content in Field Work." *Symbolic Interaction,* 2:63–78 (Fall).

Babbie, Earl R.
    1979   *The Practice of Social Research,* 2nd edition. Belmont, California: Wadsworth Publishing Company.

Barber, James David
    1972   *The Presidential Character.* Englewood Cliffs, New Jersey: Prentice-Hall, Inc.

Barnes, J. A.
    1979   *Who Should Know What? Social Science, Privacy and Ethics.* Cambridge: Cambridge University Press.

Becker, Howard S. & Blanche Geer
    1970   "Participant Observation and Interviewing: A Comparison." In William J. Filstead (ed.), *Qualitative Methodology: Firsthand Involvement with the Social World,* pp. 133–142. Chicago: Markham Publishing Company. (Originally pub. 1957.)

Becker, Howard S., Blanche Geer & Everett Hughes
    1968   *Making the Grade.* New York: John Wiley & Sons.

Becker, Howard S., Blanche Geer, Everett Hughes & Anselm Strauss
    1961   *Boys in White: Student Culture in Medical School.* Chicago: The University of Chicago Press.

Beckford, James
    1983   "Talking of Apostasy: Telling Tales and 'Telling' Tales." In M. Muklay and N. Gilbert (eds.), *Accounting for Action,* pp. 281–298. London: Greenwood Press.

Bell, Colin & Howard Newby
  1972   *Community Studies: An Introduction to the Sociology of the Local Community.* New York: Praeger Publishers.

Berger, Peter L.
  1963   *Invitation to Sociology.* Garden City, New York: Doubleday and Company.
  1971   "Sociology and Freedom." *The American Sociologist,* 6:1–5 (February).
  1979   "Sociology as a Form of Consciousness." In H. Robboy, S. Greenblatt, and C. Clark (eds.), *Social Interaction,* pp. 2–18. New York: St. Martin's Press.

Berger, Peter L. & Thomas Luckmann
  1967   *The Social Construction of Reality.* Garden City, New York: Doubleday and Company

Bernstein, Stan
  1978   "Getting It Done: Notes on Student Fritters." In John Lofland (ed.), *Interaction in Everyday Life,* pp. 17–23. Beverly Hills, California: Sage Publications.

Berreman, Gerald
  1962   *Behind Many Masks.* Society for Applied Anthropology Monograph Number 4.

Bertaux, Daniel (ed.)
  1981   *Biography and Society: The Life History Approach in the Social Sciences.* Beverly Hills, California: Sage Publications.

Beteille, Andre & T. N. Madan (eds.)
  1975   *Encounter and Experience: Personal Accounts of Fieldwork.* Honolulu: University of Hawaii Press.

Bigus, Odis E.
  1978   "The Milkman and His Customer: A Cultivated Relationship." In John Lofland (ed.), *Interaction in Everyday Life,* pp. 85–119. Beverly Hills, California: Sage Publications.

Blumer, Herbert
  1969   *Symbolic Interactionism.* Englewood Cliffs, New Jersey: Prentice-Hall, Inc.

Bogdan, Robert
  1980   "Interviewing People Labeled Retarded." In William B. Shaffir, Robert A. Stebbins, and Allan Turowetz (eds.), *Fieldwork Experience: Qualitative Approaches to Social Research,* pp. 235–243. New York: St. Martin's Press.

Bogdan, Robert & Steven J. Taylor
  1975   *Introduction to Qualitative Research Methods: A Phenomenological Approach to the Social Sciences.* New York: John Wiley & Sons.

Bok, Sissela
  1978   *Lying: Moral Choice in Public and Private Life.* New York: Pantheon Books.

Bosk, Charles L.
  1979   *Forgive and Remember: Managing Medical Failure.* Chicago: The University of Chicago Press.

Brewer, John & Albert Hunter

1983   *Introducing Multimethod Research.* Belmont, California: Wadsworth Publishing Company.

Bromley, David G. & Anson D. Shupe, Jr.

1979   *Moonies in America: Cult, Church and Crusade.* Beverly Hills, California: Sage Publications.

1980   "Evolving Foci in Participant Observation: Research as an Emergent Process." In William B. Shaffir, Robert A. Stebbins, and Allan Turowetz (eds.), *Fieldwork Experience: Qualitative Approaches to Social Research,* pp. 191–203. New York: St. Martin's Press.

Brown, Richard

1977   *A Poetic for Sociology: Toward a Logic of Discovery for the Human Sciences.* New York: Cambridge University Press.

Bruyn, Severyn T.

1983   *The Human Perspective in Sociology: The Methodology of Participant Observation.* New York: Irvington. (Originally pub. 1966.)

Burgess, Robert G. (ed.)

1982   *Field Research: A Sourcebook and Field Manual.* London: George Allen & Unwin.

Bush, Diane & R. Simmons

1981   "Socialization Processes over the Life Course." In Morris Rosenberg and Ralph Turner (eds.), *Social Psychology,* pp. 133–164. New York: Basic Books.

Caplow, Theodore & Howard M. Bahr, Bruce A. Chadwick & Margaret Holmes Williamson

1982   *Middletown Families: Fifty Years of Change and Continuity.* Minneapolis: University of Minnesota Press.

Cassell, Joan & Murray L. Wax (eds.)

1980   *Ethical Problems of Fieldwork.* A special issue of *Social Problems,* 27 (February).

Cavan, Sherri

1966   *Liquor License.* Chicago: Aldine Publishing Company.

1974   "Seeing Social Structure in a Rural Setting." *Urban Life,* 3:329–361 (October).

Charmaz, Kathy C.

1980   "The Social Construction of Self Pity in the Chronically Ill." In Norman K. Denzin (ed.), *Studies in Symbolic Interaction,* Volume 3, pp. 123–145. Greenwich, Connecticut: JAI Press, Inc.

1981   "Workshop in Methods in Symbolic Interactionism: Intensive Interviewing." Annual Meetings of the Society for the Study of Symbolic Interaction.

1982   "Intensive Interviewing." Paper presented at the Annual Meetings of the Pacific Sociological Association.

Christie, Agatha

1934   *Murder in Three Acts.* New York: Popular Library. Originally published in the U.S. by Dodd, Mead & Co., Inc.

Coelho, George, D. Hamburg & E. Murphy

1963   "Coping Strategies in a New Learning Environment." *Archives of General Psychiatry,* 9:420–429 (November).

Cohen, Stan
1980 "Ethnography Without Tears: Commentary on 'Sociology Chic.'"
Urban Life, 9:125–128 (April).

Colvard, Richard
1967 "Interaction and Identification in Reporting Field Research: A
Critical Reconsideration of Protective Procedures." In Gideon
Sjoberg (ed.), *Ethics, Politics and Social Research*, pp. 319–358.
Cambridge, Massachusetts: Schenkman Publishing Company, Inc.

Cooley, Charles Horton
1926 "The Roots of Social Knowledge." *American Journal of Sociology*,
32:59–79 (July).

Coombs, R. H. & L. J. Goldman
1973 "Maintenance and Discontinuity of Coping Mechanisms in an
Intensive-Care Unit." *Social Problems*, 20:342–355 (Winter).

Coser, Lewis
1965 *Georg Simmel.* Englewood Cliffs, New Jersey: Prentice-Hall, Inc.

Cottle, Thomas J.
1973 "The Life Study: On Mutual Recognition and Subjective Inquiry."
Urban Life, 2:344–360 (October).

Cressey, Donald R.
1971 *Other People's Money: A Study in the Social Psychology of Embezzlement.* Belmont, California: Wadsworth Publishing Company.
(Originally pub. 1953.)

Cuzzort, Ray & Edith King
1978 "Science or Rhetoric: Forms of Appeal in Sociological Literature."
Paper presented at the Annual Meetings of the American Sociological Association.

Dalton, Melville
1959 *Men Who Manage: Fusions of Feeling and Theory in Administration.* New York: John Wiley & Sons.

Danziger, Sandra K.
1979 "On Doctor Watching: Fieldwork in Medical Settings." *Urban Life*,
7:513–532 (January).

Davis, Fred
1959 "The Cabdriver and His Fare: Facets of a Fleeting Relationship."
American Journal of Sociology, 65:158–165 (September).
1961 "Deviance Disavowal: The Management of Strained Interaction
by the Visibly Handicapped." *Social Problems*, 9:120–132 (Fall).
1970 "Comment on 'Initial Interaction of Newcomers in Alcoholics
Anonymous.'" In William J. Filstead (ed.), *Qualitative Methodology: Firsthand Involvement with the Social World*, pp. 271–274.
Chicago: Markham Publishing Company. (Originally pub. 1961.)
1972 *Illness, Interaction and the Self.* Belmont, California: Wadsworth
Publishing Company.
1973 "The Martian and the Convert: Ontological Polarities in Social
Research." *Urban Life*, 2:333–343 (October).
1974 "Stories and Sociology." *Urban Life*, 3:310–316 (October).

Davis, Murray S.
> 1971 "That's Interesting! Toward a Phenomenology of Sociology and a Sociology of Phenomenology." *Philosophy of Social Science*, 1:309–344.
>
> 1973 *Intimate Relations.* New York: Free Press.

Davis, Murray S. & Catherine J. Schmidt
> 1977 "The Obnoxious and the Nice: Some Sociological Consequences of Two Psychological Types." *Sociometry*, 40:201–213 (Fall).

Denzin, Norman K.
> 1971 "The Logic of Naturalistic Inquiry." *Social Forces*, 50:166–182 (December).
>
> 1978 "Crime and the American Liquor Industry." In Norman K. Denzin (ed.), *Studies in Symbolic Interaction*, Volume 1, pp. 87–118. Greenwich, Connecticut: JAI Press.

Dexter, Lewis Anthony
> 1970 *Elite and Specialized Interviewing.* Evanston, Illinois: Northwestern University Press.

Diener, Edward & Rick Crandall
> 1978 *Ethics in Social and Behavioral Research.* Chicago: The University of Chicago Press.

Douglas, Jack D.
> 1976 *Investigative Social Research: Individual and Team Field Research.* Beverly Hills, California: Sage Publications.

Durkheim, Emile
> 1951 *Suicide.* Glencoe, Illinois: The Free Press. (Originally pub. 1897.)

Easterday, Lois, Diana Papademas, Laura Schorr & Catherine Valentine
> 1977 "The Making of a Female Researcher: Role Problems in Field Work." *Urban Life*, 6:333–348 (October).

Edgerton, R. B.
> 1967 *The Cloak of Competence: Stigma in the Lives of the Mentally Retarded.* Berkeley and Los Angeles: University of California Press.

Emerson, Robert M.
> 1969 *Judging Delinquents.* Chicago: Aldine Publishing Company.
>
> 1981a "Observational Field Work." *Annual Review of Sociology*, 7:351–378.
>
> 1981b "On Last Resorts." *American Journal of Sociology*, 87:1–22 (July).

Emerson, Robert M. (ed.)
> 1983 *Contemporary Field Research: A Collection of Readings.* Boston: Little, Brown & Company.

Erikson, Kai T.
> 1970 "A Comment on Disguised Observation in Sociology." In William J. Filstead (ed.), *Qualitative Methodology: Firsthand Involvement with the Social World*, pp. 252–260. Chicago: Markham Publishing Company.
>
> 1981 "Notes on the Sociology of Deviance." In E. Rubington and M. Weinberg (eds.), *Deviance: The Interactionist Perspective*, 4th edition, pp. 25–28. New York: The Macmillan Company.

Faulkner, Robert R. & Douglas B. McGaw
   1977   "Uneasy Homecoming: Stages in the Reentry Transition of Vietnam Veterans." *Urban Life*, 6:303–328 (October).

Feigelman, William
   1974   "Peeping: The Pattern of Voyeurism among Construction Workers." *Urban Life*, 3:35–49 (April).

Filstead, William J. (ed.)
   1970   *Qualitative Methodology: Firsthand Involvement with the Social World*. Chicago: Markham Publishing Company.

Fine, Gary Alan
   1976   "Humor in Situ: The Role of Humor in Small Group Culture." In A. J. Chapman and H. C. Foot (eds.), *It's a Funny Thing, Humor*, pp. 315–318. London: Pergamon Press.
   1979   "Small Groups and Culture Creation: The Idioculture of Little League Baseball Teams." *American Sociological Review*, 44:733–745 (October).
   1980   "Cracking Diamonds: Observer Role in Little League Baseball Settings and the Acquisition of Social Competence." In William B. Shaffir, Robert A. Stebbins, and Allan Turowetz (eds.), *Fieldwork Experience: Qualitative Approaches to Social Research*, pp. 117–132. New York: St. Martin's Press.

Fine, Gary Alan & Barry Glassner
   1979   "Participant Observation with Children: Promise and Problems." *Urban Life*, 8:153–174 (July).

Flacks, Richard
   1967   "The Liberated Generation: An Exploration of the Roots of Student Protest." *Journal of Social Issues*, 23:52–75 (July).

Freidson, Eliot
   1970   *The Profession of Medicine: A Study in the Sociology of Applied Knowledge*. New York: Harper and Row.

Freilich, Morris (ed.)
   1977   *Marginal Natives at Work: Anthropologists in the Field*. Cambridge, Massachusetts: Schenkman Publishing.

Gallagher, Patrick
   1967   "Games Malinowski Played." *The New Republic*, 17:24–26 (June).

Gans, Herbert J.
   1962   *The Urban Villagers: Group and Class in the Life of Italian-Americans*. New York: The Free Press.
   1967   *The Levittowners: Ways of Life and Politics in a New Suburban Community*. New York: Pantheon Books.
   1970   "The Ayn Rand Syndrome—A Conversation with Herbert Gans." *Psychology Today*, 3:58–62ff (March).
   1972   "The Positive Functions of Poverty." *American Journal of Sociology*, 78:275–289 (September).

Giallombardo, Rose
   1966   "Social Roles in a Prison for Women." *Social Problems*, 13:268–288 (Winter).

Gibbons, Don C. & Joseph F. Jones
 1975   *The Study of Deviance: Perspectives and Problems.* Englewood
        Cliffs, New Jersey: Prentice-Hall, Inc.

Glaser, Barney G.
 1978   *Theoretical Sensitivity.* Mill Valley, California: The Sociology Press.

Glaser, Barney G. & Anselm Strauss
 1967   *The Discovery of Grounded Theory: Strategies for Qualitative
        Research.* Chicago: Aldine Publishing Company.

Glazer, Myron
 1972   *The Research Adventure: Promise and Problems of Field Work.*
        New York: Random House.

Gmelch, George
 1971   "Baseball Magic." *Trans-action,* 9:39–41 (June).

Goffman, Erving
 1959   *The Presentation of Self in Everyday Life.* Garden City, New York:
        Doubleday and Company.
 1961   *Asylums: Essays on the Social Situation of Mental Patients and
        Other Inmates.* Garden City, New York: Doubleday and Company.
 1962   "On Cooling the Mark Out: Some Aspects of Adaptation to Fail-
        ure." In Arnold Rose (ed.), *Human Behavior and Social Processes,*
        pp. 482–505. Boston: Houghton Mifflin.
 1963   *Stigma: Notes on the Management of Spoiled Identity.* Englewood
        Cliffs, New Jersey: Prentice-Hall, Inc.
 1979   *Gender Advertisements.* Cambridge: Harvard University Press.

Golde, Peggy (ed.)
 1970   *Women in the Field: Anthropological Experiences.* Chicago: Aldine
        Publishing Company.

Gorden, Raymond L.
 1975   *Interviewing: Strategy, Techniques and Tactics,* revised edition.
        Homewood, Illinois: The Dorsey Press.

Gouldner, Alvin
 1958   "Cosmopolitans and Locals: Toward An Analysis of Latent Social
        Roles—II." *Administrative Science Quarterly,* 2:444–480 (March).
 1962   "Anti-Minotaur: The Myth of Value-Free Sociology." *Social Prob-
        lems,* 9:199–213 (Winter).
 1979   *The Future of Intellectuals and the Rise of the New Class.* New
        York: The Seabury Press.

Gray, Paul S.
 1980   "Exchange and Access in Field Work." *Urban Life,* 9:309–331
        (October).

Gusfield, Joseph
 1981   *The Culture of Public Problems: Drinking-Driving and the Sym-
        bolic Order.* Chicago: The University of Chicago Press.

Guzman, German
 1969   *Camilo Torres.* New York: Sheed and Ward.

Hannerz, Ulf
 1969   *Soulside: Inquiries into Ghetto Culture and Community.* New York:
        Columbia University Press.

Harrison, Michael
1974 "Preparation for Life in the Spirit: The Process of Initial Commitment to a Religious Movement." *Urban Life*, 2:390–401 (January).

Heilman, Samuel C.
1976 *Synagogue Life: A Study in Symbolic Interaction*. Chicago: The University of Chicago Press.
1980 "Jewish Sociologist: Native-As-Stranger." *American Sociologist*, 15:100–108 (May).

Heirich, Max
1971 *The Spiral of Conflict: Demonstrations at Berkeley 1964–1965*. New York: Columbia University Press.

Hesslink, George K.
1968 *Black Neighbors: Negroes in a Northern Rural Community*. Indianapolis: The Bobbs-Merrill Company.

Hilbert, Richard A.
1980 "Covert Participant Observation: On Its Nature and Practice." *Urban Life*, 9:51–78 (April).

Hochschild, Arlie R.
1978 *The Unexpected Community: Portrait of an Old Age Subculture*. Berkeley and Los Angeles: University of California Press. (Originally pub. 1973.)

Hoffman, Joan Eakin
1980 "Problems of Access in the Study of Social Elites and Boards of Directors." In William B. Shaffir, Robert A. Stebbins, and Allan Turowetz (eds.), *Fieldwork Experience: Qualitative Approaches to Social Research*, pp. 45–56. New York: St. Martin's Press.

Humphreys, Laud
1975 *Tearoom Trade: Impersonal Sex in Public Places*, enlarged edition. Chicago: Aldine Publishing Company.

Hunter, Albert
1974 *Symbolic Communities: The Persistence and Change of Chicago's Local Communities*. Chicago: The University of Chicago Press.
1975 "The Loss of Community: An Empirical Test through Replication." *American Sociological Review*, 40:537–552 (October).
1978 "Persistence of Local Sentiments in Mass Society." In David Street and Associates (eds.), *Handbook of Contemporary Urban Life*, pp. 133–162. San Francisco: Jossey-Bass.

Irwin, John
1970 *The Felon*. Englewood Cliffs, New Jersey: Prentice-Hall, Inc.
1980 *Prisons in Turmoil*. Boston: Little, Brown & Company.

Jacobs, Glenn, (ed.)
1970 *The Participant Observer: Encounters with Social Reality*. New York: George Braziller.

Jacobs, James B.
1974 "Participant Observation in Prison." *Urban Life*, 3:221–240 (July).

Jacobs, Jerry
1974 *Fun City: An Ethnographic Study of a Retirement Community*. New York: Holt, Rinehart and Winston.

1979 "Symbolic Bureaucracy: A Case Study of a Social Welfare Agency."
In Howard Schwartz and Jerry Jacobs, *Qualitative Sociology: A Method to the Madness*, pp. 143–155. New York: The Free Press.

Johnson, John M.
1975 *Doing Field Research.* New York: The Free Press.

Johnson, Sheila K.
1971 *Idle Haven: Community Building among the Working-Class Retired.*
Berkeley and Los Angeles: University of California Press.

Joseph, Suad
1978 "Women and the Neighborhood Street in Borj Hammoud, Lebanon." In Elizabeth Fernea and Basmia Berzirgan (eds.), *Women in the Muslim World*, pp. 541–557. Cambridge: Harvard University Press.

1983 "Working Class Women's Networks in a Sectarian State: A Political Paradox." *American Ethnologist*, 10:1–22 (January).

Junker, Buford H.
1960 *Field Work: An Introduction to the Social Sciences.* Chicago: The University of Chicago Press.

Kanter, Rosabeth Moss
1977 *Men and Women of the Corporation.* New York: Basic Books.

Kaplan, Howard, I. Boyd & S. Bloom
1968 "Patient Culture and the Evaluation of Self." In E. Rubington and M. Weinberg (eds.), *Deviance: The Interactionist Perspective*, pp. 355–367. New York: The Macmillan Company.

Karp, David A.
1973 "Hiding in Pornographic Bookstores: A Reconsideration of the Nature of Urban Anonymity." *Urban Life*, 1:427–452 (January).

1980 "Observing Behavior in Public Places: Problems and Strategies."
In William B. Shaffir, Robert A. Stebbins, and Allan Turowetz (eds.), *Fieldwork Experience: Qualitative Approaches to Social Research*, pp. 82–97. New York: St. Martin's Press.

Klapp, Orrin
1958 "Social Types." *American Sociological Review*, 23:673–681 (December).

1964 *Symbolic Leaders.* Chicago: Aldine Publishing Company.

1971 *Social Types: Process, Structure and Ethos.* San Diego: Aegis Publishing.

Kleinman, Sherryl
1980 "Learning the Ropes as Fieldwork Analysis." In William B. Shaffir, Robert A. Stebbins, and Allan Turowetz (eds.), *Fieldwork Experience: Qualitative Approaches to Social Research*, pp. 171–183. New York: St. Martin's Press.

1981 "Making Professionals into 'Persons': Discrepancies in Tradition and Humanistic Expectations of Professional Identity." *Sociology of Work and Occupations*, 8:61–87 (February).

Kleinman, Sherryl & Gary Alan Fine
1979 "Rhetorics and Action in Moral Organizations: Social Control of Little Leaguers and Ministry Students." *Urban Life*, 8:275–294 (October).

Klockars, Carl B. & Finbarr W. O'Connor (eds.)
1979   *Deviance and Decency: The Ethics of Research with Human Subjects.* Beverly Hills, California: Sage Publications.

Kochman, Thomas
1969   "Rapping in the Black Ghetto." *Trans-action*, 6:26–34 (February).

Komarovsky, Mirra
1957   "Introduction." In Mirra Komarovsky (ed.), *Common Frontiers of the Social Sciences*, pp. 1–30. Glencoe, Illinois: The Free Press.

Kornblum, William
1974   *Blue Collar Community.* Chicago: The University of Chicago Press.

Kotarba, Joseph A.
1977   "The Chronic Pain Experience." In Jack D. Douglas and John M. Johnson (eds.), *Existential Sociology*, pp. 257–272. New York: Cambridge University Press.
1980   "Discovering Amorphous Social Experience: The Case of Chronic Pain." In William B. Shaffir, Robert A. Stebbins, and Allan Turowetz (eds.), *Fieldwork Experience: Qualitative Approaches to Social Research*, pp. 57–67. New York: St. Martin's Press.

Kübler-Ross, Elisabeth
1969   *On Death and Dying.* New York: The Macmillan Company.

Lejeune, Robert
1977   "The Management of a Mugging." *Urban Life*, 6:123–148 (July).
1980   "A Note on 'The Management of a Mugging.'" *Urban Life*, 9:113–119 (April).
1981   "Commentary on a Symposium." *Urban Life*, 10:215–218 (July).

Lejeune, Robert & Nicholas Alex
1973   "On Being Mugged: the Event and Its Aftermath." *Urban Life*, 2:259–287 (October).

LeMasters, E. E.
1973   "Social Life in a Working Class Tavern." *Urban Life*, 1:27–52 (April).

Lemert, Edwin M.
1951   *Social Pathology.* New York: McGraw-Hill Book Company.
1972   *Human Deviance, Social Problems and Social Control.* Englewood Cliffs, New Jersey: Prentice-Hall, Inc.

Levin, Jack
1975   *The Functions of Prejudice.* New York: Harper & Row.

Levinson, Daniel J.
1978   *The Seasons of a Man's Life.* New York: Alfred A. Knopf.

Liebow, Elliot
1967   *Tally's Corner: A Study of Negro Streetcorner Men.* Boston: Little, Brown & Company.

Lofland, John
1966   *Doomsday Cult: A Study of Conversion, Proselytization and Maintenance of Faith.* Englewood Cliffs, New Jersey: Prentice-Hall, Inc.
1967   "Notes on Naturalism in Sociology." *Kansas Journal of Sociology*, 3:45–61 (Spring).
1969   *Deviance and Identity.* (With the assistance of Lyn H. Lofland.) Englewood Cliffs, New Jersey: Prentice-Hall, Inc.

1970 "Reply to Davis' Comment on 'Initial Interaction.'" In William J. Filstead (ed.), *Qualitative Methodology: Firsthand Involvement with the Social World*, pp. 278–282. Chicago: Markham Publishing Company. (Originally pub. 1961.)

1971 *Analyzing Social Settings.* Belmont, California: Wadsworth Publishing Company.

1976 *Doing Social Life: The Qualitative Study of Human Interaction in Natural Settings.* New York: John Wiley & Sons.

1977 *Doomsday Cult: A Study of Conversion, Proselytization and Maintenance of Faith*, enlarged edition. New York: Irvington-Wiley.

1980 "Early Goffman." In Jason Ditton (ed.), *The View from Goffman*, pp. 25–51. New York: St. Martin's Press.

1982 "Crowd Joys." *Urban Life*, 10:355–382 (January).

Lofland, John & Norman Skonovd

1981 "Conversion Motifs." *Journal for the Scientific Study of Religion*, 20:373–385 (December).

Lofland, John & Rodney Stark

1965 "Becoming a World-Saver: A Theory of Conversion to a Deviant Perspective." *American Sociological Review*, 30:862–875 (December).

Lofland, Lyn H.

1972 "Self Management in Public Settings: Parts I & II." *Urban Life*, 1:93–108 & 217–231 (April & July).

1973 *A World of Strangers: Order and Action in Urban Public Space.* New York: Basic Books.

1975 "The 'Thereness' of Women: A Selective Review of Urban Sociology." In Marcia Millman and Rosabeth Moss Kanter (eds.), *Another Voice: Feminist Perspectives on Social Life and Social Science*, pp. 144–170. Garden City, New York: Doubleday and Company.

1980 "Reminiscences of Classic Chicago: The Blumer-Hughes Talk." *Urban Life*, 9:251–281 (October).

1982 "Loss and Human Connection: An Exploration into the Nature of the Social Bond." In William Ickes and Eric Knowles (eds.), *Personality, Roles and Social Behavior*, pp. 219–242. New York: Springer-Verlag.

Lopata, Helena Znaniecki

1971 *Occupation: Housewife.* New York: Oxford University Press.

1973 *Widowhood in an American City.* Cambridge: Schenkman Publishing Company.

1979 *Women as Widows: Support Systems.* New York: Elsevier.

1980 "Interviewing American Women." In William B. Shaffir, Robert A. Stebbins, and Allan Turowetz (eds.), *Fieldwork Experience: Qualitative Approaches to Social Research*, pp. 68–81. New York: St. Martin's Press.

Lopreato, Joseph & Letitia Alston

1970 "Ideal Types and the Idealization Strategy." *American Sociological Review*, 35:88–96 (February).

Lowry, Ritchie P.

1965 *Who's Running This Town? Community Leadership and Social Change.* New York: Harper & Row.

Lyford, Joseph P.
    1964   *The Talk in Vandalia: The Life of an American Town.* Charlotte and
            Santa Barbara: McNally and Loftin.

Lynd, Robert S. & Helen Merrell Lynd
    1929   *Middletown: A Study in Contemporary American Culture.* New
            York: Harcourt, Brace and Company.

McCall, George & J. L. Simmons
    1969   *Issues in Participant Observation: A Text and Reader.* Reading,
            Massachusetts: Addison-Wesley.

McClenahen, Lachlan & John Lofland
    1978   "Bearing Bad News: Tactics of the Deputy U.S. Marshall." In John
            Lofland (ed.), *Interaction in Everyday Life,* pp. 135–156. Beverly
            Hills, California: Sage Publications.

McCoy, F. N.
    1974   *Researching and Writing in History: A Practical Handbook for Stu-
            dents.* Berkeley and Los Angeles: University of California Press.

Malinowski, Bronislaw
    1967   *A Diary in the Strict Sense of the Term.* New York: Harcourt, Brace
            and World.

Mann, Floyd C.
    1970   "Human Relations Skills in Social Research." In William J. Filstead
            (ed.), *Qualitative Methodology: Firsthand Involvement with the Social
            World,* pp. 119–132. Chicago: Markham Publishing Company.

Marshall, Victor W.
    1975   "Socialization for Impending Death in a Retirement Village."
            American Journal of Sociology, 80:1,124–1,144 (March).
    1976   "Organizational Features of Terminal Status Passage in Residen-
            tial Facilities for the Aged." In Lyn H. Lofland (ed.), *Toward A
            Sociology of Death and Dying,* pp. 115–134. Beverly Hills, Califor-
            nia: Sage Publications.

Matthews, Sarah
    1976   "Old Women and Identity Maintenance: Outwitting the Grim
            Reaper." In Lyn H. Lofland (ed.), *Toward a Sociology of Death and
            Dying,* pp. 105–114. Beverly Hills, California: Sage Publications.
    1979   *The Social World of Old Women: Management of Self-Identity.*
            Beverly Hills, California: Sage Publications.

Matza, David
    1969   *Becoming Deviant.* Englewood Cliffs, New Jersey: Prentice-Hall,
            Inc.

Melbin, Murray
    1978   "Night as Frontier." *American Sociological Review,* 43:3–22
            (February).

Mennerick, Lewis
    1974   "Client Typologies: A Method of Coping with Conflict in the Ser-
            vice Worker-Client Relationship." *Sociology of Work and Occu-
            pations,* 1:396–417 (November).

Merton, Robert K.
    1968   *Social Theory and Social Structure,* enlarged edition. New York:
            The Free Press.

Merton, Robert K., G. Reader & P. Kendall
  1957   *The Student-Physician: Introductory Studies in the Sociology of Medical Education.* Cambridge: Harvard University Press.

Mileski, Maureen & Donald J. Black
  1972   "The Social Organization of Homosexuality." *Urban Life,* 1:187–202 (July).

Mills, C. Wright
  1959   *The Sociological Imagination.* New York: Oxford University Press.

Miner, Horace
  1939   *St. Denis: A French-Canadian Parish.* Chicago: University of Chicago Press.

Moore, William Jr.
  1969   *The Vertical Ghetto: Everyday Life in an Urban Project.* New York: Random House.

Myers, James E.
  1969   "Unleashing the Untrained: Some Observations on Student Ethnographers." *Human Organization,* 28:155–159 (Summer).

Nader, Laura
  1977   "Studying Up." *Psychology Today,* 10:132 (September).

Naroll, Raoul & R. Cohen
  1973   *A Handbook of Method in Cultural Anthropology.* New York: Columbia University Press.

Paul, B. D.
  1953   "Interview Techniques and Field Relations." In A. L. Kroeber, (ed.), *Anthropology Today,* pp. 430–451. Chicago: The University of Chicago Press.

Pepinsky, Harold
  1980   "A Sociologist on Police Patrol." In William B. Shaffir, Robert A. Stebbins, and Allan Turowetz (eds.), *Fieldwork Experience: Qualitative Approaches to Social Research,* pp. 223–234. New York: St. Martin's Press.

Posner, Judith
  1980   "On Sociology Chic: Notes on a Possible Direction for Symbolic Interactionism." *Urban Life,* 9:103–112 (April).

Powdermaker, Hortense
  1966   *Stranger and Friend: The Way of an Anthropologist.* New York: W. W. Norton & Co.

Prus, Robert
  1980   "Sociologist as Hustler: The Dynamics of Acquiring Information." In William B. Shaffir, Robert A. Stebbins, and Allan Turowetz (eds.), *Fieldwork Experience: Qualitative Approaches to Social Research,* pp. 132–144. New York: St. Martin's Press.

Quarantelli, E. L. & Russell Dynes
  1968   "Looting in Civil Disorder." *American Behavioral Scientist,* 2:7–10 (July).

Radcliffe-Brown, A. R.
  1935   "On the Concept of Function in Social Science." *American Anthropologist,* 37:394–402 (July-September).

Rainwater, Lee & D. J. Pittman
1967   "Ethical Problems in Studying a Politically Sensitive and Deviant Community." *Social Problems*, 14:357–366 (Spring).

Reed, Myer S., Jerry Burnette & R. Troiden
1977   "Wayward Cops: The Functions of Deviance in Groups Reconsidered." *Social Problems*, 24:565–575 (June).

Reiss, Albert J.
1968   "The Social Integration of Queers and Peers." In E. Rubington and M. Weinberg (eds.), *Deviance: The Interactionist Perspective*, pp. 371–381. New York: The Macmillan Company. (Originally pub. 1961.)

Reynolds, Paul
1979   *Ethical Dilemmas and Social Science Research: An Analysis of Moral Issues Confronting Investigators in Research Using Human Participants*. San Francisco: Jossey-Bass.

Riecken, Henry W.
1969   "The Unidentified Interviewer." In George J. McCall and J. L. Simmons (eds.), *Issues in Participant Observation: A Text and Reader*, pp. 39–44. Reading, Massachusetts: Addison-Wesley Publishing Company.

Riemer, Jeffrey W.
1977   "Varieties of Opportunistic Research." *Urban Life*, 5:467–477 (January).

Rodale, Jerome Irving
1978   *The Synonym Finder*. Emmaus, Pennsylvania: Rodale Press.

Roth, Julius
1963   *Timetables: Structuring the Passage of Time in Hospital Treatment and Other Careers*. Indianapolis: Bobbs-Merrill Co.
1966   "Hired Hand Research." *The American Sociologist*, 1:190–196 (August).
1970   "Comments on 'Secret Observation.'" In William J. Filstead (ed.), *Qualitative Methodology: Firsthand Involvement with the Social World*, pp. 278–280. Chicago: Markham Publishing Company.
1974   "Turning Adversity to Account." *Urban Life*, 3:347–361 (October).
1977   "Review of D. Caplowitz: The Poor Pay More." *Contemporary Sociology*, 6:115 (January).

Rothchild-Whitt, Joyce
1979   "The Collectivist Organization: An Alternative to Rational-Bureaucratic Models." *American Sociological Review*, 44:509–527 (August).

Roy, Donald F.
1976   "'Banana Time': Job Satisfaction and Informal Interaction." In John Lofland, *Doing Social Life*, pp. 274–300. New York: John Wiley & Sons. (Originally pub. 1959–1960.)

Rubin, Lillian B.
1981   "Sociological Research: The Subjective Dimension." *Symbolic Interaction*, 4:97–112 (Spring).

Rubinstein, Moshe F.
1975   *Patterns of Problem Solving*. Englewood Cliffs, New Jersey: Prentice-Hall, Inc.

Sagarin, Edward

1973   "The Research Setting and the Right Not to Be Researched." *Social Problems*, 21:52–65 (Summer).

1980   "Commentary on 'Sociology Chic.'" *Urban Life*, 9:120–124 (April).

Schatzman, Leonard & Anselm Strauss

1973   *Field Research: Strategies for a Natural Sociology.* Englewood Cliffs, New Jersey: Prentice-Hall, Inc.

Schmidt, Catherine

1979   "The Guided Tour: Insulated Adventure." *Urban Life*, 7:441–467 (January).

Schneider, Louis

1975   "Ironic Perspectives and Sociological Thought." In Lewis Coser (ed.), *The Idea of Social Structure*, pp. 323–337. New York: Harcourt, Brace and Jovanovich.

Schutz, Alfred

1967   *The Phenomenology of the Social World.* Evanston, Illinois: Northwestern University Press. (Originally pub. 1932.)

Schwartz, Howard & Jerry Jacobs

1979   *Qualitative Sociology: A Method to the Madness.* New York: The Free Press.

Scott, Marvin B.

1968   *The Racing Game.* Chicago: Aldine Publishing Company.

Seidel, John V. & Jack A. Clark

1982a   "Computer Techniques for Storing, Retrieving, and Managing Ethnographic Data." Paper presented at the Annual Meetings of the Midwest Sociological Society.

1982b   "Computers and Ethnography: A Review of Recent Developments in the Use of Computers in Ethnographic Research." Paper presented at the Annual Meetings of the American Sociological Association.

Selznick, Philip

1953   *TVA and the Grassroots: A Study in the Sociology of Formal Organizations.* Berkeley: University of California Press.

1960   *The Organizational Weapon: A Study of Bolshevik Strategy and Tactics.* New York: The Free Press.

Shafer, R. J.

1969   *A Guide to Historical Method.* Homewood, Illinois: The Dorsey Press.

Shaffir, William B., Victor Marshall & Jack Haas

1980   "Competing Commitments: Unanticipated Problems of Field Research." *Qualitative Sociology*, 2:56–71 (January).

Shaffir, William B., Robert A. Stebbins & Allan Turowetz (eds.)

1980   *Fieldwork Experience: Qualitative Approaches to Social Research.* New York: St. Martin's Press.

Shupe, Anson D., Jr. & David G. Bromley

1980a   *The New Vigilantes: Deprogrammers, Anti-Cultists and the New Religions.* Beverly Hills, California: Sage Publications.

1980b   "Walking a Tightrope: Dilemmas of Participant Observation of Groups in Conflict." *Qualitative Sociology*, 2:3–21 (January).

Simmons, J. L.
   1964   "On Maintaining Deviant Belief Systems." *Social Problems*, 11:250–256 (Winter).

Sjoberg, Gideon (ed.)
   1967   *Ethics, Politics and Social Research.* Cambridge: Schenkman Publishing Company.

Smelser, Neil J.
   1976   *Comparative Methods in the Social Sciences.* Englewood Cliffs, New Jersey: Prentice-Hall, Inc.

Smith, H. W.
   1975   *Strategies of Social Research.* Englewood Cliffs, New Jersey: Prentice-Hall, Inc.

Smith, Robert B. & Peter K. Manning (eds.)
   1982   *Qualitative Methods.* Cambridge: Ballinger Publishing Company.

Snow, David & Richard Machalek
   1982   "On the Presumed Fragility of Unconventional Beliefs." *Journal for the Scientific Study of Religion,* 21:15–26 (March).

Snow, David, Louis Zurcher & Gideon Sjoberg
   1981   "Interviewing by Comment: An Adjunct to the Direct Question." Paper presented at the Annual Meetings of the Society for the Study of Symbolic Interaction.

Spector, Malcolm
   1977   "Legitimizing Homosexuality." *Society,* 15:52–56 (July/August).
   1980   "Learning to Study Public Figures." In William B. Shaffir, Robert A. Stebbins, and Allan Turowetz (eds.), *Field Work Experience: Qualitative Approaches to Social Research,* pp. 98–110. New York: St. Martin's Press.

Spradley, James P.
   1979   *The Ethnographic Interview.* New York: Holt, Rinehart & Winston.
   1980   *Participant Observation.* New York: Holt, Rinehart & Winston.

Stebbins, Robert A.
   1978   "Classical Music Amateurs." *Humboldt Journal of Social Relations,* 5:78–103.
   1979   *Amateurs: On the Margin Between Work and Leisure.* Beverly Hills, California: Sage Publications.

Stinchcombe, Arthur L.
   1975   "Merton's Theory of Social Structure." In Lewis Coser (ed.), *The Idea of Social Structure,* pp. 11–33. New York: Harcourt, Brace and Jovanovich.

Strauss, Anselm, Leonard Schatzman, Rue Bucher, Danuta Erlich & Melvin Sabshin
   1964   *Psychiatric Ideologies and Institutions.* New York: The Free Press.

Sudnow, David
   1967   *Passing On: The Social Organization of Dying.* Englewood Cliffs, New Jersey: Prentice-Hall, Inc.
   1979   "Normal Crimes: Sociological Features of a Penal Code in a Public Defender Office." In H. Robboy, S. Greenblatt, and C. Clark (eds.), *Social Interaction,* pp. 473–496. New York: St. Martin's Press. (Originally pub. 1965.)

Sundholm, Charles A.

  1973   "The Pornographic Arcade: Ethnographic Notes on Moral Men in Immoral Places." *Urban Life*, 2:85–104 (April).

  1978   *Adversary Justice: A Critical Ethnography of the Criminal Trial Process*. Ph.D. Dissertation, Department of Sociology, University of California, Davis.

Suttles, Gerald D.

  1968   *The Social Order of the Slum: Ethnicity and Territory in the Inner City*. Chicago: The University of Chicago Press.

  1972   *The Social Construction of Communities*. Chicago: The University of Chicago Press.

Sykes, Gresham & David Matza

  1979   "Techniques of Neutralization: A Theory of Delinquency." In H. Robboy, S. Greenblatt, and C. Clark (eds.), *Social Interaction*, pp. 497–504. New York: St. Martin's Press. (Originally pub. 1957.)

Thorne, Barrie

  1975a   "Protest and the Problem of Credibility: Uses of Knowledge and Risk Taking in the Draft Resistance Movement of the 1960's." *Social Problems*, 23:111–123 (December).

  1975b   "Women in the Draft Resistance Movement: A Case Study of Sex Roles and Social Movements." *Sex Roles*, 1:179–195 (June).

  1979   "Political Activist as Participant Observer: Conflicts of Commitment in a Study of the Draft Resistance Movement of the 1960's." *Symbolic Interaction*, 2:73–88 (Spring).

  1980   "'You Still Takin' Notes?' Fieldwork and the Problems of Informed Consent." In Joan Cassell and Murray L. Wax (eds.), *Ethical Problems of Fieldwork*, pp. 284–297. A special issue of *Social Problems*, 27 (February).

Turner, Ralph

  1947   "The Navy Disbursing Officer as a Bureaucrat." *American Sociological Review*, 12:342–348 (June).

Unruh, David

  1979a   "Characteristics and Types of Participation in Social Worlds." *Symbolic Interaction*, 2:115–129 (Fall).

  1979b   "Influencing Common Sense Interpretations of an Urban Setting: The Freeway Coffee Shop." *Symbolic Interaction*, 2:27–42 (Spring).

  1980   "The Nature of Social Worlds." *Pacific Sociological Review*, 23:271–296 (July).

  1983   *Invisible Lives: Social Worlds of the Aged*. Beverly Hills, California: Sage Publications.

Vidich, Arthur J. & Joseph Bensman

  1958   *Small Town in Mass Society: Class, Power and Religion in a Rural Community*. Princeton, New Jersey: Princeton University Press.

  1968   *Small Town in Mass Society: Class, Power and Religion in a Rural Community*, 2nd edition. Princeton, New Jersey: Princeton University Press.

Wallace, Samuel E.

  1973   *After Suicide*. New York: John Wiley & Sons.

Waller, Willard
  1938 *The Family: A Dynamic Interpretation*. New York: Cordon.
Wallis, Roy
  1979 *Salvation and Protest: Studies of Social and Religious Movements*. New York: St. Martin's Press.
Walton, John
  1983 *Reluctant Rebels*. Princeton, New Jersey: Princeton University Press.
Walum, Laurel
  1978 "The Changing Door Ceremony: Notes on the Operation of Sex Roles in Everyday Life." In John Lofland (ed.), *Interaction in Everyday Life*, pp. 51–60. Beverly Hills, California: Sage Publications.
Warner, W. Lloyd
  1959 *The Living and the Dead: A Study of the Symbolic Life of Americans*. New Haven: Yale University Press.
Warner, W. Lloyd & J. O. Low
  1947 *The Social System of the Modern Factory. The Strike: A Social Analysis*. New Haven: Yale University Press.
Warner, W. Lloyd & Paul S. Lunt
  1941 *The Social Life of a Modern Community*. New Haven: Yale University Press.
  1942 *The Status System of a Modern Community*. New Haven: Yale University Press.
Warner, W. Lloyd & Leo Srole
  1945 *The Social Systems of American Ethnic Groups*. New Haven: Yale University Press.
Warren, Carol A. B.
  1974 *Identity and Community in the Gay World*. New York: John Wiley & Sons.
  1977 "Fieldwork in the Gay World: Issues in Phenomenological Research." *Journal of Social Issues*, 33:93–107 (Fall).
  1980 "Data Presentation and the Audience: Responses, Ethics and Effects." *Urban Life*, 9:282–308 (October).
Warren, Carol A. B. & Paul K. Rasmussen
  1977 "Sex and Gender in Field Research." *Urban Life*, 6:349–369 (October).
Wax, Murray & Joan Cassell
  1981 "From Regulation to Reflection: Ethics in Social Research." *American Sociologist*, 16:224–229 (November).
Wax, Rosalie H.
  1971 *Doing Fieldwork: Warnings and Advice*. Chicago: The University of Chicago Press.
Webb, Eugene, Donald T. Campbell, Richard D. Schwartz, Lee Sechrest & Janet B. Grove
  1981 *Nonreactive Measures in the Social Sciences*, 2nd edition. Boston: Houghton Mifflin.
Weber, Max
  1949 *The Methodology of the Social Sciences*. Glencoe, Illinois: The Free Press. (Sections originally pub. 1904, 1910, 1917.)
Weinberg, Martin S. & Colin J. Williams
  1972 "Fieldwork among Deviants: Social Relations with Subjects and

Others." In Jack D. Douglas (ed.), *Research on Deviance*, pp. 165–186. New York: Random House.

Weppner, Robert S. (ed.)
1977 *Street Ethnography: Selected Studies of Crime and Drug Use in Natural Settings.* Beverly Hills, California: Sage Publications.

Werthman, Carl
1963 "Delinquency in Schools: A Test for the Legitimacy of Authority." *Berkeley Journal of Sociology,* 8:39–60.

West, James
1945 *Plainville, U.S.A.* New York: Columbia University Press.

West, W. Gordon
1980 "Access to Adolescent Deviants and Deviance." In William B. Shaffir, Robert A. Stebbins, and Allan Turowetz (eds.), *Fieldwork Experience: Qualitative Approaches to Social Research,* pp. 31–44. New York: St. Martin's Press.

Whyte, William F.
1948 *Human Relations in the Restaurant Industry.* New York: McGraw-Hill Co.

1955 *Streetcorner Society: The Social Structure of an Italian Slum,* enlarged edition. Chicago: The University of Chicago Press. (Originally pub. 1943.)

Williams, Thomas Rhys
1967 *Field Methods in the Study of Culture.* New York: Holt, Rinehart and Winston.

Wiseman, Jacqueline
1970 *Stations of the Lost: The Treatment of Skid-Row Alcoholics.* Englewood Cliffs, New Jersey: Prentice-Hall, Inc.
1974 "The Research Web." *Urban Life,* 3:317–328 (October).
1979 "Close Encounters of the Quasi-Primary Kind: Sociability in Urban Second-Hand Clothing Stores." *Urban Life,* 8:23–51 (April).

Wolfe, Tom
1970 *Radical Chic and Mau-Mauing the Flak Catchers.* New York: Farrar, Straus and Giroux.
1976 *Mauve Gloves and Madmen, Clutter and Vine.* New York: Farrar, Straus and Giroux.

Zablocki, Benjamin
1980 *The Joyful Community: An Account of the Bruderhof, A Communal Movement Now in Its Third Generation.* Chicago: University of Chicago Press.

Zablocki, Benjamin & Rosabeth Moss Kanter
1976 "The Differentiation of Life-styles." In Ralph Turner (ed.), *Annual Review of Sociology,* pp. 269–298. New York: Annual Reviews, Inc.

Zimmerman, Don H. & D. Lawrence Wieder
1977 "The Diary: Diary-Interview Method." *Urban Life,* 5:479–498 (January).

Zurcher, Louis, D. Scnenschein & E. Metzner
1966 "The Hasher: A Study of Role Conflict." *Social Forces,* 44:505–514 (June).

Index